Pro Sports Halls of Fame

VOLUME 6

FOOTBALL

1979–1996

Dick Butkus to Joe Gibbs

Pro Sports Halls of Fame

VOLUME
6

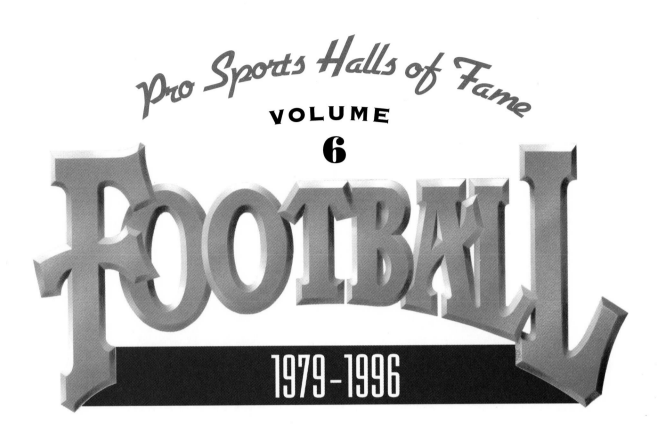

FOOTBALL
1979-1996

Dick Butkus to Joe Gibbs

Grolier Educational

SHERMAN TURNPIKE, DANBURY, CONNECTICUT

Published 1997 by Grolier Educational, Danbury, CT 06816
This edition published exclusively for the school and library market

*The publisher gratefully acknowledges permission from the following sources to
reproduce photographs:*

UPI/Corbis-Bettmann: 1, 6, 21, 23, 24, 30, 31, 37, 39, 40, 59, 61, 62,
63, 64, 65, 66, 86, 95, 107, 108, 109, 111, 112, 114, 128, 136, 138,
140, 153

Reuters/Bettmann: 12

UPI/Bettmann: 9

All other photographs courtesy of AP/Wide World Photos

A Creative Media Applications Production

Writer – Basketball: Michael Burgan
Writer – Hockey: Robin Doak
Writer – Football: Della Rowland
Writer – Baseball: Michael Teitelbaum
Editor: Matt Levine
Design and Production: Alan Barnett, Inc.
Copyeditor: Kathleen White
Copyeditor: Barbara Jean DiMauro
Researcher: David Fischer
Indexer: Lynne Karmen

Set ISBN 0-7172-7651-1
Volume 6 ISBN 0-7172-7657-0

Pro sports halls of fame.
       p.   cm.
     Includes biographical references and indexes.
     Contents: v. 1. Basketball, from Naismith to Mikan.
     Summary: Presents biographical information, career statistics,
and special achievements of people who have been inducted into
the baseball, basketball, football, or hockey hall of fame.
     ISBN 0-7172-7651-1
     1. Sports – United States – Registers – Juvenile literature.
     2. Halls of fame – United States – Directories – Juvenile literature.
     3. Halls of fame – United States – Registers – Juvenile literature.
     4. Athletes – United States – Biography – Juvenile literature.
     [1. Baseball players. 2. Basketball players. 3. Football players.
     4. Hockey players. 5. Athletes – Statistics. 6. Halls of fame.]
     I. Grolier Educational.
GV583.P756   1996
796'.0973 – dc20   96-30181
                                                         CIP
                                                          AC

Contents

The History of Football 1

The Football Hall of Fame 17

Inductees 1979–1982 33

Inductees 1983–1986 55

Inductees 1987–1989 81

Inductees 1990–1992 103

Inductees 1993–1996 125

Glossary of Football Terms 153

Index 161

The History
of Football

THE HISTORY OF PROFESSIONAL FOOTBALL
From 1951–1996

It's A New Game

The 1950s saw several dramatic changes in football. One of the biggest, the "free substitution" rule, led to the development of the game as we know it today. Adopted in 1950, the ruling brought about an era of players specializing in one position. Up until the 1950s, the players were two-way, "60-Minute Men." They routinely played both offense and defense for the whole 60 minutes of a game.

Suppose a kicker was needed for a play, but he was already in the game playing several positions, as most players did. In order to perform his kicking duty, he had to neglect one of his other duties. Free substitution meant that a coach could send in any player at any time, as long as there were only eleven men on the field. Now he could send in someone who specialized in kicking and other position duties would still be covered.

After the rule was adopted, teams were divided into offensive and defensive units. The two-way players began to specialize at one position, such as passer, receiver, blocker, or punter. This change was good for football in that it created better competition between

George Blanda (16) began his career as quarterback and placekicker in 1949, with the "age of specialization." Football's "grand old man" played 26 years, through 1975—longer than any other pro football player.

FACE MASKS: A TACKLER'S FRIEND

After his L.A. Rams were slaughtered 56-20 by the Philadelphia Eagles in 1950, Coach Joe Stydahar gave them a pep talk. "Here's why you guys can't win," he hollered. And with that he pulled a bridge of false front teeth out of his mouth. "A half-dozen of [the Eagles] are wearing these things. Nobody on this team has any guts to charge in there with his head up. From now on, I want to see…teeth flying."

But the Rams didn't get much of a chance to show the coach their stuff. Early in the 1950s, NFL teams began wearing clear Lucite face masks, but the Lucite tended to shatter. In 1954 a new ruling required players to wear face masks, and the next year a helmet with a tubular bar across the face was invented. Soon there were two, then three bars protecting a player's face. Now a tackler could really go after an opponent without worrying about changing the shape of his nose or racking up big dentist bills.

teams. If a player only had to worry about doing one job, he could do it better and make the game more entertaining. On the other hand, players were no longer as well-rounded as they had been in football's earlier days. Fans rarely ever saw exciting performances from players like Jim Thorpe or Sammy Baugh who did it all on both sides of the football.

The age of specialists brought about the decade of the quarterback in the 1950s. Football had changed from a ground game, in which a running attack was used to score, to an aerial or passing game. Now quarterbacks threw more often to receivers to score touchdowns. Strong runners still played the game, but wide-ranging receivers and bullet-throwing passers were the big stars. Quarterbacks dominated the action—especially Bobby Layne of the Detroit Lions, Otto Graham of the Cleveland Browns, and Johnny Unitas of the Baltimore Colts. The T formation, well-suited for ballhandling deception, was a natural for this kind of offense.

As the game turned up the excitement, more fans turned the turnstiles. They also began turning on their televisions to watch the game at home.

Football Finds Its Frame

Television helped establish football as a major sport during the 1950s, but in the beginning of the relationship, "the tube" was not always football's friend. The good news was that it increased the number of fans who watched the sport. The bad news was that it also decreased the number who actually went to the stadium and paid to watch a game.

For example, in 1950 the Los Angeles Rams became the first team to televise all its games. During the 1949 season, without television, the team drew 205,109 fans. The next year the Rams' attendance dropped to 110,162 because the fans were watching the games at home. In 1951 the Rams televised only their road games, and their attendance rose again to 234,110.

To keep fans coming to the stadiums, the NFL went to court in 1953 to obtain a ruling that home games would be blacked out. Three years later NFL commissioner Bert Bell reinforced that ruling. He announced that the only NFL games that could be televised were road games.

The first televised pro game was between the Brooklyn Dodgers and the Philadelphia Eagles on October 22, 1939. Allen "Skip" Walz was paid $25 to broadcast the game from Brooklyn's Ebbets Field. His crew was small—nine people with two cameras. (It takes some 200

SUDDEN DEATH

The 1958 NFL championship game between the Baltimore Colts and the New York Giants was the first sudden death overtime championship game. The league had experimented with the "sudden death" rule in 1947 and adopted it in 1955 as a way of ending tie games in the postseason. The NFL came up with this rule primarily to make the game more exciting. Rather than having teams play out a full quarter, the rule allowed the team scoring first during overtime play to win. In other words, the first team's score was "sudden death" to the other team's chance of winning.

When it was first put into effect, sudden death applied only to division and championship playoffs. In 1962, it was expanded to Pro Bowls. Finally, in 1974, it applied to all games. However, for regular and preseason games overtime was limited to fifteen minutes. After that time the game would end as a tie.

The longest game ever was a sudden death overtime in the 1971 AFC division playoff between the Kansas City Chiefs and the Miami Dolphins. That game lasted 82 minutes and 40 seconds.

One of football's first telecasts in 1939 used only two cameras— one on the sidelines and a second one in the press booth (upper left).

people to televise the Super Bowl today.) But the audience was also small. At that time there were only about 1,000 TV sets in New York.

Twelve years later millions of fans watched the 1951 championship game between the Cleveland Browns and the Los Angeles Rams. It was the first NFL game to be televised nationally. However, the 1958 championship game between the Baltimore Colts and the New York Giants was the one that put football at the top of the popularity charts.

For three quarters the Colts led 14–3. Then a couple of gamble plays backfired and the Giants wound up with a 17–14 lead. With seven seconds left, Baltimore kicked a 20-yard field goal to tie the score and the game went into sudden death overtime. After neck and neck action, the Colts finally made the first touchdown and their fans tore down the goalposts.

"The Greatest Game of All Time" was played before millions of nail-biting fans in TV land. When they turned off their sets, they knew they had just watched one of the most entertaining sports being played. And by that time it had dawned on the networks and advertisers that football would sell.

Football had found its medium. The action-packed game was perfect for the small screen. Sunday became football day in millions of U.S. households.

A Rival Hits the Field

After a decade of easy, steady growth, upheaval hit the NFL in 1959. On October 11, Bert Bell, the NFL commissioner since 1946, died at age 64. He was watching a game between the Eagles and Steelers at Philadelphia's Franklin Field, a fitting end for the NFL commissioner. His loss was keenly felt when Texas millionaire Lamar Hunt announced the formation of yet another American Football League—the fourth rival to the NFL in the league's history.

Hunt had discussed starting a team in Dallas with Bell earlier, but the commissioner didn't think the NFL was ready to expand. After he was unable to purchase a team, Hunt decided to start his own league. Throughout 1959 he met with wealthy businessmen from Houston, Minneapolis, Denver, Los Angeles, New York, Buffalo, and Boston to form the AFL.

When Hunt asked Bell if he would be commissioner for both leagues, Bell replied he would consider it. Unfortunately, when Bell died in October, the possibility of a partnership between the two leagues died with him. Lamar Hunt was named first AFL president, and Pete Rozelle, general manager of the L.A. Rams, succeeded Bell as NFL commissioner.

The war between the leagues started off the 1960s with a bang. The upstart AFL had big money in its favor as it went up against the 40-year-old NFL. Its first year, 1960, the AFL adopted a fourteen-game schedule for its eight teams. The next year the NFL increased its twelve-game schedule to fourteen in order to compete. In 1960 the AFL also signed a five-year, $10 million contract with ABC to

Using their "run to daylight" offensive strategy, the Green Bay Packers beat the Kansas City Chiefs 35–10 during the first Super Bowl in 1967.

televise its games. Rozelle was still negotiating with CBS to televise NFL games. With television investing in the AFL, it was clear the NFL's rival was there to stay. At that, both leagues began a race to place clubs in new territories.

The NFL awarded franchises to Dallas and Minneapolis-St. Paul and grew to thirteen teams. The AFL set up new teams in Boston, Denver, Houston, Oakland, and Buffalo. Then they established clubs in New York, Los Angeles, and Dallas to compete with existing NFL teams. With eight teams, the AFL played its first regular-season game in Boston before 21,597 new fans.

The two leagues carried on a fierce bidding war for players, driving the price of football talent sky high. The battle began with the AFL's first player draft in 1959. With its big bucks and growing reputation for quality playing, the AFL attracted many superior players. But it's biggest prize was "Broadway Joe" Namath. In 1965 the AFL New York Jets signed the popular and talented quarterback for an unheard-of $425,000.

After competing separately for seven years, both leagues were heading for financial ruin. Finally, in 1966, they agreed to merge. The agreement called for a championship playoff between the two leagues that season and a combined draft in 1967. By 1970 there would be a complete merger, including playing schedules.

The AFL's bitter struggle with the NFL actually produced a healthier league. Because of competition between the AFL and NFL, new clubs had been established all over the country, making football a truly national sport. Players' salaries were higher, but so were the number of fans filling the stands. And as more turned-on fans turned on their TVs, each team's television revenues also grew.

The Long View

Pete Rozelle had been working on lucrative television contracts since he was elected NFL commissioner. He had seen football's future—through the television camera. Rozelle realized that if he could represent all the teams in one TV package, the league would have more bargaining power with the networks.

First Rozelle had to convince the successful team owners that it was in their best interest to share television revenues equally, even with struggling teams. In the short run, they might not make as much, but in the long run, all the teams would benefit, making the league stronger. With this accomplished, in 1961 Rozelle had a law passed exempting football from future monopoly charges. This way the league could act as one unit instead of as individual teams.

MORE THAN ONE WAY TO BE A PRO

Figuring out how football works can sometimes be a confusing task. Even more confusing is the difference between All-Pro and Pro Bowl teams.

Two Pro Bowl teams are chosen at the end of each season, one for the AFC and one for the NFC. These teams are officially recognized by the NFL and usually hold their playoff in Hawaii two weeks after the Super Bowl. To be chosen for a Pro Bowl team is a great honor for a player.

A Pro Bowl team has 41 players, plus a "need player" who is chosen by the head coaches. (This extra guy is usually a cornerback or a safety.) Each Pro Bowl team is chosen by the coaches and players in its conference. Each team get two votes, one from the head coach and the other representing the players' choice. A team is allowed to vote only for players in its conference and voters are not allowed to vote for any members of their own teams.

Several All-Pro teams are listed each year, but only three of them are official NFL teams. Those team lists are chosen by the Pro Football Writers of America, the Associated Press, and the United Press International.

By 1962 the NFL had a two-year contract with CBS for $4.65 million a year. Then, during the merger with the AFL, the leagues negotiated a four-year contract with both CBS and NBC for $9.5 million. Beginning in 1967 the two networks would televise the AFL-NFL World Championship Games, later called the Super Bowls. In 1969, the newly combined league signed a $150-million contract with ABC. The network would televise thirteen NFL regular-season Monday night games for the next three years. Howard Cosell, Don Meredith, and Frank Gifford became the network's broadcast crew. Monday Night Football became a regular fall event.

The Defense Decides

In the 1950s and early 1960s, a football team's offense led the way to victory. By the late 1960s, it was the defense. For years, the quarterbacks, running backs, and wide receivers had thrown and carried the ball to high scores. To deal with these multiple offensive attacks, the defense went on the defensive.

Defensive coaches were hired. Defensive specialists were drafted out of college. Defensive linemen were still stout and strong, but now they were speedy too. Their speed enabled them to carry out the new "pass defense" strategy. The pass defense consisted of double-teaming the receiver and rushing the quarterback at the same time.

To avoid being rushed, the quarterback began dropping back farther behind his offensive line and getting rid of the ball quicker to the receiver. So defense put a "zone" defense on the receiver. This was a formation in which players covered an area of the field instead of an individual opponent. When a receiver was covered by a zone defense, he couldn't run far enough to get into position to catch long passes from the quarterback. Instead of throwing a long bomb, the offense had to go back to using the running attack, which had been out of fashion for years.

These new strategies allowed the defense to control the outcome of the game. For example, great offense had made the Green Bay Packers the team of the 1960s. Using Coach Vince Lombardi's "run to daylight" offensive strategy, the Pack took NFL championship titles in 1961, 1962, 1965, and 1966, then won the first two Super Bowls in 1967 and 1968. The 1970s, however, were dominated by two teams with devastating defensive units. Miami's "No-Name" defense led the Dolphins to two Super Bowls. And the Pittsburgh Steelers, by dropping their "Steel Curtain," won four.

IF I CAN'T USE MY BALL, I WON'T PLAY!

In order to bring about the merger of the AFL and the NFL, Pete Rozelle negotiated some strange compromises. One of them concerned which ball to use for the first league championship game.

The official ball of the NFL was made by Wilson. The AFL used a Spalding ball. Since the shapes of these balls were slightly different, both leagues wanted to use their own. So a compromise was arranged. During the first NFL-AFL World Championship a Wilson ball had to be used when the NFL played offense. When the AFL was on offense, the ball in play was a Spalding.

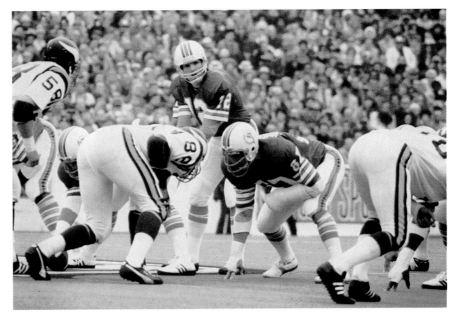

Miami quarterback Bob Griese (12) called the signals during Super Bowl VIII in 1974. But it was the Dolphins' "No-Name" Defense that beat the Minnesota Vikings 24–7.

Low Scores For Defense

The main problem with a game driven by the defense was low scores. Because of the great new defensive strategies, the quarterback wasn't passing as much to the receiver anymore. Every fan knows that the more times the ball is passed, the more exciting the game is—and the higher the score is.

By the mid-1970s, the action had slowed down so much that attendance began leveling off. So the Competition Committee decided to tinker with the rules to make them benefit the offense and hopefully bring back more passing. In 1971 the hashmarks on the field were moved in to give the offense more room to manuveur. In 1974 officials moved the goalposts back 10 yards, from the goal line to the end line. This move was meant to encourage the offense to make more touchdowns by discouraging them from kicking field goals. Teams would often kick for an easy 3 points if they were close enough to the goal instead of running another play for a 7-point touchdown. With the goalposts farther away a team would have to go for another down in order to get close enough to kick. That was exactly what the officials wanted—to keep the drive going.

When passing and scoring numbers didn't increase quickly enough, the Competition Committee cracked down harder on the defense. In 1977 the head slap was outlawed and defense was allowed to touch, or "bump," a receiver only once, within the first 5 yards off the scrimmage line.

That same year, offensive linemen were allowed "legalized holding." This meant they could extend their arms and use open hands on a pass block. Slowly these rule changes began to work, and passing stats and scoring rose.

The New NFL

In 1970, when the AFL and NFL officially merged, the new NFL was divided into two conferences—the National Football Conference and the American Football Conference. Each conference had thirteen teams and was divided into three divisions, the Eastern, Central, and Western. The teams at that time were:

AFC	NFC
Eastern Division	
Baltimore	Dallas
Boston	New York Giants
Buffalo	Philadelphia
Miami	St. Louis
New York Jets	Washington
Central Division	
Cincinnati	Chicago
Cleveland	Detroit
Houston	Green Bay
Pittsburgh	Minnesota
Western Division	
Denver	Atlanta
Kansas City	Los Angeles
Oakland	New Orleans
San Diego	San Francisco

The first two AFL-NFL championships were won by the NFL's Green Bay Packers. The Pack's victories confirmed what most folks believed: that the NFL was the superior league with the better teams. However, Joe Namath, quarterback for the AFL New York Jets, changed their minds. Just before Super Bowl III, he guaranteed that his team would win, even though the experts predicted the NFL's Baltimore Colts would win by 17 points. Everyone laughed at Namath's guarantee until he led the Jets to a stunning 16–7 upset.

Striking New Ground

After the dust of the league war had settled, things seemed to be brighter in the football world. Attendance hit a single weekend record on November 22, 1970, when 749,191 fans attended thirteen games. It was an average of 57,630 per game. A year later, the NBC telecast of Super Bowl V was the top-rated one-day sports telecast ever, with fans watching in nearly 24 million homes.

Just as things were going smoothly for the league, the players threatened to strike in 1970. They had watched team owners throw out big bucks to attract top players during the league war. Now they wanted some of that money. A strong NFL Players Association managed to negotiate a four-year agreement that put $4.5 million annually into player pension and insurance benefits. The call for a strike quieted down.

The union began renegotiating a new contract agreement with league management in 1974. Once again it threatened strikes and legal suits, this time over the "Rozelle Rule." This "ruling" gave the commissioner the right to decide how much a team could pay to acquire a free agent. It was meant to keep owners from going after other team's players, but the players felt it was keeping their salaries down. In 1977, the courts struck down the rule, and owners and players agreed to a new limited free agent system to be in effect until 1982.

The Problem with Prosperity

The 1980s saw as many football battles in the courtroom as it did on the gridiron. Football was prosperous and that was the problem.

The NFL had expanded to Tampa Bay and Seattle in 1976 and increased their regular season to 16 games two years later. By 1981 the number of fans attending NFL games had increased four seasons in a row. That same year three major television networks had signed new five-year contracts to broadcast games. Football's pot of gold was overflowing and the players wanted their share of the big bucks.

When they didn't get it, the Players Association pulled a 57-day strike in 1982. The strike demolished the schedule for October and early November. In the end the players got salary and benefit increases, and, for the first time in any professional sport, they also had severance pay.

In 1983 football's prosperity enticed another league to try to carve out a slice of the money pie. That year the United States Football League took to the gridirons during the NFL off-season, from March to July. The USFL played for three seasons with twelve

THE HUDDLE — HEAR TODAY, GONE TOMORROW

For the last 50 years, coaches and managers have been trying to get rid of the huddle. Why? Because it slows down the game. The best way to keep football exciting is to keep the offensive plays moving quickly. And when players group together to call a play, the action on the field stops.

It is believed that the huddle was first used in 1894 at Gallaudet College in Washington, D.C. Gallaudet was a school for the deaf and its students used sign language to communicate even on the football field. In order to conceal their hand signals, teams huddled together to discuss strategy and call their plays. Soon the huddle was part of the game.

Since the 1940s teams have tried to replace the huddle by simply calling plays at the line of scrimmage. Today quarterbacks wear radio helmets so their coaches can tell them directly which plays to call. Soon every player might wear one so that quarterbacks can talk to them right on the line of scrimmage. One problem is hearing calls over the noise of the crowd. The other is a player getting his helmet jerked off. But if everyone can understand each other well enough to run a successful play, the huddle may soon become extinct.

teams and lots of stars, including Reggie White, Jim Kelly, Herschel Walker, and Steve Young.

The new league had planned to start a fall schedule but it couldn't land a contract with any of the television networks. At that, the USFL slapped a $1.7 million lawsuit on the NFL. The suit claimed that the older league had a monopoly on the pro football television market, which was shutting out the new league. The courts ruled for the USFL in July 1986, but by then the league had lost most of its better players to NFL teams and it folded.

Head for the Pass

After absorbing the USFL's top performers, many NFL teams were better than ever, and so was the action on the field. All the rules the NFL had adopted in the 1970s to increase the passing game were working. By the 1980s, as one history book put it, more passes for more yards were being thrown per game than ever before. Bill Walsh's San Francisco 49ers were the passing team of the 1980s. With quarterback Joe Montana throwing short, quick passes to speedy, elusive receivers, San Francisco won four Super Bowls between 1981 and 1989. With more action to see, the fans headed back to the stands, setting an all-time attendance record of nearly 17.5 million in 1986.

Many teams used the "run-and-shoot" passing attack. Each team had its own name for variations on this innovative and popular offensive strategy. Basically, it consisted of the quarterback throwing

Quarterback Joe Montana (18) led the San Francisco 49ers to four Super Bowl victories during the 1980s.

SUM COMPARISONS

In 1977 players achieved their first limited free agency. That year an average salary was about $55,000. In 1993 restricted free agency pushed the average salary to $600,000. But that jump is nothing. Today's average salary is hundreds of times higher than the first pro salary, paid in 1892 to Pudge Heffelfinger. Heffelfinger collected $500 for his first pro game—a handsome sum for the era.

Salaries weren't the only football sums that went up over the years. The first NFL franchises in 1920 cost each member $100. In 1960 a team was worth about $2 million. In 1989 the Dallas Cowboys franchise was bought for $140 million, and two new franchises each went for the same price in 1993.

a quick pass to one of four receivers. After the ball was snapped, each receiver would use a different running pattern to get downfield. Which pattern he used depended on how he was being covered by the opposition's defense.

To stop this attack, defensive linemen began bulking up to 300 pounds and rushing the quarterback quicker and harder. The idea was to throw off the the passer's timing before he could get rid of the ball. As a result, quarterback injuries soared as high as their passes. By the mid-1990s, the run-and-shoot passing attack had passed into history. It was just too dangerous physically for the passer. And, as defensive strategies became better and more complex, the long pass became used less and less.

A Litigating League Leader

The 1980s ended with Pete Rozelle's suprise retirement in 1989. The NFL's election committee spent many hours in three different meetings around the country discussing Rozelle's replacement. On the twelfth vote, the committee finally elected Paul Tagliabue, the NFL's lawyer. It was a wise choice in a time when more and more issues were being handled by lawsuits.

During his first year Tagliabue negotiated his way across several legal tightropes. He secured a four-year television contract for $3.6 billion and strengthened the league's antidrug program. He also tackled the difficult talks with the players over labor disagreements.

Those disagreements led to several lawsuits against the NFL management by the Players Association. Money was an issue, of course, but just as important was the player's right to be a free agent, to choose his own team. As a compromise, the league created a "limited" free agency in 1989. All players except a team's most important ones were free to negotiate for new homes. Under this system, most players were free to move around, but the owners were protected because their best men could not leave.

During the first signing period, which took place in the off-season, 184 free agents changed teams. But the players still weren't satisfied. Ironically, the limited system helped the less important players more than it did the best—and often the hardest-working—ones. The average players were the ones free to move to better-paying teams while the top players weren't.

It took four more years and the threat of more lawsuits to reach a settlement that satisfied both players and owners. In January 1993 the owners got a salary cap, and in exchange the players got free

1996 NATIONAL FOOTBALL LEAGUE TEAMS

AMERICAN FOOTBALL CONFERENCE

Eastern Division
Buffalo Bills
Indianapolis Colts
Miami Dolphins
New England Patriots
New York Jets

Central Division
Baltimore Ravens
Cincinnati Bengals
Houston Oilers
Jacksonville Jaguars
Pittsburgh Steelers

Western Division
Denver Broncos
Kansas City Chiefs
Oakland Raiders
San Diego Chargers
Seattle Seahawks

agent status: Any player who had been in the league for four years was free to move to the team who would pay the most for him. Out of 484 eligible players, 120 of them took another team's money and ran—for the bank.

Expanding the Horizons

In 1993 everybody in the NFL went to the bank when a TV contract was cut for $4.35 billion. On November 14, 1993, Don Shula banked his 325th victory to become the "winningest" coach in NFL history. And the team that broke the bank was the Dallas Cowboys. After buying the franchise in 1990, new owner Jerry Jones put new coach Jimmy Johnson in charge and new superstars Troy Aikman and Emmitt Smith in the front lines. Between 1992 and 1995 "America's Team" took home three more Super Bowl trophies.

Football was popular as well as prosperous. In 1990 a new attendance record was set when over 17 million people walked through the turnstiles. Compare those numbers to 1934, the first year records were kept. A total of 492,684 people attended league games—an average of 8,211 per game.

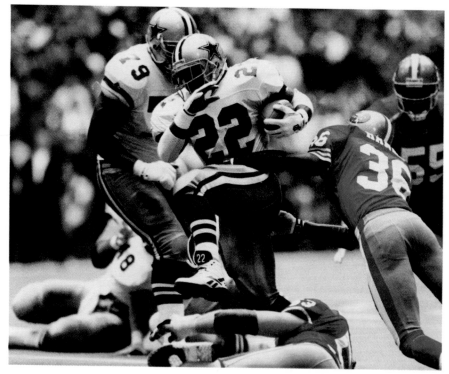

Dallas Cowboys running back Emmitt Smith (22) tore through enemy lines to help win Super Bowl trophies for "America's Team" in 1992, 1993, and 1995.

NATIONAL FOOTBALL CONFERENCE

Eastern Division
Arizona Cardinals
Dallas Cowboys
New York Giants
Philadelphia Eagles
Washington Redskins

Central Division
Chicago Bears
Detroit Lions
Green Bay Packers
Minnesota Vikings
Tampa Bay Buccaneers

Western Division
Atlanta Falcons
Carolina Panthers
New Orleans Saints
St.Louis Rams
San Francisco 49ers

In January 1994 nearly 135 million fans in 42,860,000 households cheered Super Bowl XXVIII from their armchairs. What's more, the NFL had football fans all over the world. Weekly telecasts of games appeared in more than 150 countries in the 1990s, with overseas Super Bowl audiences of 750 million.

On the home front, the NFL started two new franchises in 1995–the Carolina Panthers in Charlotte, North Carolina, and the Jacksonville Jaguars in Florida. It was the first time in nineteen years that the NFL had added any new teams. The league had come a long way since 1920 when ten owners plunked down $100 for the first franchises. Seventy years later, Jerry Jones had paid $140 million for the Dallas Cowboys. Not long after that the Fox Network had bid $1.6 billion for the rights to televise NFC games from 1994 through 1997. Football's future looked secure.

How to Get to the Super Bowl

In 1996, the NFL consisted of 30 teams–fifteen in the National Football Conference, and fifteen in the American Football Conference. Each conference was made up of three divisions–Eastern, Central, and Western. The way two of these 30 teams get to the Super Bowl is complicated. Here's how it works.

Under the present setup six teams from each conference make it to the Super Bowl playoffs. First there are the winners of the three divisions. In addition, a "wild card" spot is awarded to three other teams in each conference. These wild card teams are the three non-division champions with the best win-loss record.

In the first round of the playoffs the division winner with the poorest record in each conference plays the wild card team with the best record. The other two wild cards play the second game. The two division winners with the better records don't play the first week. Instead they get a bye–a free pass to the next round.

In the second round, the division champion with the best win-loss record plays the first-round winner with the poorest record. The second-best division champ plays the other first-round winner.

In the third round, the two winners of the second round compete for the conference championship. The two conference winners then go to the Super Bowl to determine who is the NFL's best team.

The Global Gridiron

In 1986 the NFL gridiron went global. That summer the American Bowl series played its first game in London's Wembley Stadium. More than 82,000 cheering fans packed the stands to watch the Chicago Bears play the Dallas Cowboys in a preseason battle. The first game was such a hit that the series continued for five more years, playing games in Tokyo, Berlin, Barcelona, Mexico City, and Montreal.

The American Bowl paved the way for by the World League of American Football, which formed in 1991. The U.S. made up six teams while the other four franchises included the Montreal Machine, Frankfurt Galaxy, London Monarchs, and Barcelona Dragons. The WLAF became the first sports league to hold weekly games on two continents, ending the season with the World Bowl playoffs. A crowd of 61,108 piled into London's Wembley Stadium to watch the 1991 World Bowl, and 43,789 fans attended World Bowl in 1992 at Montreal's Olympic Stadium.

After shutting down in 1993, the WLAF resumed play in 1995 as the new World League. Six franchises—in Amsterdam, Dusseldorf, Scotland, Barcelona, Frankfurt, and London—played a ten-week schedule. What began as a simple kicking game played by many ancient cultures around the world was now an organized international sport.

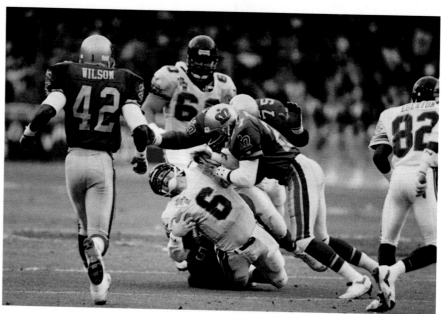

During the first World Bowl in 1991, the Barcelona Dragons took on the London Monarchs in London's Wembley Stadium.

The Football
Hall of Fame

THE FOOTBALL HALL OF FAME

Why Canton, Ohio?

The National Professional Football Hall of Fame is nestled on a 14-acre wooded parkland, a few miles west of downtown Canton, Ohio. Why Canton?

Canton was selected as the site of the Football Hall of Fame for three reasons. First, it is considered to be the birthplace of pro football. The Bulldogs, Canton's hometown team, organized in 1905, were an early pro football power. A Bulldogs player is credited with catching the first forward pass thrown in a pro football game. The team was led by "the greatest athlete of all time," Jim Thorpe. Thorpe played his first pro ball as halfback for the Bulldogs in 1915. With Thorpe leading the way, the team claimed the unofficial world championships in 1916, 1917, and 1919. The Bulldogs became the first champions of the National Football League in 1922 and claimed the title again in 1923.

The second reason is that the National Football League was organized in Canton. On September 17, 1920, Ralph Hay—owner of the Bulldogs—met with other owners and players to organize the NFL. The meeting was held at Hay's Jordan and Hupmobile showroom in the Odd Fellows' Building in downtown Canton. Jim Thorpe was the league's first president.

The National Professional Football Hall of Fame opened its doors in 1963.

Richard McCann, general manager of the Washington Redskins, became the Hall of Fame's first director.

Other towns might have a legitimate claim to the title "The Birthplace of Football." Latrobe, Pennsylvania, was the site of the first professional football game in 1895. In fact Latrobe made a bid for the Hall too, as did Green Bay, Los Angeles, and Detroit. But there is a third reason the Hall is in Canton: The city was determined to have it.

"Pro Football Needs a Hall of Fame...."

Beginning in the early 1960s, the citizens of Canton launched a campaign to build the Football Hall of Fame in their city. Germane Swanson, sportswriter for the *Canton Repository*, is credited as the first person to champion the people's idea that the Hall be in Canton. He first discussed it with Harold Sauerbrei, manager of the Cleveland Browns, who pledged his full support to the drive.

With the Browns behind the movement, Swanson and the *Repository*'s editor, Clayton Horn, ran a feature story in the *Repository* with the headline "Pro Football Needs a Hall of Fame...and Logical Site Is Here." After reading the story, the football-loving citizens of Canton lost no time in moving on the issue. Civic groups, businesses, industries, and labor unions all got behind the project. People volunteered to do legwork. Soon pledges of support and money began pouring in.

On January 25, 1961, Canton made its formal bid for the Hall. As representative of the city, William E. Umstattd attended the NFL owners' meeting. He asked the NFL to name Canton as the site for a pro football hall of fame. On April 27 the NFL handed down good news.

The Call Goes Out

Soon after getting the okay from the NFL, Dick McCann was named the Hall's first director. McCann was a sports columnist from Washington, D.C., and later the general manager of that city's Redskins team. Using his connections, the friendly, energetic McCann generated national interest in the Hall. He also established the selection process to determine who would decide who would be inducted. Then he went to work contacting press, television, and radio journalists to persuade them to participate in the yearly selection activities.

McCann also put out the call for the priceless items that would go into the football museum. Much of what is on display there was gathered through McCann's efforts. Moving from Washington, D.C., he set up shop in a small office in the Onesto Hotel in Canton. There he began the gigantic task of sorting through the thousands of football mementoes that had been carefully collected. There were Jim Thorpe's uniform and Otto Graham's shoulder pads; there were shoes, books, balls, programs, photos, newspaper clippings, and much, much more. McCann painstakingly compiled and archived each and every item.

As McCann slowly collected exhibition items, the city donated a wooded parkland for the Hall's site. By February 1962 more than $400,000 had been raised. On August 11, 1962, groundbreaking ceremonies were held. A little more than a year later, on September 7, 1963, the Hall opened its doors to the public. In two and a half years the citizens of Canton had gone from wanting a Football Hall of Fame to seeing it dedicated.

The First Immortals

Its first year the Pro Football Hall of Fame inducted seventeen charter members. These original inductees—a combination of players, coaches, and commissioners—were: Sammy Baugh, Bert Bell, Joe Carr, Dutch Clark, Red Grange, George Halas, Mel Hein, Pete "Fats" Henry, Cal Hubbard, Don Hutson, Curly Lambeau, Tim Mara,

*During the induction ceremony on the steps of the Hall,
each inductee is presented with a bronze bust.*

"It's an honor for me to be here. Most of us got together for a little while last night to compare notes and talk over old times....If any of you people doubt that we're not great, you should have been there.... The longer you're away from the sport the greater you become, and it thrills me to death to think how great I'll be when I'm a hundred years old." —*Mel Hein*

"It took me 20 years to catch up and meet Don Hutson, and it is a great pleasure and honor for me to say a few words about him today. Don Hutson set records for pass catching and scoring, which only legislation can wipe out. He is a football yardstick." —*Dante Lavelli, Cleveland Browns end and future Hall of Famer, introducing Don Hutson*

"To me the people who should be honored are the owners who stayed with it back in those days when they weren't making money....They still loved the game and thought enough of it to stay there... until the game became what it is today. A player didn't have too much to lose. When you start putting your own money up and not having anything in return, friend, you've got a little courage then." —*Sammy Baugh*

George Marshall, Johnny "Blood" McNally, Bronko Nagurski, Ernie Nevers, and, of course, Jim Thorpe.

Of the seventeen immortalized, twelve were still alive. Relatives or friends accepted for the late Bert Bell, Tim Mara, Fats Henry, Joe Carr, and Jim Thorpe. The only living member who wasn't there was George Marshall; he was in Georgetown Hospital in Washington, D.C., too ill to attend.

Before the very first induction ceremonies, the living members wandered through the Hall, looking at the paintings of one another and reliving old times. Each mural honored a superstar in some scene that represented his achievements. Bronko Nagurski is hurtling through a line of opponents. "The Galloping Ghost," Red Grange, is about to gallop off on one of his spectacular runs. Barrel-shaped Fats Henry is doing what he did best–kicking a field goal. Sammy Baugh is throwing a pass, and Don Hutson is catching one.

George Halas and Curly Lambeau–two players who became coaches–were overheard talking in front of Halas's mural. "That's a characteristic pose, George," Lambeau told Halas, pointing to his painting. "They caught you arguing with the officials."

"I never argue with officials," Halas retorted. "I admit I sometimes try to help out the poor boys and show them their mistakes. But argue with them? Never!"

The First Induction Ceremony

A week before the induction ceremony the town started celebrating with Canton Future Week. The induction day itself began with a parade. Thousands of people thronged the streets of the small city. The Hall of Famers rode down the streets of Canton in convertibles, waving at their fans. Among the marchers were members of the town's chamber of commerce wearing gigantic football helmets. It was like a carnival in Canton that day.

After the parade the crowds gathered in Fawcett Stadium across the street from the Hall. They quieted down, ready to listen to the inductees' acceptance speeches.

The program for the event paid tribute to the citizens of Canton: "Pro Football's Hall of Fame is more than a monument to the mighty men of the gridiron...more than a repository of their relics. It is a tribute to the selfless citizens of a town without a team who seized upon an idea and formed Football's Greatest Team to bring it to reality."

Each inductee was introduced by someone he had chosen–a friend, a teammate, or a coach–and presented with a bronze bust. After

"I come here to talk about Jim Thorpe....To me he was the greatest football player that it has ever been my pleasure to know and one of the greatest athletes the world has ever produced....His figure stands out as a beacon light to all young men aspiring to be great athletes and good citizens of these United States."
—*Henry Roemer, Canton businessman, presenting Jim Thorpe's award*

"When you stand in a place like this you must wonder to yourself, how did I get here? The first thought that occurs to me is that you have to have great luck [in order to compete in a game and in a league like this and to last long enough to get into this Hall of Fame]....Now when you get here you can't get here at 21, or 31, or 41, so you kind of qualify as a senior citizen. I think of some lines [from Shakespeare] that struck me once. 'The tumult and the shouting dies; the captains and the kings depart. Still stands that ancient sacrifice—a humble and contrite heart.'" —*Johnny "Blood" McNally*

On the big day, the Hall of Famers are honored with parades and award luncheons.

all the members had been enshrined, all the speeches had been made, and all the tears had been dried, the crowd settled back for—what else?—a football game! As the Cleveland Browns and the Pittsburgh Steelers took their places on the gridiron, all was right with the world in Canton. The game was the second in a series that continues today between the American Football Conference and the National Football Conference.

More Elbow Room—An Expanding Role

Erected in 1963, the original building that housed the Hall of Fame was 19,000 square feet. Since then there have been a number of major expansions—in 1971, 1978, and 1995. Together the expansions have increased the exhibition space to its current size of more than 82,000 square feet and five buildings. Without additional space, the growing amount of relics, players' shrines, and exhibits would have become quite crowded!

Since the Hall's doors opened, more than 6 million people have walked through them. In 1964 the Hall's first full year of being open, about 63,000 people wandered around the hallowed halls of football. Attendance reached a high of 330,000 in 1973, then leveled off to around 200,000 a year during the 1990s. Fans from every state have made the pilgrimage to football's holiest shrine, and as American football continues to become more popular overseas, visitors from 60 to 70 foreign nations have also come.

"Football's Greatest Weekend"

Many fans think football's greatest weekend happens during the Super Bowl. But not at the Hall of Fame. At the Hall Football's Greatest Weekend is the annual celebration for the induction of a new group of Hall of Famers. The event occurs in the summer, on either the last Sunday in July or the first Sunday in August, depending on when the NFL has scheduled the football preseason to begin.

Led by the Canton Chamber of Commerce, the festivities draw more than 200,000 outsiders as well as almost everybody in town. There are fashion shows, luncheons, a banquet honoring the inductees, and a parade through Canton. The two major events are the induction ceremonies and the preseason game between the American Football Conference and the National Football Conference. Millions watch the game and the highlights of the ceremony on TV.

The induction ceremonies usually take place on the steps of the Hall. Afterward the annual Hall of Fame game is played across the street at Fawcett Stadium. This Canton city high school stadium seats 22,375, with standing room for 1,500. Needless to say, every year sees a sellout crowd.

Bronko Nagurski was one of the first players to be inducted into the Hall of Fame.

The first Halll of Fame game was played in 1962, the year before the Hall of Fame opened. Each year different teams are selected on a rotating basis. The AFC-NFC series began in 1971 and over the next fourteen years all 28 NFL teams got to play. The NFL now has 30 teams, so a new rotation schedule will continue through 1999.

Visiting the Pro Football Hall of Fame

The Pro Football Hall of Fame is located a few miles west of downtown Canton, Ohio. Canton is about 58 miles south of Cleveland on Interstate Highway 77 at Exit 107-A. Interstate Highway 77 intersects many principal highways, such as Interstates 70, 76, and 80.

For the air traveler, the Akron-Canton airport is just a ten-minute drive from the Hall. The Hall can give you information on bus tours that are available.

The Football Hall of Fame is open every day of the year except Christmas. From Memorial Day through Labor Day its hours are 9 a.m. to 8 p.m. For the remainder of the year it is open from 9 a.m. to 5 p.m.

Parking is free but admission prices change. An adult ticket is under $10 and a child's is under $5. Family rates are available for under $25, and groups of ten or more and senior citizens receive reduced rates.

For further information, contact the Hall's Visitor Information Center at 330-456-8207, or write to 2121 George Halas Drive, NW, Canton, Ohio 44708.

Election Procedures

Any fan can nominate his or her favorite player just by writing a letter to the Hall of Fame. There are only a few requirements. Players must be retired for at least five years. Coaches must be retired, but there is no time limit. And owners, executives, and other contributors to the game do not have to be retired.

People who watch football for a living—sportswriters and broadcasters—decide who gets into the Hall. The Hall of Fame Board of Trustees selects one journalist for each city that has a team in the NFL. In 1995 there were 30 journalists. (New York City had two since there are two teams there.)

In addition to these 30 members, there are five at-large delegates. These are reporters who cover football nationally—not just in one or two cities. The final member is the president of the Pro Football Writers Association. That makes a total of 36.

Journalists are chosen as judges because they regularly see the players in action while covering the games. They are also chosen because as journalists they are supposed to be objective. Coaches, players, and owners are not judges because they might be prejudiced toward their own teams. The judges have to be fair to maintain the integrity of the Hall's induction process. And they are expected to take their responsibility very seriously.

How Are the Hall of Famers Picked?

Football's Hall of Fame election process is different from that of any other sport. For example, the journalists who select the Baseball Hall of Famers mail their decisions in. The football selectors do their judging in person. Each year they meet on the Saturday morning before the Super Bowl. They gather somewhere in the Super Bowl city to discuss and vote on that year's list of nominees.

The judges are expected to be objective, but they are not shy about promoting their favorite candidates. According to *Sports Illustrated* writer Michael Silver, "The debates over who is worthy can be provincial, political, personal, petty, and downright nasty."

When all the "selling and yelling" is over, a candidate needs a yes vote from at least 80 percent of the judges to be inducted into the Hall. That high percentage ensures a fair call for each nominee. No fewer than four and no more than seven are enshrined each summer.

In addition, a senior nominee is chosen by a special committee of five senior members of the Board of Selectors. The senior nominee is often a player whose career was over before the 36 regular judges could have seen him in action. He is selected to ensure that younger writers and broadcasters don't overlook the contributions of players they may not be familiar with. A senior nominee must have completed 70 percent of his career 25 years prior to the selection date. So a 1997 candidate would have to have finished 70 percent of his playing days by 1972.

Selectors are interested only in the candidate's pro football performance—not his college career or most of his activities off the field. Statistics and playing records are important, of course, but so are the contributions the individual has made to the game. Joe Namath, for instance, who was inducted into the Hall in 1985, had a good playing record with the New York Jets, but he made some enduring contributions to the game off the field as well. Just as important to the game was his signing with the American Football League for a huge salary. For the AFL to sign such an important player for so much money gave that league credibility. Three years after he was signed, Namath's Jets beat the NFL's Baltimore Colts in

Super Bowl III. That victory let the football world know the AFL teams were a force to be reckoned with. Both events helped bring about the merger of the AFL and the NFL. That merger in turn helped strengthen and solidify the sport and moved it toward its greatest era of growth and prosperity.

Players and coaches in the modern era must retire and players must wait five years before they can be considered for induction. But many players and coaches are expected to be inducted. Don Shula, former coach of the Baltimore Colts and Miami Dolphins, is probably a shoo-in for the honor, as are quarterbacks Joe Montana and Dan Marino, receiver Jerry Rice, and running backs Marcus Allen and Emmitt Smith.

Voting

Early in the morning on the day before the Super Bowl, the selectors have just a few hours to make their decisions. All voting for the Pro Football Hall of Fame is secret. The ballots are counted by a certified accounting firm to ensure secrecy and to make sure the results have not been tampered with. Secrecy is important to the judges as well as to the judging process. The judges are sportswriters whose jobs depend largely on getting good interviews. If a judge vetoed a hometown player and that got around, he or she would obviously be in big trouble at home. But worse, a writer might never get another important interview again.

The judges' first task is to discuss the senior nominee, who has already been selected. Next they cast their votes to narrow the list of candidates—which has been as high as 90—down to fourteen. They vote a simple yes or no on each candidate.

Each of the fourteen remaining nominees is discussed in order of position—offense and then defense one year, defense and then offense the next. After those discussions the selectors bring the list down to ten, and then to six. The final vote is on the remaining six, plus the senior nominee. The mission of the selectors is to choose no fewer than four and no more than seven to be enshrined in the Hall of Fame the following summer.

Each time a vote is cast, the accounting firm collects the ballots, counts them, and returns the verdicts to the judges. After the final vote the results are sealed in an envelope. No one but the accounting firm knows the results.

Announcing the Winners

At noon on the day before the Super Bowl, a press conference is scheduled at the stadium where the Super Bowl will be played. Just

ITEMS FOUND IN THE FOOTBALL HALL OF FAME

The Hall of Fame has thousands of relics from pro football's past and present. Here are a few, some of which are rather unusual:

- the blanket Jim Thorpe used to keep warm during the few moments he sat on the bench while playing for the Canton Bulldogs

- the worn-out equipment trunk of Ernie Nevers, used during his 112-day, 17,000-mile road trip in 1926, his rookie year with the Duluth Eskimos

- a bronze casting of Sammy Baugh's right hand—the hand that threw 1,693 complete passes

- a piece of the goalpost from the 1958 NFL championship game, called the greatest game ever played after going into eight minutes and fifteen seconds of overtime

- a pair of ice tongs that Red Grange used to deliver huge blocks of ice during his college summers; he said carrying all that heavy ice kept him in shape to play football

- a football-shaped trophy made from a piece of coal presented to the 1925 Pottsville Maroons by their loyal coal miner fans; the fans felt their team had been gypped out of the 1925 NFL championship title so they made the Maroons a worthy trophy

like at the Academy Awards, the sealed envelope is handed to the president of the Hall of Fame Board of Trustees. Before a crowd of fans he opens the envelope and pulls out the results. Then and only then do the judges—and everyone else—learn who has been judged worthy of entering the Football Hall of Fame.

Inside the Pro Football Hall of Fame

Driving up to the Pro Football Hall of Fame, you first see the 52-foot-high football-shaped dome pointing skyward. The dome rises up from the exhibition rotunda, the Hall's original building. Inside the rotunda you are greeted by a 7-foot bronze statue of Jim Thorpe, the greatest football player of all time. Standing tall beneath the dome, Thorpe is wearing a leather helmet and moleskin pants. This was the uniform at the turn of the century, when "Big Jim" played.

Then walk up the curving ramp that begins at Jim Thorpe's feet. Get ready to feast your eyes on thousands of priceless football treasures. There are uniforms, lockers, and equipment from the sport's earliest days. Special exhibits highlight achievements of players and teams or famous events. There's the Jim Thorpe/Canton Bulldogs display, showing football's greatest hero and the hometown team of the birthplace of pro football. There's also the jacket Thorpe wore when he competed in the 1912 Olympics.

There are exhibits showing the development of football over the years. "The Evolution of the Uniform" shows how uniforms have changed since the 1920s. Early uniforms included nose guards and ear guards but no helmets!

Other exhibits include:

- **Pro Football Today:** Outside the rotunda is the Pro Football Today display, honoring each of the current 30 NFL teams. Each display contains a team's helmet and history.

- **The Enshrinement Galleries:** The twin enshrinement galleries are housed in the outer rooms of the second and third buildings. Here, each member of the Hall is honored with a bronze bust, an "action" mural depicting a highlight in his career, and a brief biography. Special video presentations are located in the center hub of each gallery. The *Kickoff* series shows some of the players in action. In the *Legends of the Game* series you can listen to actual interviews with some of the Hall of Famers.

- **The Pro Football Photo Art Gallery:** Each year the Hall holds a contest for professional photographers who cover NFL games.

*A 7-foot bronze statue of Jim Thorpe
greets visitors to the Pro Football Hall of Fame.*

The Pro Football Photo Art Gallery, occupying the interior room of the second building, features the winning shots.

- **The Pro Football Adventure Room:** This exhibition inside the third building tells the story of the NFL's rival football leagues. Eight leagues challenged the NFL during its history, which began in 1920 in Canton. Major attention is given to AFL number four, which merged with the NFL in 1966. The Adventure Room includes an exhibit on the many teams that have played in the NFL. There are mementoes from the modern era, along with the video *16 Fantastic Finishes,* showing games with spectacular endings.

- **The Enshrinees Mementoes Room:** The fourth building, added in 1978, contains the Enshrinees Mementoes Room. Here each Hall of Famer is grouped with his team and honored again with a picture and some personal item. One of the teams included is the Green Bay Packers of the 1930s, with Arnie Herber, Clark Hinkle, and Don Hutson. There is a second exhibit of the 1960s Packers team, featuring Bart Starr, Jim Taylor, and Paul Hornung. The Cleveland Browns teams of the 1940s and 1950s, starring Otto Graham, Marion Motley, and Dante Lavelli, are included, and Johnny Unitas, Lenny Moore, and Raymond Berry are highlighted in the Baltimore Colts of the 1950s and 1960s. This room also holds the Top Twenty display, which shows the teams and

Each Hall of Famer has his own niche, with a bronze bust,
a short biography, and a mural showing some highlight of his career.

players with the best statistics in the league. This exhibit changes each week during the football season.

- **The Super Bowl Room:** Located in the fifth building, this room houses the Vince Lombardi Trophy, which is awarded to the winning Super Bowl team each year. You can also see replicas of the Super Bowl rings given to winning team members. Check out Bronko Nagurski's ring to see how big this Chicago Bears fullback was. The ring's diameter is the size of a half dollar! This area also contains just about every statistic for both individuals and teams ever compiled for the "Big Game." There are video summaries of each Super Bowl game, a list of its Most Valuable Players, a special exhibit on Hall of Famers who played in Super Bowls, and a huge collection of Super Bowl mementoes.

- **The GameDay Stadium:** Also located in the fifth building is the Hall's latest attraction, the GameDay Stadium. Here you can watch the many *100-Yard Universe* films in a two-sided rotating theater. First you watch the Locker Room Show to see how the teams prepare for a game. Then the seating area rotates 180 degrees to the Stadium Show, so you can watch a game in larger-than-life Cinemascope. The films run continuously throughout the day.

Also featured in the Hall, on the ground floor, is the NFL Films Theater, which shows a different NFL action movie every hour. A special exhibit honoring the contributions of African Americans to pro football and a salute to officials are found in this area. On this floor you can enjoy video monitors and interactive computer games, and visit the snack area and the museum store. Researchers and writers are invited to use the Hall's Research Center and Library.

The first football immortals, the Hall of Fame's 1963 charter members.
From left to right, in the back row are Sammy Baugh, Cal Hubbard,
Bronko Nagurski, George Halas, Red Grange, and Ernie Nevers. In the front row are
Dutch Clark, Curly Lambeau, Mel Hein, John "Blood" McNally, and Don Hutson.

Inductees

1979–1982

A TIGER ON THE FIELD

Dick Butkus once described how he wanted to be known as a tackle. "When I hit a guy," he said, "I wanted him to know who hit him without his ever having to look around and check a number. And I wanted him to know I'd be back. I wanted him to think about me instead of what he was supposed to be doing."

RICHARD MARVIN BUTKUS

1942–
Position: linebacker
Team: Chicago Bears
Inducted: 1979

As the middle linebacker of the Chicago Bears, Dick Butkus terrorized NFL quarterbacks and ballcarriers from 1965 to 1973. During his nine seasons with the Bears he performed in the Pro Bowl for eight of them and was All-NFL for seven. In 1970 the NFL coaches voted Butkus the first player they would choose if they were putting together a brand-new team.

At 6 feet 3 inches and 245 pounds, Butkus was a rib-cracking tackler and the most intimidating defender in pro football history. He popularized the middle linebacker position with his sneering, frenzied, all-consuming passion. Playing like a man possessed, he used his powerful body as a weapon to wreak havoc on opponents.

Butkus was born on December 9, 1942. He was one of nine children of Lithuanian immigrants. He grew up on the tough south side of Chicago. By the eighth grade Butkus had already decided on a pro football career, and he devoted his life to achieving that goal. He went to Chicago Vocational High School because it had a good football program. Then he chose the University of Illinois because it belonged to the Big Ten Conference.

His senior year, as captain of the team, Butkus led Illinois to the Big Ten title and a 17–7 victory over Washington in the 1964 Rose Bowl. Butkus was flooded with postseason honors: College Lineman of the Year, All-America team for the second time, Player of the Year, and third place for the Heisman Trophy—an unusual honor for a linebacker, since the Heisman usually goes to a quarterback or running back.

A first-round draft choice in 1965, Butkus joined his hometown team, the Chicago Bears. His contract for $200,000 was a record sum for a defensive player. In his first game, Butkus recorded 11 unassisted tackles. Five games later the team presented him with his first game ball for his outstanding performance. The rookie guided Chicago to victory in nine of its last eleven games. That season, he led the club in fumble recoveries and pass interceptions with 5 each.

After learning the Bears' complicated defensive strategies, Butkus

DICK BUTKUS			
Interceptions	22	**Average Gain**	7.5
Yards	166	**Touchdowns**	0

SIDESWIPING TACKLES

It seems that almost all of Dick Butkus's opponents have a story to tell about his sideswiping tackles. In a 1967 game Butkus targeted St. Louis Cardinals running back Johnny Roland. Butkus tackled Roland so hard that he shattered Roland's face mask and gave the Cardinal a puffy lip.

In a 1969 game Butkus tackled Detroit Lions tight end Charlie Sanders. During the tackle, he poked his fingers through Sanders's face mask and into his eyes. During that game, the Lions accused Butkus of starting three fights. Butkus was even accused of biting a referee during an on-field skirmish.

Another story involves the Baltimore Colts. Following a game with the Bears, the Colts were on their way to the airport in the team bus. When the bus stopped short in traffic, the vehicle behind the bus smashed into its rear end. The dazed Colts looked at one another, then said together: "Butkus!"

became a superb pass defender, making 22 career interceptions. He was also a master at causing fumbles by stripping the ball from an opponent's grasp–then he would recover the loose ball. Butkus was so fast with his hands that he seemed to tackle the runner and search him for the ball at the same time. During his career, Butkus recovered 25 opponents' fumbles, an NFL record for the time.

At middle linebacker, Butkus acted as the "quarterback" of the defense. He controlled the game from his position. He had a nose for the ball–an instinct for being in the right place at the right time to break up a play or to tackle a ballcarrier. And he was a savage tackler. In a 1969 game against Pittsburgh, Butkus made 15 solo tackles, assisted on 10 others, and scored a 2-point safety. During his nine-year career, he averaged 12.6 tackles a game. In the 1990s a player had a terrific game if he had 10.

In 1973 an injured knee caused Butkus to retire. He was inducted into the Pro Football Hall of Fame in 1979. An annual award honoring outstanding college linebackers is named after him.

Chicago Bears linebacker Dick Butkus (51) moves in on the opposition runner.

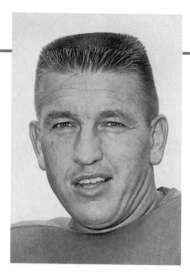

JOHN CONSTANTINE UNITAS

1933–
Position: quarterback
Teams: Baltimore Colts, San Diego Chargers
Inducted: 1979

COOL "MR. CLUTCH"

Johnny Unitas had a reputation for being calm under pressure. That's why he was nicknamed "Mr. Clutch" and why he was the spark behind so many last-minute wins.

In 1957 Unitas's 52-yard touchdown pass beat the Redskins in the last 25 seconds of a game. Three years later he defeated the Lions with a 38-yard touchdown pass with only fourteen seconds remaining. In the 1961 Pro Bowl he gave the West a 31–30 win in the final ten seconds. And Unitas also beat the Rams with a touchdown pass at the last moment in the 1962 season opener.

The list of come-from-behind victories goes on. There were few teams who didn't suffer because of Unitas's patience and steady arm.

The only thing Johnny Unitas wanted to be when he was growing up in Pittsburgh, Pennsylvania, was a pro football player. Reaching that goal wasn't easy, but when Unitas finally made it, he became one of the greatest quarterbacks of all time.

When he retired, Unitas held most major records for quarterbacks, including career passing yardage (40,239) and touchdown passes (290). But he was more than an accurate passer. "What made Johnny great," said another quarterback, "[was] the willingness to gamble and take chances." To Unitas, what he did wasn't so risky: "When you know what you're doing, you don't get intercepted."

Unitas had a tough road before he reached the pros. He was born on May 7, 1933. His father died when he was five. To help his mother, Unitas shoveled coal into bins for 75 cents per ton. He also worked on construction gangs during summers when he was in high school.

The hard work made Unitas strong, but he was thin. In his senior year he was 6 feet tall but weighed only 145 pounds. That wasn't big enough to get a scholarship to Notre Dame or any of the Big Ten Conference schools he wanted to play for. Instead, Unitas went to the University of Louisville.

Louisville didn't have a great team, but Unitas played well enough to be noticed. The Pittsburgh Steelers drafted him in the ninth round of the 1955 draft, but then they let him go before the season began. The Steelers coach said he thought Unitas would never be smart enough to call plays for a pro team.

Unitas then signed with the semipro Bloomfield Rams for $6 a game. Since he had a wife and a young child to support, he also worked a construction job, getting up at four in the morning. But a fan noticed Unitas's quarterbacking ability when he was with Bloomfield and wrote to the Baltimore Colts about him. The Colts needed a backup quarterback, so Coach Weeb Ewbank did some checking. When he received good reports on Unitas, Ewbank signed

JOHNNY UNITAS			
Passing Attempts	5,186	Average Pass Gain	7.76
Passing Completions	2,830	Touchdown Passes	290
Passing Percentage	54.6	Passes Intercepted	253
Passing Yards	40,239		

THE GREATEST GAME EVER PLAYED

In 1958 Johnny Unitas led the Colts in what some people call the greatest game ever played. It was a 23–17 overtime win over the New York Giants for the NFL championship. Baltimore was leading 14–3 early in the game, but with two minutes left to play, New York went ahead 17–14. Unitas started the Colts on a long march, completing 4 of 7 passes. A Baltimore field goal tied the score.

New York won the toss and elected to receive to open the first-ever overtime period in an NFL championship game. The Giants hoped to score the sudden death touchdown before the Colts even touched the ball. But Baltimore gained possession at its own 20-yard line.

Ten plays and 72 yards later, Unitas had directed the Colts to the Giants 8-yard line. He knew New York would be expecting a field goal attempt or a safe ground play, so he did something daring. He threw a pass, connecting with tight end Jim Mutscheller at the 1-yard line.

On the next play, fullback Alan Ameche rolled into the end zone to give the Colts a 23–17 win. Unitas explained later that he'd rather win an important game by a touchdown than a field goal.

Unitas to a $7,000 contract.

Unitas got his first chance to play pro football in the fourth game of the 1956 season. Starting Colts quarterback George Shaw had been injured in a game against the Chicago Bears, so Unitas finally got called in. His very first pass in that game was intercepted and returned for a touchdown, but his long line of hard luck ended there. From that point on, his career as a pro quarterback took off. His 55.6 pass completion percentage was the highest ever for an NFL rookie at that time.

Unitas filled the books with records and awards, but perhaps his most amazing accomplishment was throwing at least 1 touchdown pass per game over a four-year period. The streak started late in his rookie year and continued for a record 47 consecutive games. Each season from 1957 through 1960, Unitas led the league in touchdown passes.

Unitas's talent won him NFL Player of the Year honors in 1959, 1964, and 1967. He also led the Colts to the 1958 and 1959 NFL championships and helped his team win Super Bowl V in 1971. In ten Pro Bowl Games, he was named the MVP three times.

Unitas spent his last season, 1973, with the San Diego Chargers. When he retired, he held the record for the most games with more than 300 yards passing (26), as well as most pass attempts (5,186) and completions (2,830). Unitas was also known as a good runner, and he finished his career with 450 rushing attempts for 1,777 yards and 13 touchdowns.

The Pro Football Hall of Fame welcomed Unitas in 1979. His determination to be a pro player had definitely paid off.

Baltimore Colts quarterback Johnny Unitas is considered one of football's greatest passers.

1979–1982

ROBERT LEWIS LILLY

1939–
Position: defensive tackle
Team: Dallas Cowboys
Inducted: 1980

Known as "Mr. Cowboy," Bob Lilly was the key man in the Dallas Cowboys' fabled "Doomsday Defense." Lilly was feared whether he was rushing a scrambling quarterback or crunching a running back. Amazingly, he often did his work with the opposition's guard, center, and sometimes fullback hanging off him. Even triple-teamed, Lilly was rarely stopped.

Lilly started his fourteen-season career as a defensive end, then moved to tackle after his second season. He was selected for eleven Pro Bowls and was a consensus All-NFL choice for six straight years, from 1964 through 1969, then again in 1971 and 1972. Lilly played in 196 consecutive regular-season games with the Cowboys—a team record. In the postseason, he appeared in five NFL championship games and two Super Bowls.

Lilly was born on July 26, 1939, about 150 miles northwest of Dallas in the rural town of Olney, Texas. Economics forced the family to move to Pendleton, Oregon, Lilly's senior year in high school. Lilly was All-State in football and basketball. He attended Texas Christian University, where he was a consensus All-America tackle. In 1961 he was picked by Dallas as the team's first-ever draft choice.

At defensive end, Lilly was good enough to win Rookie of the Year honors. But when Coach Tom Landry shifted him inside to defensive right tackle, Lilly blossomed into a superstar. "An end has more responsibility as far as containing plays. A tackle can just go for the football," said Landry. "Because of Bob's great recovery ability, he can charge straight ahead and not worry about a definite responsibility on every play. We have been able to more or less turn him loose and let him have more freedom, and this makes Bob a better player."

"Most good pass rushing comes from outside," said George Allen, former coach of the L.A. Rams and the Washington Redskins. "But some top players are able to provide it from inside. Lilly was one who did. He made plays all over the field."

Most defensive linemen don't usually score touchdowns, but Lilly did. He made 4 of them—1 on an interception return and 3 on fumble returns. Altogether, he recovered 16 fumbles during his career.

Lilly helped make the Cowboys one of the top teams in the NFL, but some critics said the team couldn't win the big games. The Cowboys lost two NFL championship games in the late 1960s; a few

A NOT-SO-MEAN MACHINE

At 6 feet 5 inches and 260 pounds, Bob Lilly was a tower of strength. "There isn't any use arguing with him if he gets hold of your jersey," said Dolphins quarterback Bob Griese after Super Bowl VI. "You just fall wherever Lilly wants." Lilly had just sacked Griese for a stunning 29-yard loss, the biggest loss on a sack in Super Bowl history. Lilly and the rest of the Doomsday Defense held the Dolphins to just one field goal that day—the first time a team had failed to score a touchdown in a Super Bowl.

Lilly, though a terror on the field, wasn't really a mean player. "Being mean just wasn't his style," explained Cowboys coach Ernie Stautner. "He tried it, but being roughhouse just didn't work for him. He just couldn't do it. But you can't argue with the results he got being the way he was."

HELPING HANDS

Three men helped shape Bob Lilly's career. The first was his father, Buster, who was crippled in an accident when he was seventeen. "From the time I was five years old, my father worked with me to become a football player. We worked every day," Lilly said. "He couldn't run or anything, but he could pass the ball to me. He went to every home game I played in high school, college, and with the Cowboys until he died the year we went to our first Super Bowl. I'll never forget what he did for me."

Lilly's second mentor was Abe Martin, his college coach. "He was sort of like a father away from home," Lilly explained. "If you had any problems with school or anything else, he'd come by and talk, and it helped."

Finally, there was his Dallas coach, Tom Landry. As a struggling rookie, Lilly was under a lot of pressure to perform, and he especially appreciated Landry's understanding then. "Tom never faltered from his ideals and his goals, and he instilled that in all of us," Lilly attested.

years later, they lost Super Bowl V 16–13 to the Baltimore Colts. In the dramatic final second, Lilly threw his helmet 40 yards in a rage. "If we were beaten by 40 points, you could just say we were whipped. But we had every opportunity to win," said Lilly.

The next year the Cowboys silenced their critics when they beat Miami 24–3 in Super Bowl VI. Winning that game was Lilly's greatest pro football thrill.

Two years later, in 1974, Lilly was told that a neck injury could do permanent damage, and he retired at the end of that season. The first year he was eligible, Lilly was voted into the Pro Football Hall of Fame.

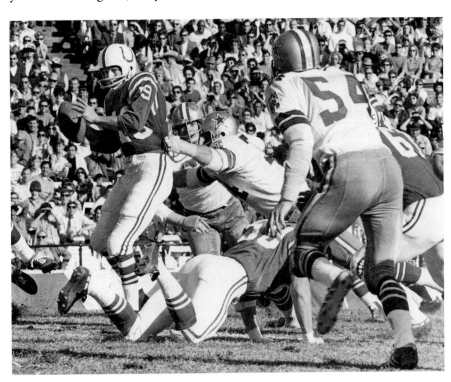

As Johnny Unitas gets ready to throw, Dallas Cowboys defensive tackle Bob Lilly grabs his jersey to bring him down.

JAMES EDWIN OTTO

1938–
Position: center
Team: Oakland Raiders
Inducted: 1980

Almost no one but Jim Otto thought he'd make the pros, and when he did make it, no one thought he'd last. But not only did Otto last, playing fifteen years with the Oakland Raiders, he also excelled at center, one of the toughest positions in football. When Otto retired, he was the most honored offensive lineman in pro football.

Otto was famous for his toughness and his speed off the line of scrimmage. Literally using his head as a weapon, Otto wore out four helmets a year. And like all the greats, Otto gave his maximum effort on the field.

Otto's amazing dedication to football started in Wausau, Wisconsin, where he was born on January 5, 1938. Otto was a second team All-Wisconsin center at his high school and then he headed to the University of Miami to play college ball. Otto played middle linebacker at Miami and set a school record for career tackles. Center, however, was his favorite spot. But at 6 feet 2 inches and 205 pounds, Otto was considered too small for pro football. When he graduated from Miami in 1960, not one NFL team drafted him or offered him a free agent contract.

Otto was finally picked by the Raiders, of the newly formed American Football League. The odds of the Raiders or the AFL surviving weren't great, but this was Otto's only chance to play pro football, and he took it.

Otto reported to the Raiders training camp with two small suitcases, two pairs of football shoes, a helmet, and an intense desire to stay. This desire took over immediately. At the start of camp, he was a skinny 210-pounder. By the end of his rookie season, he had built himself up to 240 pounds. At the height of his career he reached 260 pounds.

In the pros, Otto always played center. Usually buried under a pile of linemen, centers don't often get much attention. Otto, however, did stand out, partly because of his unusual uniform number, *00,* but mostly because he played his position so well. At the end of Otto's rookie year, the NFL teams that had previously ignored him tried to convince him to leave the Raiders. But Otto stayed in Oakland.

The Raiders lost nineteen straight games during Otto's second and third seasons. Then in 1963, under new coach Al Davis, the

A NO-ERROR EXAMPLE

Jim Otto was called the ultimate team leader. He was a quiet player who inspired his teammates because he always performed at his peak. "He loved to win. He led by example, and he set the tempo," said teammate George Blanda. "He gave the Raiders an image of hard discipline, hard work, and hard-nosed football."

The Raiders gave Otto the additional assignment of calling blocking signals for the offensive line. In one season the Raiders ran about 650 plays. It was estimated that, amazingly, Otto made only about four errors during all of those plays. "We don't make many mental errors, and Otto is the main reason," said offensive line coach Ollie Spencer.

STAND BY YOUR LEAGUE

The early days of the AFL were tough for dedicated players like Jim Otto. In the beginning, the AFL could offer only poor practice facilities and substandard travel accommodations. "Once, in Boston," Otto said "a Boy Scout troop chased us off the practice field we had picked." The Raiders were paid low salaries and had low turnouts at their games. What was more, they were shuffled from stadium to stadium like unwanted orphans during their first seven years.

Otto could have left after his first year. The NFL teams who had rejected him were offering him loads of money to quit the Raiders. "What are you waiting for?" one NFL owner asked him. "You'll make much more money with us." But Otto was loyal to the league and to the team that had given him the opportunity to play pro ball.

team bounced back with a 10–4 record. For the rest of Otto's career, Oakland had the best win-loss record in pro football. In his fifteen seasons the Raiders won seven division titles and the 1967 AFL championship.

Throughout this period, the Raiders had a well-balanced team, but their offensive line was outstanding. Otto was the anchor on their offense. A superior blocker, he often went after opposition players who were beyond the small area a center usually handled.

From 1960 to 1969 Otto was an AFL All-Pro every year—the only All-AFL center in the league's history. Then for the next three years, he was All-AFC. He played in each of the AFL's nine All-Star Games and the first three AFC-NFC Pro Bowl Games.

Otto might have played even longer than fifteen seasons if not for injuries. He constantly battled bone chips in his elbow, suffered ten broken noses, a broken jaw, numerous concussions, dislocated fingers, a dislocated knee, and a pinched neck nerve. He had three operations on his left knee and six on his right. The final operation in 1974 left him with an artificial right knee.

The injuries finally did Otto in. Early in the 1975 preseason he left a game and didn't return. "I didn't have to quit," he said. "I thought I played well, but not well enough to play with the Raiders an entire season. I know I have to quit when I am still on top."

The experts who once thought Otto couldn't play pro football now realized how great he had become. In 1980, the first year he was eligible, Otto was the first Raider inducted into the Hall of Fame.

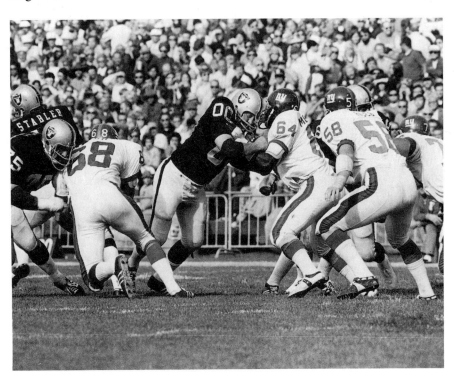

Jim Otto (00) was a top center for the Oakland Raiders for fifteen seasons.

I CANNOT TELL A LIE

For pro football fans, it's a good thing that Willie Davis disobeyed his mother. Growing up in Texarkana, Arkansas, Davis was one of three children raised in a single-parent home by their mother, Nodie. Nodie pleaded with Davis not to play football. "My mother was afraid I would get hurt," he remembered.

Davis played anyway, without his mother's knowing. "I played my first two high school games without her knowing I was on the varsity," he said. "The only reason she found out was that our third game was on the road, and there was no way I could stay out that late without her knowing what was going on."

WILLIE DAVIS

1934–
Position: defensive end
Teams: Cleveland Browns, Green Bay Packers
Inducted: 1981

Willie Davis was one of the cornerstones of the great Green Bay Packers defense during the 1960s. It was the second era of glory for the Packers, this time under Vince Lombardi. Davis had what Lombardi considered the most important qualities for a successful lineman: speed, agility, and size. "Give a man any two of those dimensions, and he'll do okay," Lombardi said. "Give him all three, and he'll be a great football player."

Willie Davis had all three of these qualities and more. Playing both the run and the pass, he was considered a model for the modern-day defensive end. Linemen don't often capture the headlines. Fighting off blocks or rushing the passer isn't as glamorous as throwing a long bomb or rushing for 100 yards per game. Davis, however, had big-play performances year after year.

Colliding with other linemen at the line of scrimmage on every play is rough work. Defensive linemen need strong legs to overpower their opponents or to spin and fake moves. Most defensive linemen are huge, weighing up to 300 pounds. At 6 feet 3 inches and 245 pounds, Davis was not the biggest or even the strongest defensive end. But he was one of the quickest.

Davis used his speed to win All-Pro honors five times, in 1962 and from 1964 to 1967. He also played in five Pro Bowls and helped the Packers win five NFL championships and two Super Bowls. By the end of his twelve-year career, he had recovered 21 fumbles—an all-time Packers record.

Davis was born on July 24, 1934, in Lisbon Louisiana. He grew up in Texarkana, Arkansas, and in high school he starred in football, basketball, and baseball. At Grambling State University, Davis was the football team's captain for two years and an National Association of Intercollegiate Athletics All-America player.

Despite his college success, the Cleveland Browns didn't pick Davis until the seventeenth round of the 1956 draft. Before joining the Browns, he served two years in the Army. Returning to the Browns in 1958, Davis played both offense and defense until 1960, when he was traded to Green Bay. Lombardi put Davis at defensive end, where he excelled for a decade.

In 1961 Green Bay won its first NFL title since 1944. An exceptional defense was responsible for the shutout in the Packers' 37–0

GETTING DOWN TO BUSINESS

Willie Davis's trade from Cleveland to Green Bay was a turning point in his entire life, not just in his career. "I had been working my way up in Cleveland, and suddenly I was gone," he said. "I realized how frustrating it would be when I couldn't play football and would have to face the world with a reduced salary and no talents."

Davis decided to make sure he'd have the talents he'd need to survive. He had been an industrial arts major at Grambling State University and, in 1968, he earned a master's degree in business from the University of Chicago. After that he had dozens of job offers.

Davis turned down several NFL assistant coaching jobs and even a head coaching job at Harvard. He felt it was better for African American kids to "remember me as a player who moved on to success in business." Two years before he retired from football, he entered the Schlitz Brewing Company management training program. After he retired from football in 1970, he took over the company's L.A. distributorship. He was successful in many business ventures, including part-ownership of a school supply company.

win over the New York Giants. Davis, however, was one of the few Packers who did not make any All-NFL listing that year. He made no bones about his anger. "I still feel that I deserved All-League recognition," he said.

Davis once said, "I want to be recognized as the best, and that will always be in my thinking." When he was told he had been inducted into the Pro Football Hall of Fame in 1981, he said, "I think back on Coach Lombardi's comments about 'earned success.' [This] is an honor that I also feel I earned."

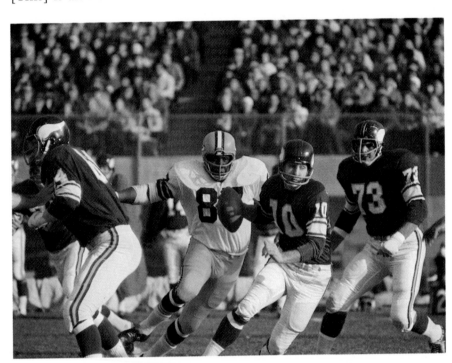

Green Bay Packer defensive end, Willie Davis (87), chases Fran Tarkenton (10), Minnesota Vikings quarterback.

MERLIN JAY OLSEN

1940–
Position: defensive tackle
Team: Los Angeles Rams
Inducted: 1982

Merlin Olsen was the perfect defensive lineman—a combination of size, spirit and brains. "He was calculating and collected, one of the most intelligent men ever to play the game," said George Allen, Olsen's coach. "He knew what was going on at all times and took advantage of every weakness the opposition had and every mistake that was made."

The Rams' first-round draft pick in 1962, Olsen was an instant hit in Los Angeles. He quickly became a key man in one of football's all-time best defensive lines: Rosey Grier at right tackle, Lamar Lundy at right end, David "Deacon" Jones at left end, and Olsen on left tackle. This defensive quartet, known as "the Fearsome Foursome," dominated football from 1966 to 1970.

In his fifteen-year pro career, Olsen was named to the Pro Bowl squad fourteen times, missing only his last season. No player has been in more Pro Bowl Games. During his career, Olsen helped the Rams win six division titles. Olsen was named the Rams MVP in 1970 and 1972, their outstanding defensive lineman four times, and was voted to their all-time team. He finished his career as the Rams' all-time leader in tackles, with 915.

Olsen was 6 feet 5 inches and 270 pounds. His brawn didn't come from lifting weights. Instead, he said he got his size and strength from doing chores as a youngster in Logan, Utah, where he was born on September 14, 1940. When he entered high school, Olsen weighed over 200 pounds.

At Utah State University, Olsen was All-America twice and won the 1961 Outland Trophy as the nation's best collegiate interior lineman. He was equally gifted off the playing field, earning Phi Beta Kappa honors.

Olsen was tough and was never afraid to throw himself into the action. However, in his rookie year with the Rams, he realized that sheer strength wasn't as important in the pros as it had been in college. Headwork counted too. "A good defensive man has to be part charging buffalo and part ballet dancer. And he has to know when to be which," Olsen once said. "He must keep his emotions in control and have the ability to concentrate."

Since they both played on the left side of the line, Olsen and Deacon Jones worked together closely. Jones was actually partly

PLAYING WITH PRIDE

Football has always been a rough game. "They don't call the middle of the line 'the pit' for nothing," Merlin Olsen once said. "We really do get like animals, trying to claw one another apart in there…. We get so bruised and battered and tired, we sometimes wind up playing in a sort of coma. By the end of the first half your instincts have taken over. By the end of the game, you're an animal."

But Olsen never thought a player had to hate his opponents in order to get in the right emotional state to beat them. "How can you feel antagonistic toward someone who is great in the profession you have chosen for yourself?" Olsen said. "If you are motivated by pride and the desire to win, you will want to dominate your opponent, but that is a lot better thing on which to tie your success than hatred."

"DEAC" AND "OLE" SIDE BY SIDE

Merlin Olsen and Deacon Jones played side by side for ten years and were good friends off the field. In many ways they were different. Jones was a southern-born African American; Olsen was a Mormon from Utah. Jones was rambunctious and spectacular; Olsen was quiet and steady. While Jones was an instinctive and enthusiastic player, Olsen was more methodical.

Jones was one of pro football's most famous sack men, but Olsen made some of the Deacon's most thrilling plays possible. "He knew what to expect from me; and I, from him," said Olsen. "He was quicker than I. That meant that sometimes he would be leaving some territory uncovered. I accepted the responsibility of covering that territory. I'd see him give a head fake and go hard outside, and I knew I had to take the inside."

"They used to flip-flop positions at times and work highly successful stunts, alternating on the pass rush and keeping the opposition off balance," said Rams coach George Allen."

"I think one of the reasons that Deacon and I played so well together was that we were close personally," said Olsen.

responsible for Olsen's playing defense. When Olsen arrived at his first training camp, the offensive and defensive coaches both wanted him. At first they put him at guard, working against Jones, but on one play Jones nearly ripped off the rookie's head. The coaches decided Olsen fit in better on defense, working *with* Jones instead of opposite him.

By 1964, the Fearsome Foursome defensive unit was in place. Olsen's responsibility was helping to mesh all four talents into one unit. By the late 1960s Olsen was the only original member left. As younger, less experienced players replaced the other three, Olsen was the glue that held the line together. However, the new players were more conservative than the former players, giving Olsen a chance to take risks after so many years of being the rock.

Between 1962 and 1976, Olsen played in 198 consecutive games. He was named a member of the All-Pro squad for the decade of the 1960s and received the 1974 Maxwell Club of Philadelphia NFL Player of the Year Award—a top honor for any player. In 1982, the first year he was eligible, Olsen was inducted into the Pro Football Hall of Fame.

L.A. Rams defensive tackle Merlin Olsen (74) dumps an opposition quarterback with a shirt tackle.

ROBERT YALE LARY

1926–1986
Positions: safety, punter
Team: Detroit Lions
Inducted: 1979

His soaring long-distance kicks made Yale Lary one of the best punters in pro football history. Lary was born on November 24, 1930. He attended Texas A&M, where he was a two-sport star before signing with the Detroit Lions in 1952. At first he was slotted as an offensive back, but that didn't work. So Coach Buddy Parker put him on defense. His main job was right safety. It was exactly right for Lary, and he helped lead the Lions to the championship title his first two seasons and again in 1957.

The Army interrupted Lary's football career for two years. In 1956 he returned to the Lions, playing with them through 1964. His defensive skills got the 5-foot 11-inch, 189-pound Lary on four All-NFL teams and in nine Pro Bowl Games. He racked up 50 career interceptions, the fifth-best record at the time he retired in 1965. He also returned 126 punts for 758 yards and 3 touchdowns.

Lary is best remembered for his kicking skills. His opponents averaged less than 1 yard per return on his kicks. He punted 503 times for an average of 44.3 yards per kick—second only to Sammy Baugh's 45.1 average at the time. In 1963 Lary's 48.9-yard average was the highest single-season average after Baugh's 51.4, which was posted in 1940. Lary led the league in punting three times.

In 1979, Yale Lary became only the fifth defensive back to be inducted into the Pro Football Hall of Fame.

YALE LARY			
Interceptions	50	Average Gain	15.7
Yards	787	Touchdowns	2

RONALD JACK MIX

1938–
Position: offensive tackle
Teams: Los Angeles Chargers, San Diego Chargers, Oakland Raiders
Inducted: 1979

It wasn't until Ron Mix had played pro football for a couple of years that he actually decided he liked it. Mix, an intelligent man, said he hated the game in high school and college, but he knew he was good at it. In fact, he was better than good. "The Intellectual Assassin" was one of the best offensive tackles in the history of the American Football League. Mix was the second player from the AFL and only the sixth offensive lineman to be elected to the Pro Football Hall of Fame in 1979.

In 1960, when Mix entered pro football, the AFL and the NFL were bitter enemies. The two leagues were often competing in many of the same cities and usually for the same players. Mix was the first-round draft choice of the NFL Baltimore Colts, but instead he chose to sign with the AFL Los Angeles Chargers. The next year, the club moved to San Diego.

Mix stood 6 feet 4 inches tall and weighed 255 pounds, with broad shoulders and a narrow waist. His body made Mix ideal for the tackle position, and he was considered the strongest offensive lineman of his era. Fast and smart, Mix had only two holding penalties called on him in ten years. He was a crunching run blocker, and it was almost impossible to get around him as he protected the passer.

Mix was born on March 10, 1938, in Los Angeles, California. At 5 feet 5 inches and 115 pounds, he made the high school football team his sophomore year. By his senior year, he had grown to 6 feet and weighed 155 pounds. He did well enough as a receiver to win a football scholarship to the University of Southern California.

Because of a slight vision problem, Mix was moved from end to tackle in college. He began wearing contact lenses to improve his sight, and he started lifting weights to build up his body until he weighed 250 pounds. In his senior year he was co-captain of the team and earned All-America honors.

Mix wound up earning universal recognition as one of the best tackles to play the game. For eight of nine seasons he was an All-AFL choice. He played in five of the first six AFL championship games and was on the winning team in 1963. When the Hall of Fame picked the All-Time AFL team, Mix was chosen by unanimous vote.

HERBERT A. ADDERLEY

1939–
Position: cornerback
Teams: Green Bay Packers, Dallas Cowboys
Inducted: 1980

Herb Adderley had the perfect attitude for a cornerback: He loved to gamble on the field. Positioned in the defensive backfield, the cornerback's main job is to prevent the receiver from catching a pass. Adderley, though, wasn't content just to stop a reception—he wanted the ball himself. "If I can see the football and feel something happening ahead of time, I go for it," he said.

In twelve pro seasons Adderley snared 48 interceptions and returned 7 for touchdowns. He was also an excellent kickoff returner and once returned a kickoff 103 yards. Adderley's speed and quick reflexes made him a valuable asset to his teams.

Adderley was born on June 8, 1939, in Philadelphia, Pennsylvania. He attended Michigan State University, where he majored in physical education. An All–Big Ten running back, he was Green Bay's number one draft choice in 1961. He came to be known as a big-play star–someone who could turn defeat into victory.

As a Packer Adderley was All-NFL five times and played in five straight Pro Bowls from 1963 through 1967. He was an important part of the Green Bay teams that won the first two Super Bowls. In Super Bowl II he returned an interception 60 yards for a touchdown

In 1970 Green Bay traded Adderley to Dallas for two players. The Cowboys used a more complicated defense than the Packers did. In Dallas one side of the defense played man-to-man, and the other played in a zone. The alignment changed depending on how the offense was set up. As a result Adderley became more of a team player, forming a powerful combination with right cornerback Mel Renfro.

In Adderley's first year with Dallas, the 6-foot 1-inch, 200-pound speedster allowed only 1 touchdown reception and the Cowboys reached the Super Bowl. The next season, Adderley gave up only 3 touchdowns and picked off 6 interceptions. Dallas once again reached the Super Bowl and this time won, giving Adderley his third championship ring. In 1980 he was inducted into the Pro Football Hall of Fame.

HERB ADDERLEY			
Interceptions	48	Average Gain	21.8
Yards	1,045	Touchdowns	7

DAVID "DEACON" JONES

1938–
Position: defensive end
Teams: Los Angeles Rams, San Diego Chargers, Washington Redskins
Inducted: 1980

Deacon Jones was a different kind of defensive end. The way he played made the crowds watch him as much as they did the quarterback. Jones was one of the first defenders to go from sideline to sideline on every play. "It used to be that the big defensive linemen just sat in one place and waited for the play to come to them," he said. "But mobility is what makes a football player exciting, so I make myself exciting."

To aid his mobility as a pass rusher, "the Secretary of Defense" came up with the "head slap," which was later outlawed. At the snap, he would slap the blocker's helmet to distract him. That gave him time to get the extra step needed to break free.

From the beginning of his pro football career, Jones was determined to grab as much attention as he could. When he signed with the Rams in 1961, he listed his name as *Deacon*, rather than *David*, because he thought people would better remember it.

Jones came up with the term *sack*, which is commonly used to describe tackling the quarterback behind the line of scrimmage. "Like, you know, you sack a city—you devastate it." And the 6-foot 5-inch, 260-pound Jones was a master sacker. In 1967 Jones was credited with 26 sacks and the next year he had 28 (although sacks were not counted as an official statistic until 1982).

Despite Jones's description of football as "a game of civilized violence," he was a clean player. He once injured his ankle to avoid hitting a quarterback who had just released the ball. He declared, "If you play the game right, you can protect yourself from physical harm." In his case that was true. He played fourteen seasons without a "zipper," or stitches, and missed only three out of 196 games.

During Jones's eleven years with L.A., the Rams had the top defensive team in the NFL. Jones was part of their famous "Fearsome Foursome" front line. But it was a fluke that he was even drafted. Jones was born in Eatonville, Florida, on December 9, 1938. He played average high school football but made All-Conference tackle and Most Valuable Lineman at South Carolina State as a sophomore in 1958. He wound up at Mississippi Vocational in 1960, just in time to be spotted by two Rams scouts. They were looking at some films of a

defensive back when they realized a defensive lineman was outrunning the defensive back. That lineman was Jones.

After he left the Rams in 1971, Jones played two seasons with the San Diego Chargers. His last season, 1974, was spent with the Washington Redskins. He made All-League teams six straight years, from 1965 through 1970, and he played in eight Pro Bowls. Twice he was named the NFL's Outstanding Defensive Player by his teammates. Then in 1980 he received his greatest professional honor: a niche in the Pro Football Hall of Fame.

MORRIS "RED" BADGRO

1902–
Position: end
Teams: New York Yankees, New York Giants, Brooklyn Dodgers
Inducted: 1981

It took Red Badgro 45 years to be inducted into the Pro Football Hall of Fame. Although he was always outstanding on the field, he was often overlooked because he was so modest off the field. He was so modest that he didn't even keep a scrapbook.

When Badgro played, the game of football was quite different than it is today. Many players were used on both offense and defense and played the whole 60 minutes of a game. Today players specialize in one position and are rarely on the field for a whole game.

Playing two-way end, Badgro was a powerful tackle on defense, a stonewall blocker on offense, and a talented receiver. His catches were often a major factor in his team's victory. In 1934 he tied for the NFL individual pass catching title with 16 receptions. This was a significant number in those days. This was before the age of high-scoring offensive players, when football was more of a running sport than it is today.

Badgro was born on December 1, 1902, in Orilla, Washington. In high school he lettered in basketball, baseball, and football. The University of Southern California awarded him a basketball scholarship in 1921, but he wound up starring in baseball and football as well. His senior year at USC he was selected as an All-America honorable mention in football.

In 1927 the 6-foot, 190-pounder signed with the New York Yankees. Around midseason the team went into a slump, and the rookie left to play baseball for the St. Louis Browns. But Badgro found he missed football, and in 1930 he joined the New York Giants.

During his six-year career with the Giants, Badgro was named to the All-NFL team from 1931 to 1934. In the NFL's first championship game between Eastern and Western division winners, he scored the first touchdown.

In 1981, at age 78, Badgro was finally recognized for his outstanding play so many years before when he was inducted into the Pro Football Hall of Fame.

RED BADGRO			
Pass Receptions	48	Average Gain	16.3
Pass Receiving Yards	784	Touchdowns	6

GEORGE FREDERICK BLANDA

1927–
Positions: quarterback, placekicker
Teams: Chicago Bears, Houston Oilers, Oakland Raiders
Inducted: 1981

At an age when most players have long since left the gridiron, George Blanda was still thrilling football fans. In 1970 the 43-year-old Blanda won or tied five straight games for the Oakland Raiders by throwing for touchdowns

or kicking field goals and extra points; he was named Male Athlete of the Year and the American Football League Player of the Year.

That season was just one highlight in Blanda's 26-year career, the longest of any pro football player. As a quarterback he threw 4,007 passes for 26,920 yards and 236 touchdowns. As a placekicker he kicked 943 extra points and 335 field goals for a total of 1,948 points. Combined with the 9 touchdowns he scored as a quarterback, Blanda wound up with a record total of 2,002 points—303 more than the runner-up, Jan Stenerud

Blanda was born on September 17, 1927, in Youngwood, Pennsylvania, the son of a coal miner. He attended the University of Kentucky, where Coach George Halas of the Chicago Bears noticed him. Blanda signed with the Bears in 1949, but he was only used as a regular for two seasons there. When Chicago decided to use him only as a kicker in 1959, he retired.

The next year, however, the American Football League formed, and Blanda joined the AFL Houston Oilers. During the next seven years in Houston, he threw for 19,149 yards and 165 touchdowns. In 1961 the 6-foot 2-inch, 215-pounder threw 36 touchdowns—a record that stood for 23 years. He also led the Oilers to their second straight AFL championship and was named AFL Player of the Year.

In the mid-1960s the Oilers started to decline, and Blanda was blamed for the losses. The Oakland Raiders traded for him in 1966, and Blanda began the third stage of his pro football career. In Oakland Blanda was the placekicking specialist and backup quarterback. He handled both roles excellently, kicking more than 100 points during each of his first three seasons with the team. He was surprised and hurt when the Raiders put him on waivers just before the 1970 season. Oakland assured Blanda they intended to use him just as before, but he wasn't convinced and seriously considered retiring again. After all, he had already had a nineteen-year career—longer than most players. But he decided to stick it out and went on to have one of his best years ever.

In 1976 the Raiders finally let 49-year-old Blanda go, even though he had scored at least 1 point in each of his last 69 games. This time he retired for good.

During his career, George Blanda set several records (many of which have been broken since), including most games played (340), most field goals made in a career (335), most kicking points scored (1,948), most interceptions thrown in a career (277), and most consecutive games played (224). In 1981, the first year he was eligible, Blanda was inducted into the Pro Football Hall of Fame.

GEORGE BLANDA

Passing Attempts	4,007	Extra Point Attempts	959
Passing Completions	1,911	Extra Points	943
Passing Percentage	47.7	Field Goal Attempts	638
Passing Yards	26,920	Field Goals	335
Average Pass Gain	6.72		
Touchdown Passes	236		
Passes Intercepted	277		

JAMES STEPHEN RINGO

1931–

Position: center
Teams: Green Bay Packers, Philadelphia Eagles
Inducted: 1981

Jim Ringo gave the credit for his successful pro football career to his high school football coach in Phillipsburg, New Jersey. The coach switched him from fullback to center. Some 35 years later Ringo was inducted into the Pro Football Hall of Fame as a center.

After a successful college career at Syracuse University, Ringo was drafted by the Green Bay Packers. When he came to training camp, he panicked when he saw all the bigger players competing for the center position. After two weeks at camp, he packed up and went home to Easton, Pennsylvania. His wife and his father, however, urged him to go back. Ringo did, and he became the Packers' regular center for the next eleven seasons.

Ringo was born on November 21, 1931, in Orange, New Jersey. He played pro football from 1953 to 1967, at the end of an era when linemen did not look like bodybuilders. Even at 6 feet 1 inch and 235 pounds, Ringo wasn't as big as the other players, so he had to learn to use his quickness to outmaneuver larger opponents.

Ringo was the pivot-man on the offensive unit. A sportswriter described him as the key man in an offensive play who was always "up front calling blocking assignments for the interior linemen, keying the start of each play, and then leading the blocking downfield or setting up to protect the passer."

During Ringo's first six years with the Packers, the team had a miserable record. Then Vince Lombardi took over as head coach in 1959, and Green Bay's record went from 1–10–1 to 7–5–0 his first season. After the 1960 division championship, the Packers took NFL titles in 1961 and 1962. Then in 1964, Lombardi traded the 32-year-old Ringo to the Philadelphia Eagles.

In his career, Ringo was All-NFL six times and was named the top NFL center of the 1960s. During his fifteen-year career, he played in ten Pro Bowls. When he retired, the highly durable Ringo held the record for most consecutive games played (182).

DOUGLAS LEON ATKINS

1930–
Position: defensive end
Teams: Cleveland Browns, Chicago Bears,
New Orleans Saints
Inducted: 1982

To Doug Atkins, his main job as defensive end was to make life miserable for the opposition quarterbacks. And for seventeen years and 205 games the 6-foot 8-inch, 275-pounder did just that. One of his favorite tricks was to throw a blocker into the quarterback. Even players who had a good day against Atkins wouldn't admit it to the press. They were afraid it would make Atkins mad. This "Paul Bunyan of football" did his job so well that he became the model example of what a defensive end should be. Thirteen years after his retirement, he was inducted into the Pro Football Hall of Fame.

Atkins was born on May 8, 1930, in Humboldt, Tennessee. As a teenager his favorite sport was basketball, not football. A basketball scholarship took him to the University of Tennessee, where he was a good all-around athlete. Filling in on the track team one year, he won a high jump title with a 6-foot 6-inch leap. Later, on the pro football field, he used this jumping ability to leapfrog over blockers in order to get to the quarterback.

On the college basketball court, Atkins caught the eye of the football coach, who was amazed at how well such a big man could move. The football coach persuaded Atkins to switch to football. He did, and in 1953, after his senior year, the Cleveland Browns chose him as their number one pick in the college draft.

Atkins was a regular on the Browns defensive team as they took the division title in 1953 and the NFL championship in 1954. Then, just before the 1955 season, he was traded to the Chicago Bears. In no time he became an important member of one of the most overpowering defensive units of that era. He won All-NFL

honors from 1960 to 1962 and started in the Pro Bowl eight of his last nine years with the Bears. He was voted Most Valuable Lineman in the 1959 Pro Bowl.

In spite of twelve successful years with Chicago, Atkins never got along with Bears coach George Halas. After the 1966 season he asked to be traded, and Halas sent him to the New Orleans Saints. Happy in his new home, Atkins played with the energy of a rookie and the wisdom of a veteran. He spent three great years with the Saints and played the best season of his career in 1968, when he was 38 years old.

After suffering a broken leg, Atkins retired in 1969. During his seventeen seasons, he racked up two damaged knees, torn biceps, several cracked ribs, a broken leg, a broken collarbone, broken hands, sprained ankles, and a ripped groin muscle. But that was nothing compared with the damage he inflicted on every quarterback he tackled.

ROBERT LEE "SAM" HUFF

1934–
Position: linebacker
Teams: New York Giants, Washington Redskins
Inducted: 1982

If it hadn't been for football, Sam Huff might have ended up a coal miner like his dad. Instead, he became one of the best-known linebackers in football. Huff was born on October 4, 1934, in Morgantown, West Virginia, and attended high school in Farmington. When he was a junior, the coach from West Virginia University came to look at another student. As it turned out, Huff was recruited, and the other kid wound up in the mines. In 1955 Huff was an All-America selection.

In 1956 the New York Giants drafted Huff but didn't know where to play him. He was too small for tackle and not quick enough for offensive guard. Discouraged, Huff was on his way to the airport when Vince Lombardi, an assistant coach with the Giants, intercepted him. After lecturing Huff on guts and determination, Lombardi persuaded him to return to the Giants.

Huff soon became the leader of the Giants defense. Huff was best known for his tough play near the scrimmage line. When Huff played, a linebacker had to be big enough to stop power runners, fast enough to catch halfbacks, and quick enough to cover receivers. Huff had all those qualities, plus a built-in instinct for finding the ball. He intercepted 30 tosses during his career. Twice he returned stolen passes for touchdowns.

Huff was one of the first defensive players to become a national idol. In his second season with the Giants, the 6-foot 1-inch, 230-pounder appeared on the cover of *Time* magazine. In 1959 he was named the NFL's top linebacker and voted to the NFL's All-1950s team. And in 1960, he was the subject of a TV special titled *The Violent World of Sam Huff.* The show focused on the "hard-hitting realities of pro football." It emphasized Huff's fierce duels with great running backs Jim Brown and Jim Taylor. Almost overnight Huff became a public sensation.

During Huff's eight years with the Giants, the team reached the NFL title game six times (1956, 1958, 1959, and 1961–63), winning the championship in 1956. As a Giant, Huff played in four of his five Pro Bowl Games and was All-NFL four times. When the Giants traded him to the Redskins in 1964, Huff was angry and bewildered.

After Washington welcomed him with an excellent contract, Huff settled in and quickly became a team leader. When a severe ankle sprain put him on the bench in 1967, he retired. However, a year later he was back as a player-coach under Lombardi. His primary job was to train his successor at middle linebacker. After Lombardi's death the next summer, Huff quit football for good.

In 1982 Huff was inducted into the Pro Football Hall of Fame. When told he had been elected to the Hall, Huff did what he had done when he was traded and when he announced his first retirement—he cried.

SAM HUFF			
Interceptions	30	Average Gain	12.7
Yards	381	Touchdowns	2

GEORGE FRANCIS MUSSO

1910–
Positions: guard, tackle
Team: Chicago Bears
Inducted: 1982

George Musso was born on April 8, 1910, in Collinsville, Illinois. When he finished grade school, he was expected to join his father working in the coal mines. However, neighbors persuaded his father to let him attend high school, where he excelled in four sports. Those neighbors later persuaded his father to let him play football at Millikin University. In 1933 the concern of those neighbors paid off, when Musso began a twelve-year career with the Chicago Bears.

At 6 feet 2 inches and 270 pounds, "Moose" Musso was one of the "biggest" stars of the Chicago Bears' "Monsters of the Midway." He started his career as an offensive tackle and won All-NFL honors in 1935. Two years later, he switched to middle guard on defense and won All-NFL honors at that position, becoming the first player to win All-NFL honors at two positions. In his fourth year with the Bears, he was elected team captain, a position he held until he retired.

Musso was a perfect example of the powerful lineup that the Bears had put together. His size and strength made it impossible for a ball-carrier to run through him. And he was fast for such a big man. It seemed that no one could get out of the line quicker to lead interference for his quarterback.

During Musso's twelve-year career with the Bears, Chicago won seven division titles and four NFL championships. Their regular-season record for those years was 104–26–6. Musso anchored the Bears' five-man line and specialized in what was called the "big play." In other words, whatever was necessary to stop the opposing team—a blocked kick, a last minute tackle—Moose could do it.

Thirty-eight years after his last football game in 1944, the efforts of George Musso's neighbors to help him escape the coal mines were rewarded once again. In 1982 Musso was given football's highest honor when he was inducted into the Pro Football Hall of Fame.

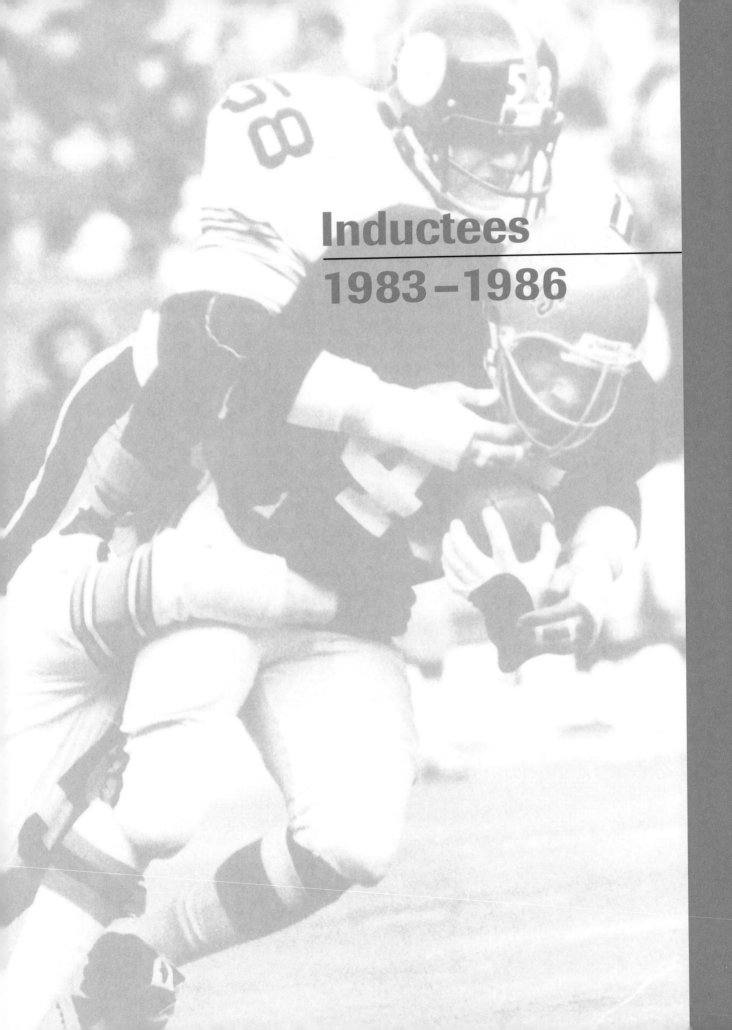

Inductees
1983–1986

PAUL D. WARFIELD

1942–

Position: wide receiver
Teams: Cleveland Browns, Miami Dolphins
Inducted: 1983

THE STATS CAN LIE

When he retired, Paul Warfield had caught only 427 receptions—more than 200 fewer than other leading wide receivers, such as Charley Taylor, Don Maynard, and Raymond Berry. Warfield's average of 2.6 catches per game was far smaller than the averages of today's great receivers. But Warfield gained 8,565 yards, and he averaged 1 touchdown for every 5 receptions.

"[Warfield] didn't catch a lot of balls in a game, but he did a lot with the ones he caught," said one pro coach. "He was a receiver you had to double-team. You did it as much to discourage the passer from throwing to him as you did to contain him, because it was extraordinarily difficult to contain him."

Paul Warfield was inducted into the Pro Football Hall of Fame the first year he was eligible. Looking at his stats, one might wonder why. Although he was one of the best wide receivers in pro football, he never led the league in receptions. But there is much more to Warfield's pro story than just numbers. Warfield, who was 6 feet and 188 pounds, played much of his career for a team that used the forward pass mostly to make the ground game more effective. But even though Warfield's catches were few, his yardage total was great. He wound up with a stunning 20.1 yards per catch.

In college Warfield starred on both offense and defense. Playing for football powerhouse Ohio State, Warfield was All-America and played in the College All-Star Game. The Cleveland Browns made him their number one draft pick in 1964. Coach Paul Brown put Warfield at wide receiver because of his speed and his ability to leap into the air to catch the ball.

His rookie year, Warfield caught 52 passes for 920 yards and 9 touchdowns—a tremendous pro start. He suffered a double fracture of the collarbone, which sidelined him for all but one game in 1965. The following year he rebounded with a respectable 36 receptions for 741 yards—an average of 20.1 yards per catch. Warfield's next three years were outstanding, with 1968 being his best. On 50 catches, he gained 1,067 yards—a 21.3-yard average—and led the league with 12 touchdowns.

Able to make quick moves at top speed, Warfield never gained fewer than 700 yards a season as part of Cleveland's air game. So everyone was stunned in 1970 when Warfield was traded to Miami for the team's number one draft choice. Miami hadn't had a winning season since the team's formation in 1966. However, Don Shula took over as head coach in 1970, and the Dolphins' record improved that year to 10–4. Warfield contributed 28 receptions for 703 yards and a career-high 25.1-yard average. The next year the Dolphins won their first AFC championship, and Warfield snagged

PAUL WARFIELD			
Pass Receptions	427	**Total Points**	516 (86 touchdowns)
Pass Receiving Yards	8,565		
Average Gain	20.1		
Touchdowns	85		

GOING FULL CIRCLE

When he began his pro career, Paul Warfield was thrilled to be playing for the Cleveland Browns. He gave his team a superstar performance, and in return, the Browns gave him to Miami. "I had made a positive contribution to the team," he told the press. "I wasn't a troublemaker, and I felt that wasn't the way to reward an employee who had done a good job." The fans were more loyal. In 1973, when the Dolphins played in Cleveland, 80,000 fans gave Warfield a standing ovation.

Warfield never felt Miami's ground game utilized his receiving talents. "The Dolphins [could] have one of the most dangerous long-strike, big-play offenses in existence," wrote one observer. "Warfield is a tremendous key to all this."

Warfield split to play in the new World Football League, hoping to see more passes coming his way. When the league crumbled, Browns owner Art Modell asked Warfield to come back to Cleveland. Ironically, Modell was the one who had traded Warfield to Miami in the first place.

43 catches for 996 yards, a 23.2-yard average, and 11 touchdowns that season.

Miami lost Super Bowl VI, but came back in 1972 with the NFL's only perfect season. The Dolphins finished the year 17–0, capping if off with a 14–7 victory over Washington in Super Bowl VII. Miami went on to repeat as Super Bowl champs the following year. Warfield, however, was deeply dissatisfied with the way he was being used in the club's passing game. The Dolphins built their offense around the powerful running game of Larry Csonka, Mercury Morris, and Jim Kiick. In Super Bowl VII quarterback Bob Griese threw just 7 passes. Consequently, Warfield caught only 2 passes for 33 yards.

In 1975 Warfield jumped to the Memphis Southmen of the new World Football League, but the league folded after only ten games. In 1976 the Browns brought Warfield back to his NFL roots for his last two seasons. In his thirteen-year career, Warfield was named to All-NFL teams five years and played in eight Pro Bowls.

Wide receiver Paul Warfield (42) pulls in a pass for the Miami Dolphins.

CHARLES ROBERT TAYLOR

1941–
Position: wide receiver
Team: Washington Redskins
Inducted: 1984

FAMOUS FOREVER

A magazine poll once revealed that NFL players believed Charley Taylor was one of the most underrated players in the league. It wasn't the first time Taylor was overlooked.

Taylor was born on September 28, 1941, in Grand Prairie, Texas, a short distance from Dallas. In spite of an excellent high school record, he didn't get any attention from colleges—probably because his high school was segregated. A local booster took him to the Cowboys office to help him get a scholarship.

"It's hard to believe that Charley wasn't eagerly sought by a lot of colleges," said Gil Brandt, the Dallas personnel director. "As luck would have it…an ASU coach just happened to be in our offices at the time." Eventually Taylor wound up at Arizona State, in the NFL record books, and in the Hall of Fame. No one is ignoring Charley Taylor anymore.

When Charley Taylor joined the Washington Redskins in 1964, he made a name for himself as a sleek halfback who could also catch more than his share of passes. Two years later the Redskins wanted to move Taylor to split end. He resisted the move, but it turned out to be a blessing in disguise. When he retired in 1977, Taylor held the record for career pass receptions.

Playing on both offense and defense at Arizona State, Taylor won MVP honors in the East-West game his senior year and again for his College All-Star Game performance. He was the Redskins' number one draft choice in 1964, but no one knew quite where to put the 6-foot 3-inch, 210-pound speed burner. Some said to make him a cornerback; others said he was a natural return specialist. But most voted for him to be a halfback, so Taylor began his pro career in the backfield. He led the Redskins with 755 yards rushing and added 53 receptions. Those stats earned him Rookie of the Year honors. Even with a bad ankle his second year, he led his team in rushing yards, with 402.

In spite of Taylor's outstanding performance at halfback, Redskins coach Otto Graham decided to use him at both halfback and split end. Taylor vehemently opposed the change. He had dreams of being an outstanding running back—perhaps as good as Jim Brown. Taylor was so unhappy over the change that he lost 15 pounds. "After you have set out to do something and come so close," he said, "to lose it all of a sudden, it's got to take something out of you." What's more, he wasn't doing well as either a running back or a receiver.

Then in the ninth game of his third season, Graham used Taylor just as a split end. That game he caught 8 passes for 111 yards and a touchdown. A week later he made a record-tying 11 catches in one game. Three weeks after that, he grabbed 4 catches for 145 yards and a touchdown. Something was happening. Taylor ended the 1966 sea-

CHARLEY TAYLOR			
Pass Receptions	649	Rushing Attempts	442
Pass Receiving Yards	9,140	Rushing Yards	1,488
Average Gain	14.1	Average Gain	3.4
Touchdowns	79	Touchdowns	11
		Total Points 540 (90 touchdowns)	

CHARLEY'S CATCHES

In his new position as wide receiver, Charley Taylor immediately began catching high numbers of passes in 1966. After a few weeks of this, he realized this was the position he played best. Once he found enough room to run beyond the line of scrimmage, he could break free of tackles.

"I've got a favorite pattern I like to run," Taylor said. "I like to cut toward the sideline a couple of times. The man who's guarding me sneaks closer so he can step in front of me and intercept the ball. When he's close, I shoot by him to catch the ball and there's nothing else in front of me but touchdown-land."

son leading the league with 72 catches. A year later he caught 70 passes to lead the league again.

Taylor kept racking up an average of about 60 receptions a year. At the end of the 1975 season his career total was 635. For the first time in his outstanding career, he was getting the attention he deserved. When a reporter asked how he would feel about achieving a place in football history, he answered, "When you stop playing, nobody remembers you. If your name is in the record book, though, that's proof that you did play and people will remember."

A shoulder injury benched Taylor for the entire 1976 season. He returned in 1977, his final year. Taylor finished his career with a total of 649 catches and is among the all-time reception leaders. After his retirement, Taylor became the Redskins receiver coach. The wide receiver job that he so bitterly opposed had been his ticket to the record books. In 1984 it also took him into the Pro Football Hall of Fame.

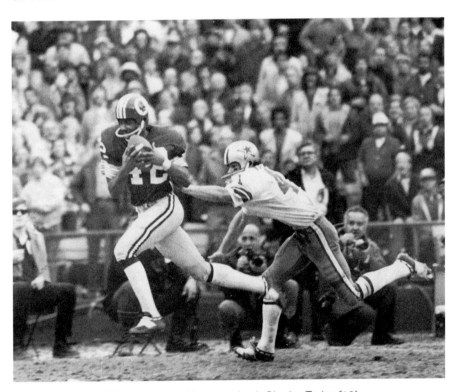

Wide receiver and running back Charley Taylor (42) makes another great catch for the Washington Redskins.

JOSEPH WILLIAM NAMATH

1943–
Position: quarterback
Teams: New York Jets, Los Angeles Rams
Inducted: 1985

THOSE GIMPY KNEES

Joe Namath always had knee problems. He had his first knee surgery just 23 days after signing his Jets contract in 1965. He was back in the hospital a year later and again in 1968 and 1971.

But after that last hospital stay, Namath came back strong. In his first game back in 1971, against the San Francisco 49ers, he threw for 358 yards and 3 touchdowns. The next season Namath continued to dazzle, with two 400-yard passing games. Perhaps the finest game of Namath's career came that year against Baltimore, when he threw for 496 yards and 6 touchdowns.

During his career, a wrist injury and a separated shoulder also benched Namath for weeks. But his gimpy knees were more famous. He had a total of five knee operations, and he finished his career playing with braces on both legs. In 1977 those bad knees forced him to retire.

Joe Namath is best remembered for his guarantee that the New York Jets would win Super Bowl III against the Baltimore Colts in 1969. His outrageous boast made front-page news. But then, Namath was always in the news.

This handsome, fun-loving quarterback was one of football's most colorful personalities. Namath wore his hair long at a time when most players sported crewcuts. Partying all night at trendy Broadway clubs in New York City earned him the nickname "Broadway Joe." He was the hottest celebrity seller on TV, appearing in commercials for everything from popcorn poppers to panty hose.

Namath's guarantee that the Jets would win the Super Bowl made news. And so did the Jets' 16–7 upset over the Colts. Namath led his team to victory, completing 17 of 28 passes for 206 yards and was voted the game's Most Valuable Player. Always the showman, he left the stadium with a woman on each arm and two police escorts with guard dogs. Broadway Joe was going out to celebrate.

Namath was born on May 31, 1943, in Beaver Falls, Pennsylvania. He started throwing a football with his brothers when he was six years old. His older brother Bobby showed him how to grip the ball and throw from behind his ear. "He taught me…the quick release, although neither of us had ever heard of the expression then," remembered Namath. Namath was a three-sport star in high school. After graduating he attended the University of Alabama. He led the Crimson Tide to four postseason bowl games and was the star of the 1965 Orange Bowl. Though Alabama lost, the All-America passer threw for 255 yards and 2 touchdowns.

Namath graduated at the height of the war between the established National Football League and its upstart rival, the American Football League. His pro football career began in an uproar when he signed a three-year contract with the AFL Jets for $425,000 in 1965. It was the most any football player had ever been paid.

JOE NAMATH			
Passing Attempts	3,762	**Average Pass Gain**	7.35
Passing Completions	1,886	**Touchdown Passes**	173
Passing Percentage	50.1	**Passes Intercepted**	220
Passing Yards	27,663		

A few days before Super Bowl III, Joe Namath told a crowd in a swanky Miami restaurant, "Most people don't give us a chance." He was right. Most sports experts were predicting the Colts would cream the Jets by at least 17 points. But Namath went on to pronounce that the Jets would win. "I guarantee it," he proclaimed.

Furious over Namath's bragging, the Colts came on the field ready to mow down the Jets. But in the first half, the Colts blew two good chances to score. After the Jets intercepted a Colts pass, Namath led the team on a 80-yard touchdown drive. At halftime the score was 7–0. An odd thought occurred to the Colts and the fans: Maybe Namath had been right.

During the third quarter, the Jets kicked 3 field goals, making the score 16–0. The Colts were desperate enough to send in their top gun, Johnny Unitas, who was sidelined with injuries. In the last three and a half minutes, Unitas helped the Colts score a touchdown, but even he couldn't change the final outcome. The clock ran out on a 16–7 Jets upset.

In the dressing room afterward, Namath lay on the massage table, grinning. "I told you so," he said to reporters. And winning Super Bowl III was not a victory just for Joe Namath and the Jets—it was also a victory for the American Football League. Very few fans took the AFL seriously until the Jets signed Namath and went on to win the Super Bowl.

One of the best passers football had ever seen, Namath could throw a ball as swift and as straight as a bullet. His ability to call plays as well as his superior passing arm spurred his team to name him captain in 1968, 1969, 1970, and 1972, and team MVP three times. The 6-foot 2-inch, 200-pounder had 300 and 400 yards passing in games at a time when those stats were rare. In 1967 he became the first passer ever to top 4,000 yards passing in one season. Others have done it since, but not in a fourteen-game season.

Namath's list of awards and honors is a long one. He was AFL Rookie of the Year and AFL All-Star MVP his first year in the pros. He was named co-MVP in the All-Star Game two years later. In 1968 he was a unanimous All-AFL selection and the Super Bowl MVP. He also won the Hickok Belt, given to the top professional athlete of the year. In 1972 he was a unanimous All-Pro quarterback.

Perhaps Namath's one weakness was his confidence in his ability to complete any pass he threw. Because of this confidence, he would throw even when his receivers faced double coverage, increasing the risk of an interception. But that confidence is also what made Namath great.

Quarterback Joe Namath (12) gets ready to throw another bullet pass for the New York Jets.

ALVIN RAY "PETE" ROZELLE

1926–
NFL Commissioner
Inducted: 1985

THEN AND NOW

Pete Rozelle was inducted into the Pro Football Hall of Fame 25 years to the day after he was elected NFL commissioner. During that period, the NFL grew and changed considerably. Comparing the NFL in 1960 and in 1985, some aspects show astonishing changes.

In 1960 there were only thirteen NFL teams and 500 pro players. By 1985 more than 1,500 players were employed by 28 teams. The average attendance at an NFL game in 1960 was a little more than 40,000 fans. In 1984 the average was 59,811 fans.

When Rozelle took office, the players' share for winning the NFL title game was $5,116 apiece. The year Rozelle was inducted into the Hall of Fame, each member of the San Francisco Super Bowl XIX championship team took home $36,000. An NFL team's share of television revenues grew from $330,000 annually in 1962 to about $14 million annually under contracts that ran through 1986.

In January 1960, twelve NFL team owners sat in a room trying to decide on a successor for Commissioner Bert Bell. The league's popular leader had died three months earlier; his shoes would be hard to fill. The marathon meeting was at a standstill until Wellington Mara of the New York Giants and Paul Brown of the Cleveland Browns came up with Pete Rozelle's name. Choosing the 33-year-old general manager of the L.A. Rams was perhaps the most important decision made in the league's 65-year history.

Until the fateful day he was named NFL commissioner, Rozelle's football career had been limited to six years with the Rams. His first three were spent handling the team's public relations, then he moved up to general manager. Most veterans thought he was too much of a nice guy to handle the strong-willed owners. But Rozelle's polite and patient negotiating style was his strength and always brought the owners around to an agreement.

Rozelle realized that television was a force that football had to reckon with. Right away he moved the NFL office from a Philadelphia suburb to the media hub of New York City. His first act of business was to negotiate a contract with a major television network. To accomplish that, he first had to convince the team owners in large metropolitan cities that they would benefit from sharing TV revenues with teams from smaller market areas. Then he lobbied for a limited antitrust exemption for the NFL. This legislation would allow the league to act as a single enterprise when negotiating the television contract.

After the sports legislation bill was signed into law, Rozelle signed a contract with CBS. The network had the rights to broadcast NFL games for $4,650,000 a year, to be divided equally among the NFL teams. It was a huge sum of money at the time. Rozelle's deal was farsighted. For one thing, it improved the NFL's financial outlook. It also helped to attract millions of new fans to pro football. Largely as a result of television, NFL attendance rose from 2 million in 1950 to nearly 5 million by the early 1960s.

In 1963 allegations about players gambling on NFL teams landed on Rozelle's desk. After careful investigation he suspended two very popular players. The suspensions were lifted at the end of the 1963 season, but the integrity of pro football was assured for much longer.

The same year Rozelle was named NFL commissioner, the American Football League was formed. The rival AFL competed

WHO IS PETE ROZELLE ANYWAY?

Pete Rozelle never played football, but he always had an interest in sports. Rozelle was born on March 1, 1926, in South Gate, California. He played tennis and basketball in high school. He entered Compton Junior College in 1946, where he was the school's sports information director. He also worked as a "stringer" (freelancer) for the *Long Beach Press Telegram* and picked up 50 cents for each Compton sports score he phoned in to the L.A. papers. That year he also began editing the L.A. Rams' game programs.

In 1948 Rozelle transferred to the University of San Francisco, where he majored in English. While a student there, he worked as the school's sports publicity director. After graduation he briefly served as the school's assistant athletic director. Rozelle planned to take a job as a sports editor with the *Los Angeles Times,* but in 1952 his plans changed.

Tex Schramm, chief assistant to L.A. Rams president Dan Reeves, offered Rozelle a job handling public relations for the Rams. Rozelle took it. Three years later he left to join an international public relations firm that was promoting the 1956 Summer Olympics in Australia. By 1957, however, he was back with the Rams as general manager, and there he stayed until January 1960, when he became the NFL commissioner.

"For me, timing was just good," he said modestly.

heavily with the NFL for players and fans. A bidding war for players drained both leagues, bringing several clubs to the brink of collapse. The war had to end. In 1966 Rozelle helped negotiate the successful merger of the two leagues, to take place in 1970. After the merger, he kept all 26 owners in a 36-hour marathon meeting until they reached another agreement. This one was to form two thirteen-team conferences.

The Super Bowl was another product of the AFL-NFL merger. Thanks to Rozelle's handling of television coverage, the Super Bowl became the most-watched TV sports event of all time.

During the 1970s and 1980s Rozelle presided over player strikes, court cases challenging the NFL's organizational structure, and antitrust legislation. In 1989, after 30 years at the helm, he retired.

NFL commissioner Pete Rozelle led the league for 30 years.

ORENTHAL JAMES SIMPSON

1947–
Position: running back
Teams: Buffalo Bills, San Francisco 49ers
Inducted: 1985

THE ELECTRIC COMPANY TURNS ON THE JUICE

The Buffalo Bills offensive linemen were once asked why they called themselves "the Electric Company." Guard Reggie McKenzie answered, "We turn on the Juice."

"Juice" was O.J. Simpson's nickname. From 1972 through 1976, when Simpson made and broke his records, the Electric Company turned on the Juice hundreds of times.

The last game of the 1973 season was a snowy, wind-blown day at Shea Stadium. "At the end of the third quarter," Simpson recalled, "Joe Ferguson, our quarterback, came down the bench.... He said, 'Juice only needs 50 yards for 2,000. Let's get it.'"

At the end of the game, Simpson had 200 yards and 2,003 for the season. He was carried off the field by his ecstatic teammates. At his press conference after the game, the Juice insisted the entire Electric Company offensive line be there when the flashbulbs and spotlights were turned on. "I wouldn't be here without them," he said.

Slicing through the line and breaking tackles, O.J. Simpson was one of the most electrifying running backs in history. After a brilliant college career at the University of Southern California, Simpson eventually became the greatest pro ball carrier of his era. Combining strength with explosive speed, Simpson won four rushing titles and was the first NFL back to run for 2,000 yards in a season.

Simpson first showed his athletic talents in high school in San Francisco, where he was born on July 9, 1947. At USC he was All-America twice, he won the Heisman Trophy, and he led the Trojans to consecutive Rose Bowls. He became one of history's most famous rookies when the Buffalo Bills made him the number one draft pick in the 1969 draft.

But after signing with the Bills, Simpson didn't do well during his first three seasons in Buffalo. His slow start was partially due to his playing on weak teams. But most of the blame lies with the way Bills head coach John Rauch chose to use Simpson. It was pointed out to Rauch that Simpson could probably carry the ball 30 or 40 times a game, but Rauch didn't care. "That's not my style," he stated. "I wouldn't build my offense around one back, no matter how good he is. It's too easy for the pros to set up defensive keys. O.J. can be a terrific pass receiver, and we expect him to block too."

So for the next three years, Simpson was a runner, a receiver, and a kickoff return man. Although he led his team in rushing each year, his totals didn't stack up with those of other players in the league. To make matters worse, he suffered a severe knee injury while carrying out the dangerous assignment of returning kickoffs. His bum knee kept him out of eight games in 1970.

Simpson was ready to retire when Lou Saban took over as head coach in 1972. Saban preferred strong running games and intended to remake Buffalo's offense around Simpson. In Saban's first year

O.J. SIMPSON			
Rushing Attempts	2,404	Pass Receptions	203
Rushing Yards	11,236	Pass Receiving Yards	2,142
Average Gain	4.7	Average Gain	10.5
Touchdowns	61	Touchdowns	14
		Total Points	456 (76 touchdowns)

AND THE STATS PLAYED ON

One story says that growing up, O.J. Simpson was the fastest boy on the block and was always cocky about his speed. One day he saw Jim Brown leaving the San Francisco stadium after Brown's team had just smashed the 49ers. O.J. was only fourteen, but he walked right up to Brown and said, "Mr. Brown, one day I'm going to break all your records."

Simpson's single-season rushing record has since been surpassed, by Eric Dickerson, as have many of his other records. But here's a listing of some of O.J.'s impressive career achievements.

• First all time in games with 200 or more yards rushing: 6

• Second all time in rushing yards in a season: 2,003 (1973)

• Second and third all time in rushing yards in a game: 273 (in 1976) and 250 (in 1973)

• Second all time in games with 100 or more yards rushing in a season: 11 (1973)

• Third all time in consecutive seasons with 1,000 or more yards rushing: 5 (1972–76)

About the only thing Simpson didn't do was play in a Super Bowl.

Simpson led the league in rushing for the first time, with 1,251 yards.

Saban went to work building a good offensive line. If Simpson was going to run his best he needed strong blockers in front of him. In 1973 that line was ready. That year Simpson rushed for more than 100 yards in eleven of fourteen games, including three games of 200 yards or more. His 250 yards against New England were a record at the time. By the last game of the year, he needed just 61 yards to pass Jim Brown's rushing mark of 1,863 yards in one season. Simpson ran for 200 yards to finish with 2,003.

As great as 1973 was, 1975 was Simpson's finest campaign. He rushed for 1,817 yards, with another 428 yards on receptions, including 7 touchdown catches. His 2,245-yard combined net yardage total was 172 yards more than his 1973 combined net yardage total, and he scored a record 23 touchdowns.

In 1976 Saban abruptly left Buffalo. Shaken, Simpson asked for a trade to a West Coast team but was turned down. His next season, he rushed for 1,503 yards, his third-best mark, and broke his own single-game rushing record with 273 yards.

In 1979 Simpson was traded to his hometown team, the San Francisco 49ers. With the 49ers, he was hoping to beat Jim Brown's all-time rushing record. Injuries, however, forced Simpson to retire that year, and he wound up more than 1,000 yards short of Brown's career mark.

In 1985, the first year he was eligible, Simpson was elected to the Pro Football Hall of Fame. Waiting for him there were the ball he carried and the jersey he wore during the game in which he broke 2,000 single-season rushing yards.

Buffalo Bills running back O.J. Simpson (32) broke old NFL records and set several new ones.

ROGER THOMAS STAUBACH

1942–
Position: quarterback
Team: Dallas Cowboys
Inducted: 1985

A SCRAMBLING SAILOR

Roger Staubach was born in Cincinnati, Ohio, on February 5, 1942. He was a football star in Ironton, Ohio, where he grew up. Several major universities recruited him, but he chose to attend the U.S. Naval Academy.

Staubach arrived at Annapolis in 1961. Coach Wayne Hardin was using a drop-back passing attack at the time. But it wasn't long before the coach changed his entire offensive strategy to take advantage of Staubach's scrambling style of running. While taking long strides, Staubach would perform a series of quick wiggle-and-jerk movements with his hips and shoulders. His scrambling was so effective that the Navy team wound up with a 9–1 record for 1963, and Staubach was awarded the Heisman Trophy.

After scrambling his way to Heisman heights, "the Jolly Roger Dodger" eventually scrambled to All-Pro status and Hall of Fame history.

Roger Staubach was one of the greatest "two-minute-drill" quarterbacks in football history. He had an uncanny ability to come up with some kind of daring play in the last minutes of a game. He was responsible for no less than 23 come-from-behind victories. Fourteen of them were in the last two minutes of the game.

Perhaps the most famous example of Staubach's never-say-die style of playing came in a 1972 playoff game against San Francisco. After shoulder surgery, Staubach had played in just four games and thrown only 20 passes that season for the Dallas Cowboys. He entered the game in the fourth quarter. Dallas was behind 28–16 with the clock down to 78 seconds. Staubach threw a 20-yard touchdown pass to make the score 28–23. After Dallas recovered an onside kick, Staubach needed just three plays to win the game. He clinched it on a 10-yard pass that gave the Cowboys a 30–28 victory.

Staubach even pulled off a nail-biting victory in his final regular-season game. In the last 140 seconds he threw 2 touchdown passes to beat the Washington Redskins 35–34.

Neither his fans nor the opposing team nor his coaches ever knew what Staubach was going to do when he took the snap from the center. He might hand off, pass, or run. If his receivers weren't open and he saw a sliver of daylight, he would often tuck the ball under his arm and take off. Once he did, his scrambling ability—long strides with quick, jerky hip and shoulder movements—made him difficult to catch.

"[Staubach] was the most difficult quarterback to intercept I ever coached against," said Redskins coach George Allen. "He had the discipline to accept having the signals called for him. And when it was called for, he improvised brilliantly and still led the team."

ROGER STAUBACH			
Passing Attempts	2,958	Rushing Attempts	410
Passing Completions	1,685	Rushing Yards	2,264
Passing Percentage	57.0	Average Gain	5.5
Passing Yards	22,700	Touchdowns	20
Average Pass Gain	7.67		
Touchdown Passes	153		
Passes Intercepted	109		

THE "HAIL MARY" PASS

Roger Staubach is responsible for one of football's most famous terms to describe a play. He coined it after some typical last-minute heroics in the 1975 NFC division playoffs.

The Cowboys were trailing the Minnesota Vikings 14–10. With 32 seconds to play, Dallas had the ball on the Vikings 32-yard line. On second down, Staubach took the snap, faked to his left, then turned to his right and fired a pass to wide receiver Drew Pearson. Vikings cornerback Nate Wright was also right under Staubach's pass. Pearson cut inside Wright— causing him to lose his balance and fall—and grabbed the ball. Hugging the ball to his hip, Pearson ran the remaining 5 yards for the winning touchdown.

No one could believe what Staubach had done. "Our only hope was to throw and hope for a miracle," said Coach Tom Landry.

"It was just a Hail Mary pass," Staubach said. "You throw it up and pray he catches it."

Ever since, the term *Hail Mary pass* has been used to describe a very, very lucky play.

Staubach's running skills caused many teams to overlook his forward passing. He could throw accurate bullets with his unusually strong arm. He finished his career with a 57.0 completion percentage.

A U.S. Naval Academy Heisman Trophy winner, 6-foot 3-inch, 202-pound Staubach joined the Dallas Cowboys in 1969 after serving four years in the Navy. He split his job as passer with Craig Morton his first two years. In the eighth game of 1971, with the Cowboys' record at 4–3, Staubach was promoted to starter. The Cowboys didn't lose another game that season and went all the way to Super Bowl VI. Staubach led the league in passing and was named NFL Player of the Year. He finished his first starting year as Super Bowl MVP.

During the eight full years Roger Staubach was the starting quarterback for Dallas–from 1972 to 1979–the Cowboys enjoyed their greatest success. They won 85 games and lost 32, for a .726 win percentage. Staubach led Dallas to the playoffs each season but one. He was the Cowboys' winning quarterback in four NFC championship games and in Super Bowls VI and XII.

Staubach finished his eleven-year career with many honors. He was All-NFC four times and played in four Pro Bowls. Concussions eventually caused Staubach to call it quits in 1980. Five years later the Pro Football Hall of Fame elected him to football immortality.

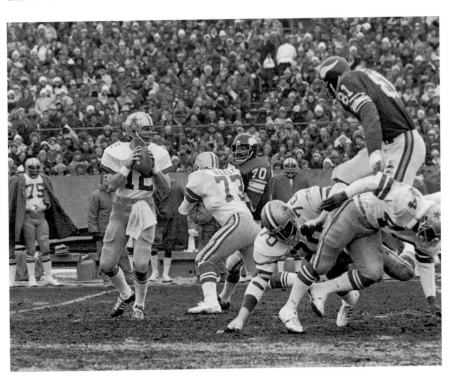

Dallas Cowboys quarterback Roger Staubach (12) looks for a receiver while an opposition lineman leaps toward him.

PAUL VERNON HORNUNG

1935–
Positions: running back, placekicker
Team: Green Bay Packers
Inducted: 1986

Paul Hornung could do it all—rush, pass, receive, block, kick, and put points on the scoreboard. Known as "the Golden Boy" for his good looks and charming manner, Hornung was one of football's most versatile players ever. Despite his skills, it took the Hall of Fame Selection Committee 20 years to induct him, largely because of a gambling scandal that tainted his career.

But before that scandal, Hornung helped the Green Bay Packers become one of the most feared teams in the NFL. In 1960 Hornung set a scoring record with 176 points (15 touchdowns, 15 field goals and 41 extra points), a mark that few experts think will ever be beat. The next two seasons, Hornung and the Packers won the NFL championship, and after sitting out the 1963 season, he returned to help Green Bay win two more NFL titles.

Hornung was born on December 23, 1933, in Louisville, Kentucky. In high school Hornung lettered in three sports. Football, however, was his first love, and as quarterback he led his high school team to the state championship

Hornung then went to Notre Dame, where he was All-America and won the Heisman Trophy. In 1957 he was drafted by the Green Bay Packers in the first round. For two dismal years he played three different backfield positions, never knowing which position he would be asked to play. In spite of this confusing coaching, Hornung led the Packers in scoring in 1958, with 67 points, but the Packers had a 1–10–1 record.

Everything turned around in 1959 when Vince Lombardi took over Green Bay as head coach. In studying the films, Lombardi realized that Hornung had many of the same talents as Frank Gifford, a multitalented halfback Lombardi had coached with the New York

PAUL HORNUNG			
Rushing Attempts	893	Pass Receptions	130
Rushing Yards	3,711	Pass Receiving Yards	1,480
Average Gain	4.2	Average Gain	11.4
Touchdowns	50	Touchdowns	12
		Total Points	760 (62 touchdowns, 66 field goals, 190 extra points)

THE LOSING WINNER

Paul Hornung's success in high school led nearly three dozen colleges to offer him football scholarships. Hornung chose his mother's favorite university, Notre Dame.

As a sophomore, Hornung played fullback and backup quarterback, and the Fighting Irish had a 9–1–0 record. His junior year, as starting quarterback, Hornung led Notre Dame to an 8–2 season. His last year, 1956, was a fabulous one for Hornung. Notre Dame sank to a miserable 2–8 record but Hornung won the Heisman Trophy, college football's highest honor.

Usually, the Heisman winner is the player who has had an outstanding year with an outstanding team. However, the voting committee decided Hornung deserved it based solely on *his* performance. It was the first and only time the Heisman Trophy was awarded to a player from a losing team.

Giants. In Hornung, Lombardi saw speed, power, fabulous running instincts, and toughness. And Hornung could handle Lombardi's favorite play—the pass-run option.

Playing halfback, the 6-foot 2-inch, 220-pound Hornung blossomed, leading the Packers in the big plays during the big games. In 1959 he made 152 rushes for a career-high 681 yards. The Packers, who hadn't had a winning season since 1947, won seven of their twelve games.

Over the next three years, Hornung used his running, catching, and kicking skills to win the NFL scoring title with 94, 176, and 146 points. Hornung was Green Bay's placement specialist, and in six seasons he missed only 4 of 194 conversion-point attempts.

In 1961, in a game against the Colts, Hornung scored 4 touchdowns and kicked a field goal and 6 extra points to score a career-high 33 points in one game. That year the Packers won their first league championship since 1944.

In both 1960 and 1961 Hornung was named to the All-Pro team and selected to the Pro Bowl Game. He was also named the NFL's Player of the Year in 1961. But two years later things turned black for football's Golden Boy. In 1963 Hornung was suspended for the season for gambling on the Packers. He sat out the entire year.

Following his return to football, Hornung was plagued by injuries. A leg injury forced him to give up placekicking, and a pinched nerve in his neck caused his left arm to atrophy. His injuries finally made it impossible for Hornung to play.

Hornung is best remembered as a clutch performer who "had a nose for the end zone." "He may not be the greatest football player in the world," Lombardi once said, "but Paul has the special ability to rise to the occasion and to be the greatest of the great when the games are on the line."

*Halfback for the Green Bay Packers, "Golden Boy"
Paul Hornung (5) covers ground to get by the opposition.*

ROBERT LEE BELL

1940–
Position: linebacker
Team: Kansas City Chiefs
Inducted: 1983

Take a 6-foot 4-inch, 225-pound frame that's built like an upside-down pyramid—with massive shoulders tapering down to a 32-inch waist. Add exceptional speed and agility, plus the ability to take and dish out punishment. Put all those qualities together and you have Bobby Bell—the perfect outside linebacker.

Bell was born on June 17, 1940, in Shelby, North Carolina. He realized early on that football might be his only road of escape from racism's dead-end alley. An All-State quarterback in high school, Bell drew attention from Notre Dame and Michigan State. However, Jim Tatum, coach at the segregated North Carolina University in Shelby, heard about the offers. He knew both of those teams would be playing against North Carolina, and he didn't want Bell as an opponent. Tatum called the coach at the University of Minnesota and told him about Bell's talents. Bell became the first scholarship player to be accepted at Minnesota sight unseen.

Starting out as a quarterback, Bell was shifted to tackle his sophomore season. At first he didn't even know how to get into a lineman's stance, but he learned quickly and won All-America honors his junior and senior years. In 1962 Bell won the Outland Trophy as the nation's top college interior lineman.

The following year Bell was drafted by the AFL Kansas City Chiefs. He could have played several positions for Kansas City, either on offense or defense. In spite of the fact that he weighed only 210 pounds his rookie season, he played defensive end and became one of the top pass rushers in the AFL. Bell even snapped the ball on punts and kickoffs, a skill he had learned at college.

At defensive end, Bell won All-AFL honors his second year. But he didn't always stay on the line. To take advantage of Bell's quickness and strength, Chiefs coach Hank Stram sometimes had Bell drop back and become a fourth linebacker. Stram called this the "stack defense." Today the four-linebacker alignment is a common formation.

Of all the positions he could play, Bell's favorite was outside linebacker. "Linebacker is one of the most difficult and challenging positions to play," he once said. "You have to worry about the pass, the run, man-to-man coverage, containing the play, screens, and draws. It's a spur of the moment position."

Bell eventually made a permanent switch to linebacker and went on to superstardom. He starred on two AFL championship teams and played in Super Bowls I and IV. He was also chosen to play in the last six AFL All-Star Games and the first three AFC-NFC Pro Bowl Games. After twelve seasons, Bell retired in 1974 and in 1983 he became the first outside linebacker inducted into the Hall of Fame.

BOBBY BELL			
Interceptions	26	Average Gain	18.4
Yards	479	Touchdowns	6

SIDNEY GILLMAN

1911–
Coach
Teams: Los Angeles Rams, Los Angeles Chargers, San Diego Chargers, Houston Oilers
Inducted: 1983

Sid Gillman began his pro coaching career in 1955 with the Los Angeles Rams. When he retired from coaching in 1974, his 123–104–7 record put him among the top dozen coaches in all-time career wins.

Gillman was born on October 26, 1911, in Minneapolis, Minnesota. In Gillman's first year with the Rams, the team won their division—an impressive start for a rookie coach. But the next few years were tough for the Rams, and Gillman was let go after the 1959 season. Still, by surviving five years in Los Angeles, Gillman proved his coaching talents; before Gillman, the Rams had gone through six coaches in eleven years.

Gillman was immediately offered a position with the Los Angeles (later San Diego) Chargers, a member of the newly organized American Football League. Most experts felt that the AFL was a much weaker league than the NFL. In no time, however, Gillman's coaching experience, along with superior players such as Lance Alworth, brought respect for the Chargers and the AFL.

As usual, Gillman surrounded himself with talented assistants. His ultraprofessional scouting department had orders to build the team with new players, not NFL rejects. The Chargers took the AFL Western Division title five of Gillman's first six years with the team, making him the first coach to win division titles in both the NFL and AFL. In 1963 the Chargers slaughtered the Boston Patriots 51–10 to win the championship.

Gillman was considered an expert on the forward pass. When he started coaching, most of his peers felt that running the ball was a much safer way to score than throwing it. Teams rarely passed more than half a dozen times a game. Gillman, however, believed that big plays came from using the pass. He taught his offense to use the entire field, making it difficult for the opposing defense to cover the five receivers sent out on every play. Soon most teams were using pass plays that Gillman had developed, with receivers running precise patterns.

Two years after he resigned from the Chargers in 1971, Gillman was called to Houston. The Oilers had 1–13 seasons in 1972 and 1973. But in 1974, with Gillman in charge, their record improved to 7–7. After leaving the Oilers, Gillman worked with a number of pro teams as a special consultant; the game never seemed to pass him by.

SID GILLMAN			
Wins	123	Ties	7
Losses	104	Win Percentage	.526

CHRISTIAN A. "SONNY" JURGENSEN III

1934–
Position: quarterback
Teams: Philadelphia Eagles, Washington Redskins
Inducted: 1983

Sonny Jurgensen was one of the finest passers of his time. During his eighteen seasons in pro football he played on only eight winning teams, but football fans knew Jurgensen was better than his teams' records might show.

In five different seasons Jurgensen passed for more than 3,000 yards. He racked up more than 300 passing yards in a game 25 times, and more than 400 passing yards in a game five times. He tossed at least 1 scoring pass for 23 straight games, and twice he threw 5 touchdowns in one game.

Jurgensen's stats were even more of an achievement because the enemy defenses concentrated on stopping him. There was no need for the opposing defense to go after any other player. Jurgensen's passing arm was his team's main weapon. The 6-foot, 203-pounder was a classic drop-back passer. "All I ask of my blockers is four seconds," he explained. "I beat people by throwing, not running."

Jurgensen was born on August 23, 1934. He played high school football, basketball, and baseball in his home town of Wilmington, North Carolina. Football earned him a scholarship to Duke University. In 1957 he was signed by the Philadelphia Eagles.

His first years with the Eagles, Jurgensen was a sub for Norm Van Brocklin. When Van Brocklin retired in 1961, Jurgensen led the

Eagles to a 10–4 record and proved he was an outstanding passer. In 1961 his 235 completions, 2,723 yards passing, and 32 touchdown tosses led the NFL.

Even though Jurgensen continued to excel, the Eagles had a two-year slump. When they put Jurgensen up for trade in 1964, the Redskins snapped him up, eager for a quarterback known for his superb passing skills, his ability to be calm under fire, his intelligence off the field, and his fierce determination.

Vince Lombardi took over the Redskins in 1969. "In five days I learned more from [Lombardi] than I had in twelve years of pro football," said Jurgensen. In 1970 Lombardi's untimely death set the Redskins' progress back. Still, Jurgensen had a good year, with 23 touchdown passes. Then in 1971, injuries began to limit his playing time. By 1973 the 39-year-old star was used only in emergencies.

Jurgensen made a great comeback in 1974, completing 64 percent of his passes and winning the NFC passing title. In 1975 he reluctantly retired at age 41. The Redskins retired his jersey number, 9, then sent his whole uniform to the Pro Football Hall of Fame, confident that he would follow.

SONNY JURGENSEN			
Passing Attempts	4,262	Average Pass Gain	7.56
Passing Completions	2,433	Touchdown Passes	255
Passing Percentage	57.1	Passes Intercepted	189
Passing Yards	32,224		

ROBERT CORNELIUS MITCHELL

1935–
Positions: wide receiver, halfback
Teams: Cleveland Browns, Washington Redskins
Inducted: 1983

When Bobby Mitchell was drafted by the Cleveland Browns in 1958, he had had his sights set on the 1960 Olympics. But he had a new family to care for, and he felt he should take the salary and run. And run is what he did, for eleven seasons. During four years with the Browns and seven with the Redskins, Mitchell played halfback and flanker. He was one of the best catch-run yardage makers in the NFL and a breakaway threat as a punt and kickoff returner.

Mitchell was born on June 6, 1935, in Hot Springs, Arkansas. He played football and basketball and ran track in high school. The St. Louis Cardinals offered him a baseball contract, but he turned it down for a football scholarship to the University of Illinois. After graduation Mitchell signed with Cleveland. The Browns were impressed with his tremendous speed, his ability to shift his weight without faltering, and his ability to stop and start at full speed.

Coach Paul Brown put the 6-foot, 195-pounder at halfback, as a running mate for Jim Brown. From 1958 to 1961 Mitchell racked up 2,297 yards rushing, 1,463 yards receiving, 607 yards on punt returns, and 1,150 yards on kickoff returns. He also scored 38 touchdowns.

In 1962 Coach Brown wanted running back Ernie Davis, the 1961 Heisman Trophy winner. Washington had first pick in the draft and was sure to snap up Davis, so Brown worked a deal with Redskins owner George Preston Marshall and sent Mitchell to Washington. Mitchell was agreeable to the trade when he learned he would be full-time flanker.

That year, 1962, he led the NFL with 72 receptions for 1,384 yards and 11 touchdowns. His stats the next year were equally impressive: 69 catches, 1,436 yards, and 7 touchdowns.

Mitchell was All-NFL in 1962 and 1964 and was chosen for four Pro Bowls. In the 1964 Pro Bowl, he was the top pass catcher. When he retired in 1969, he had racked up 699 yards and 3 touchdowns on 69 punt returns, 2,690 yards and 5 touchdowns on 102 kickoff returns, and was one of the all-time leaders in touchdowns, with 91. Mitchell's 14,078 combined yards are among the top totals of all time.

BOBBY MITCHELL			
Pass Receptions	521	Rushing Attempts	513
Pass Receiving Yards	7,953	Rushing Yards	2,735
Average Gain	15.3	Average Gain	5.3
Touchdowns	65	Touchdowns	18

WILLIAM FERDIE BROWN

1940–

Position: cornerback
Teams: Denver Broncos, Oakland Raiders
Inducted: 1984

The cornerback position is a difficult one to learn, but Willie Brown was a natural. In addition to speed and strength, his quick reactions enabled him to second-guess a receiver's moves and intercept the ball.

Brown often gave a receiver lots of room in order to tempt the opposition's quarterback into throwing to his area. Then, quick as lightning, he'd step in at just the right second to steal the ball. Lance Alworth, the San Diego Chargers star receiver, described playing against Brown: "He reacts so fast, he doesn't…have to follow all your moves. You can waste a lot of fakes on Willie."

Brown combined his excellent football instincts with lots of hard work. He spent hours studying films every week. "Every receiver has some kind of little move that tips off where he's going, and if you study the film long enough, you'll see it," he said.

Brown was born on December 2, 1940, in Yazoo City, Mississippi. He was a blocking tight end at Grambling State University. After graduating in 1963, Brown was ignored by both the NFL and AFL. Finally, the Houston Oilers called him. They had tagged him for defensive back, a new position for Brown. He struggled in training camp and was cut before the season began.

Within days, Denver signed Brown, and he made 1 interception his rookie year. The next season he made 9 for 140 yards. After his first All-Star Game in 1964, he was named the game's MVP on defense. But in 1967, after several injuries, the Broncos traded him to Oakland.

Being traded was a blow to Brown, but it was also his big break. For the next decade, the 6-foot 1-inch, 210-pounder was the leader of the Raiders secondary. He constantly talked to his men on the field, making sure they knew what was coming. He also inspired his line with his willingness to play hurt. In the 1981 season Brown played with his arm in a cast, a pulled groin muscle, and a broken thumb.

During his career Brown intercepted at least 1 pass in each of his sixteen seasons. He had 54 regular-season steals, plus 7 in postseason games. One of his career highlights was a 75-yard interception return for a touchdown in Super Bowl XI. That run is still a Super Bowl record for an interception.

In 1984, the first year he was eligible, Brown was inducted into the Pro Football Hall of Fame.

WILLIE BROWN			
Interceptions	54	Average Gain	8.7
Yards	472	Touchdowns	2

MICHAEL McCORMACK JR.

1930–
Position: tackle
Teams: New York Yankees, Cleveland Browns
Inducted: 1984

"Big Mike" McCormack's pro career was spent mostly with the Cleveland Browns. But he got to that team in a very strange way. He began his pro career with the New York Yankees in 1951. He entered the Army the next year, and in 1953 the Yankees disbanded and assigned him to the Baltimore Colts. That year Cleveland coach Paul Brown traded ten players to the Colts for McCormack and four other players. The 6-foot 4-inch, 250-pound McCormack was the key player in Brown's trade, even though he still had to serve another year in the Army.

His first year with the Browns–1954–McCormack plugged a hole in the Browns defense created by the retirement of the team's superstar middle guard, Bill Willis. At that time the middle guard position was the forerunner of the middle linebacker position. In addition to size and strength, the middle guard's job called for speed and the ability to figure out the opposition quarterback's plays. McCormack had all these qualities and helped the Browns get to the 1954 NFL championship against the Detroit Lions. Detroit had beaten Cleveland in the past two title games, and the Browns were tense. Early in the 1954 game, McCormack snatched the ball out of Lions quarterback Bobby Layne's hand as Layne dropped back to throw. McCormack's steal set up an important touchdown and gave the Browns the heart needed to rack up a 56–10 winning score.

In 1955 McCormack was moved to offensive tackle. He was just as good at opening up holes for a running back as he was at protecting a quarterback. He helped his team take the championship title again that year.

McCormack was born on June 21, 1930, in Chicago, Illinois. He attended high school in Kansas City, Missouri. He lettered in football as a fullback and tackle and in basketball as a center. During his four years at the University of Kansas, he played tackle and guard. His senior year, 1950, he was an All–Big Seven tackle, as well as the team captain.

After the New York Yankees drafted him, McCormack had an excellent rookie year, playing tackle on offense and linebacker on defense. That season he won his first Pro Bowl spot as offensive tackle. His reputation as a player continued while he was in the Army–enough to inspire Paul Brown's fifteen-player trade.

McCormack's playing courage was put to the test late in his career, when he tore up his knee during training camp. Most players would have been out for the season. For six weeks after surgery, McCormack worked with his trainer from early in the morning to eleven o'clock at night. By the second game of the season, he was ready to play.

From 1955 on, McCormack was team captain for the Browns. During his ten-year career, he was named to All-Pro teams almost every year and was selected to play in six Pro Bowls. In 1984 he entered the Pro Football Hall of Fame.

ARNIE WEINMEISTER

1923–
Position: defensive tackle
Teams: New York Yankees, New York Giants
Inducted: 1984

Arnie Weinmeister played only six seasons of pro football in the U.S. before he went with a Canadian team, but other players say that Weinmeister was to the defensive tackle spot what Gale Sayers was to the halfback position. He was in a class by himself.

Weinmeister's career began in 1948 with the New York Yankees. The Yankees belonged to the All-America Football Conference, a rival to the National Football League. His rookie year, Weinmeister won All-AAFC honorable mention, and the next season he won first team All-AAFC honors. When the AAFC folded after the 1949 season, Weinmeister moved to the New York Giants, where he stayed until 1954. He was a unanimous All-NFL selection and played in the Pro Bowl all four years he was with the Giants.

Weinmeister was born on March 23, 1923, in Rhein, Saskatchewan, Canada. His family moved to Portland, Oregon, when he was a baby. He was an All-City tackle for two years in high school. After graduating, he received a football scholarship to the University of Washington, where he played end, fullback, and guard.

Weinmeister's biggest asset was his great speed. He was fast enough to outrun most backs and zipped all over the field to make tackles. He became one of the first defensive players the fans loved to watch as much as they loved watching the ballhandlers.

Weinmeister, at 6 feet 4 inches and 235 pounds, was the key to New York's defense. His defensive charges were so explosive and so fast that the opposition quarterbacks were forced to get rid of the ball too quickly. In addition, he had a natural ability to figure out opposition plays and stop them. He was inducted into the Pro Football Hall of Fame in 1984.

FRANK GATSKI

1922–

Position: center
Teams: Cleveland Browns, Detroit Lions
Inducted: 1985

The center position in the T formation is considered one of the most important—and one of the toughest—jobs in football. Once the ball is snapped, the center has to hold off the opposi-tion's interior defensive linemen long enough to let the quarterback get in position to pass. Frank Gatski, at 6 feet 3 inches and 240 pounds, carried out this assignment on every down of every game during his twelve-season career.

From 1946 to 1956 Gatski played with the Cleveland Browns, then finished his career with the Detroit Lions. And although there are no stats for centers, Gatski was a winner wherever he went. He played in eleven championship games in twelve years, with his teams winning eight times.

"Gunner," as Gatski was nicknamed, never missed a game or a practice and never even called a timeout in 20 years of high school, college, and pro football. His toughness came from working in the coal mines of Number Nine Coal Camp, which was near the town in which he grew up.

Gatski was born on March 18, 1922 in Farmington, West Virginia. He played four years of football in high school. When he made the Marshall College football team, Gatski felt very lucky. It was "the only chance I had to get out of the mines," he said.

Later, a teammate from Marshall arranged for Gatski to try out for the Browns. After beating out some better-known players to make the team, Gatski waited almost two years to start. But when he did, he didn't stop. With Gatski at center, the Browns won the 1950, 1954, and 1955 NFL titles. When the team slumped in 1956, the Browns traded Gatski to the Detroit Lions in 1957. That season, Gatski's last, the Lions smashed the Browns 59–14 in the title game.

A good center is rarely noticed unless he makes a bad snap. During his pro career Gatski did such a good job of making his teams' offense click that no one really paid any attention to him. In 1985 the Pro Football Hall of Fame changed all that by inducting him into football immortality.

KENNETH RAY HOUSTON

1944–
Position: safety
Teams: Houston Oilers, Washington Redskins
Inducted: 1986

In high school Ken Houston played tuba, trombone, French horn, and trumpet in the school band. After his freshman year, he noticed that the football players—not the band members—attracted all the girls. Besides, Houston needed a scholarship to get into college. He decided to sign up for football. The music world's loss was football's gain.

Houston became one of the NFL's greatest safeties ever. He was a natural for the position. His long, graceful stride gave him excellent speed. His 6-foot 3-inch, 198-pound frame made him an ideal pass defense player. And his strength made him a punishing tackler.

Ken Houston was born on November 12, 1944, in Lufkin, Texas. After making his transition from band to football in high school, Houston ended up at Prairie View A&M. As a middle linebacker Houston earned the reputation as "the monster man." In 1966, his senior year, the Houston Oilers noticed he was a hard-hitting tackler for his size (he was only 190 pounds). In 1967 the Oilers drafted Houston and began using him at safety. Learning a new position was so difficult that Houston almost quit, but by the end of the year, he was a completely different player. His hard-nosed play helped the Oilers win the AFC East Division title.

The highlight of Houston's career with the Oilers came on December 19, 1971, when he stole 2 passes for touchdowns. His performance that day also tied the season record of 4 scoring returns and the single-game record of 2 scoring returns. Houston finished the season with 5 touchdowns (the fifth came on a fumble return) and he was named to the All-AFC team for the first time.

But after intercepting 25 passes during his first five years, Houston had none in 1972. The Oilers were also having a bad year, with a 1–13 season. That year Houston and a draft pick were traded to the Redskins for five of Washington's veteran players. With the Redskins Houston became a team leader, a co-captain, and a defensive signal caller. He was named All-Pro or All-NFC for seven straight years, from 1973 to 1979.

In fourteen seasons, Houston achieved Pro Bowl status an amazing twelve straight times (1968–79)—five as an Oiler and seven as a Redskin. He finished his career with 49 interceptions, which he returned for a total of 898 yards and an 18.3-yard average per return. Houston still holds the NFL career record for most touchdowns off interceptions, with 9. He also scored 1 touchdown each on a blocked field goal return, a fumble return, and a punt return. In 1986, the first year he was eligible, Houston was elected to the Pro Football Hall of Fame.

KEN HOUSTON			
Interceptions	49	Average Gain	18.3
Yards	898	Touchdowns	9

WILLIE EDWARD LANIER

1945–
Position: linebacker
Team: Kansas City Chiefs
Inducted: 1986

In high school Willie Lanier was a 200-pound guard and linebacker. He had a reputation for tackling so hard that some accused him of playing dirty. Not so, Lanier said. "In high school and college, I tried to be a big hitter because I believed pro coaches like hitters, and I wanted to play pro football."

Lanier realized his dream and became one of the top middle linebackers in the game. He kept his reputation as a powerful hitter, but he also knew how to cover receivers, grabbing 27 interceptions in his career.

Lanier was born on August 21, 1945, in Clover, Virginia, and raised in Richmond. In college, at Morgan State, he was team captain and an All-America selection. The Kansas City Chiefs drafted him in 1967.

The Chiefs also chose another middle linebacker that year—Jim Lynch from Notre Dame. Who would win the starting position—a black player from a little-known college or a white player from a university famous for its football? Lanier was sure it wouldn't be him. By midseason, however, Lanier was starting middle linebacker, and Lynch was shifted to right linebacker. With Bobby Bell at left linebacker, this awesome threesome formed one of history's finest linebacker squads.

At first Lanier played with his old reckless style. Then he struck his head diving over a blocker to grab a ballcarrier. A few days later he wandered into the wrong huddle and collapsed. He had a severe concussion, which left him with double vision for months. The next season, Lanier's playing was more careful. "I began to select the hits," he said. "If I was off balance or at a bad angle, I just made the play without excessive force." After suffering the concussion, Lanier wore a special padded helmet. He also became more of a thinker than a basher. "Playing middle linebacker is sort of a science," he said. "It involves mathematics, geometry, and angles."

Off the field Lanier was easygoing and quick to smile, but on the field he was an awesome sight to the quarterback lined up against him. Lanier was 6 feet 1 inch and 245 pounds. He had a 20-inch neck, a 50-inch chest, and a 34-inch waist. One player remembered a bone-crushing tackle from Lanier. "Part of me landed one place; and the rest of me, someplace else. I pulled myself together and went on just like a mountain had never fallen on me."

Except for 1969, Lanier was All-Pro, All-AFL, or All-AFC every year from 1968 through 1976. He played in AFL All-Star Games in 1968 and 1969 and was defensive MVP in the 1971 Pro Bowl. In nine of eleven seasons he intercepted at least 2 passes, and he recovered 15 opponents' fumbles during his career.

Lanier retired in 1974 to enter private business, then changed his mind and signed another contract with the Chiefs. He retired for good after the 1977 season.

WILLIE LANIER			
Interceptions	27	Average Gain	16.3
Yards	440	Touchdowns	2

FRANCIS ASBURY TARKENTON

1940–
Position: quarterback
Teams: Minnesota Vikings, New York Giants
Inducted: 1986

For the Minnesota Vikings, 1961 promised to be a rough season. New to the NFL that year, the club played its first game against the Chicago Bears, an original league member with a tradition of excellence. And running the inexperienced Vikings offense was a rookie quarterback—Fran Tarkenton. But if Tarkenton was nervous he didn't show it.

The 6-foot, 185-pound quarterback passed for 250 yards and 4 touchdowns and ran for 1 touchdown, leading the Vikings to an amazing 37–13 upset over the Bears. The Vikings won only two more games that year, but Tarkenton was on the way to superstardom. A quarter of a century later, he became the first Viking to enter the Pro Football Hall of Fame.

Tarkenton had a running style of twisting and turning and retreating before throwing a pass. He was described as running "as if he is in a basketball game." This method of scrambling was exciting to watch, and it was out of the ordinary. At that time, most quarterbacks stayed securely in the pocket behind their blockers.

When Tarkenton finally did throw the ball, he connected. By the year he retired, 1978, he had thrown 342 touchdowns—an NFL career record. Tarkenton also set career records for passing attempts, completions, and passing yards—records that stood for more than fifteen years.

Tarkenton was born on August 3, 1940, in Richmond, Virginia. He began developing his scrambling skills in high school in Athens, Georgia, and later, at the University of Georgia. The Vikings had just formed when they picked him in the third round of the 1960 draft. His first year he passed for 4 touchdowns in three different games. His 58.1 completion percentage was a rookie record.

In 1967, after a stormy relationship with Vikings coach Norm Van Brocklin the year before, Tarkenton was traded. The New York Giants wanted him, hoping Tarkenton would spark publicity as well as throw for touchdowns. The Giants were in hot competition with the New York Jets and their star quarterback, Joe Namath. Tarkenton's best season with New York was 1970, when he led the Giants to a 9–5 record. After a salary dispute in 1971, he asked to be traded, and Minnesota took him back.

Starting in 1973, the Vikings won six straight NFC Central Division championships, with a 62–22–2 record, and made it to three Super Bowls. During that period Tarkenton was All-NFC once, All-Pro twice, and was invited to three Pro Bowls. In total, he was elected to nine Pro Bowls, playing in six. He suffered a serious leg injury in 1977, but went on to play his best—and last—season in 1978, with 345 completions for 3,468 yards and 25 touchdowns. After an eighteen-year career with the Vikings and Giants, Tarkenton's combined rushing and

passing total was 50,677 yards—nearly 29 miles, or 500 football fields.

FRAN TARKENTON			
Passing Attempts	6.467	Rushing Attempts	675
Passing Completions	3,686	Rushing Yards	3,674
Passing Percentage	57.0	Average Gain	5.4
Passing Yards	47,003	Touchdowns	32
Average Pass Gain	7.27		
Touchdown Passes	342		
Passes Intercepted	266		

DOAK WALKER

1927–
Position: halfback
Team: Detroit Lions
Inducted: 1986

Doak Walker had a short but spectacular career with the Detroit Lions—just six seasons. At 5 feet 11 inches and 172 pounds, Walker was thought to be too small for the pros, but he proved to be a versatile offensive threat, twice leading the NFL in scoring.

Walker was born on January 1, 1927, in Dallas, Texas. He was a three-time All-America halfback and a 1948 Heisman Trophy winner at Southern Methodist University. Despite his size, the Lions took a chance with him, and Walker quickly rewarded their confidence.

In his rookie year—his best season—Walker led the league in scoring, with 128 points. Twice he scored all his team's points in a game, in victories over Green Bay and Pittsburgh. He caught 35 passes, rushed for 386 yards, was named Rookie of the Year and All-NFL, and played on the Pro Bowl team.

Walker went on to lead the NFL in scoring again in 1955, with 96 points. He made a total of four All-NFL teams and played in five Pro Bowl Games. Doak was a key offensive threat for the Lions when they won back-to-back NFL titles in 1952 and 1953.

In 1956, when a successful business venture demanded his time, Walker left the Lions and pro football. In addition to his rushing and receiving achievements, some of his other numbers include 18 punts returned for 284 yards and a touchdown, 38 kickoffs returned for 968 yards, 183 extra points kicked, and 49 field goals kicked. In 1986 Walker was inducted into the Pro Football Hall of Fame.

DOAK WALKER			
Rushing Attempts	309	Pass Receptions	152
Rushing Yards	1,520	Pass Receiving Yards	2,539
Average Gain	4.9	Average Gain	16.7
Touchdowns	12	Touchdowns	21

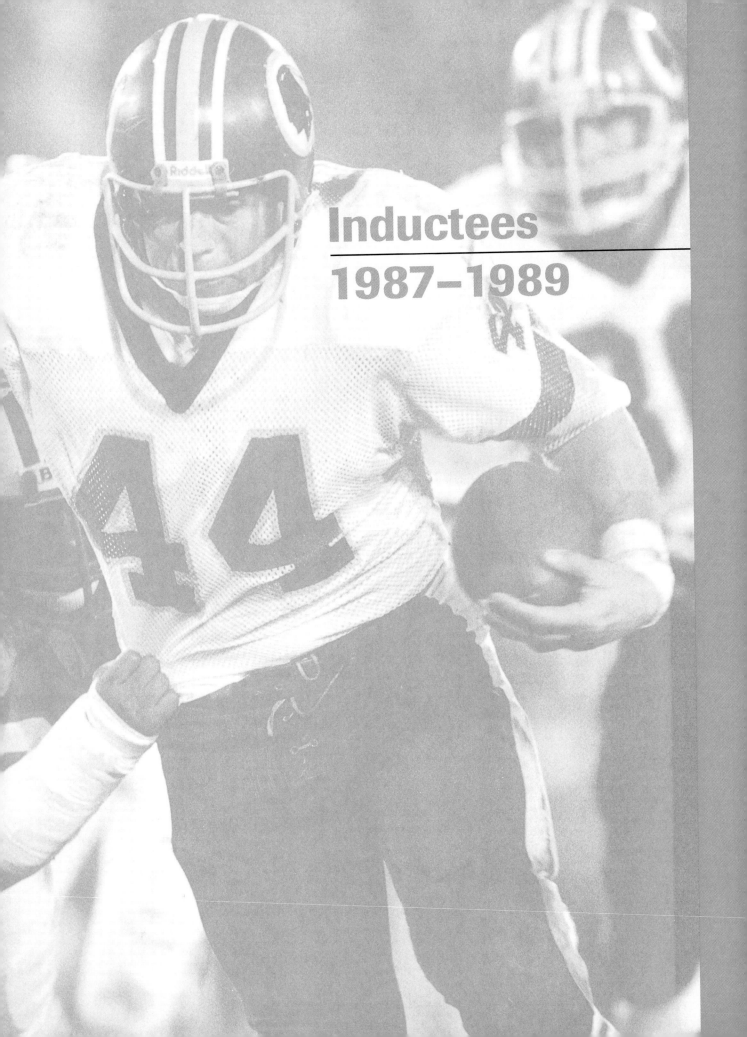

Inductees
1987–1989

LAWRENCE RICHARD CSONKA

1946–
Position: fullback
Teams: Miami Dolphins, New York Giants
Inducted: 1987

HE WON'T WORK ZONKED

Larry Csonka took lots of pounding to achieve his impressive stats. In addition to several concussions, he suffered a broken nose a dozen times, plus a cracked eardrum. He had surgery to repair an elbow and a knee. Through all of this, he refused to take painkillers.

"I don't like to take novocaine," he said. "If I can't control the pain with my head, I shouldn't be playing. I'm willing to play hurt, though. I have an obligation to my teammates to do that. The desire to play, however, must come from within. It is based on pride and determination."

Larry Csonka talked casually about his role as a line-smashing ballcarrier. "My job is no big deal. I am a fullback, a power back whose assignment is to establish an inside running game." In 1987 the Pro Football Hall of Fame decided that Csonka's work had been a big deal—enough to ensure his induction.

Csonka's eleven-year career stats weren't amazing, though he did have three seasons with 1,000 or more yards rushing. And he was sure-handed, fumbling just 21 times in almost 2,000 career carries. But what made Csonka truly valuable were his endurance, strength, and willingness to do anything to help his team. Miami coach Don Shula called him "the modern-day Bronko Nagurski."

Csonka was born on Christmas Day, 1946, in Stow, Ohio. He attended Syracuse University. An All-America player, the 6-foot 3-inch, 235-pound "Zonk" continued the great tradition of Syracuse runners: Jim Brown, Ernie Davis, Jim Nance, and Floyd Little. Csonka was the AFL Miami Dolphins' number one draft choice in 1968, the team's third year in the league.

During Csonka's first two years with Miami, the Dolphins had a losing record. Then Don Shula arrived in 1970, and Miami's record went to 10–4. In Shula's first five years with the Dolphins, the team compiled a sensational 57–13–1 record. Miami won four AFC East titles, three AFC championships, and two Super Bowls. In 1972 the team won 17 straight games on its way to a Super Bowl championship, becoming the only team to finish a season undefeated.

Shula's strategy called on the running game about two out of every three plays. Csonka and halfbacks Jim Kiick and Mercury Morris carried the load on those plays. Kiick was a great ballcarrier as well as pass catcher, and Morris was the outside runner. Csonka was the inside workhorse, leading the team in both carries and yards during each of Shula's first five years.

LARRY CSONKA

Rushing Attempts	1,891	Pass Receptions	106
Rushing Yards	8,081	Pass Receiving Yards	820
Average Gain	4.3	Average Gain	7.7
Touchdowns	64	Touchdowns	4
		Total Points	408 (68 touchdowns)

ZONK'S KIND OF JOB

A heavy-duty workhorse, Larry Csonka was an excellent ballcarrier. When he didn't have the ball, he was a punishing blocker. But he didn't think of himself as a great all-around athlete who made contributions to many facets of the game. He described his role as if he were a simple worker who had a job to do every day to feed his family.

"My role is to make the power running game work. A lot of plays I run are momentum plays. They are not designed for long gains. If you make 4 or 5 yards, everyone is happy. It's not a spectacular strategy, but I've lived and breathed it, and I know it works."

In 1971 Csonka joined the 1,000-yard club for the first of three straight seasons. Those three seasons he was named either All-Pro, All-AFC, or both. He was also picked for five straight Pro Bowls. In Super Bowl VII Csonka was the game's top rusher, with 112 yards on 15 carries. The next year he carried 33 times for a Super Bowl record 145 yards, scored 2 touchdowns, and was named the game's Most Valuable Player.

In 1975 Csonka and two other Dolphins joined the Memphis Southmen of the newly formed World Football League. When the WFL folded midseason, Csonka was a free agent, and he joined the New York Giants. A regular fullback all his three years in New York, he didn't dominate the ballcarrying as he had under Shula. His rushing total dropped to 311 yards in fourteen games by 1978 and the Giants released him.

There was a happy reunion in 1979 when Csonka signed once more with the Dolphins. That year he carried a career-high 220 times for 827 yards and 12 rushing touchdowns. He ended his career after being named the NFL Comeback Player of the Year.

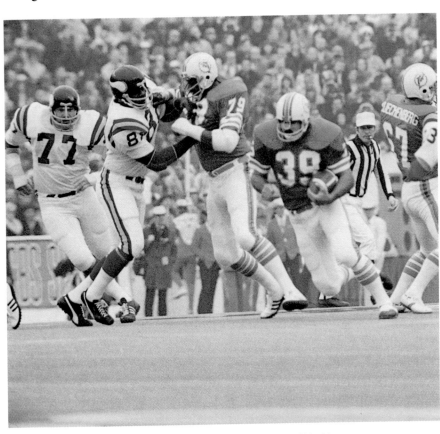

Fullback Larry Csonka plows through the Washington Redskins' line to score for the Miami Dolphins.

CHARLES E. "JOE" GREENE

1946–
Position: defensive tackle
Team: Pittsburgh Steelers
Inducted: 1987

WHAT'S IN A NAME?

Joe Greene's varsity team at North Texas State was called "the Mean Green Machine." Sportswriters quickly added the name to North Texas's star player. And for good reason. Greene's rookie season he was thrown out of two games—once for starting a fight and once for landing a late tackle on Giants quarterback Fran Tarkenton. Greene hit Tarkenton so hard that the crash was heard all the way up in the press box.

During a 1977 AFC playoff game, Greene dealt a Denver guard a vicious uppercut to the stomach. During a losing game against the Eagles, he thought he was being held on every play. Frustrated, he heaved the ball into the stands and stomped off the field.

A gentle man off the field, Greene didn't like his nickname. When he retired, he said, "I just want people to remember me as being a good player and not really mean."

When Coach Chuck Noll was hired to rebuild the Pittsburgh Steelers in 1969, he made a defensive lineman—not a quarterback or running back—the cornerstone of the team. But "Mean Joe" Greene wasn't just any defensive lineman. At 6 feet 4 inches and 260 pounds, Greene became the leader of the awesome defensive unit called "the Steel Curtain." Fearless and strong, Greene was also clever. He perfected a way of lining up at an angle between the center and guard, a tactic that interfered with the opposition's blocking assignments. The imposing tackle helped turn the Steelers from one of the worst teams in the NFL into the winners of four Super Bowls in six years.

As a rookie Greene watched the Steelers hit rock bottom with a 1–13 record. Greene, however, showed his talents, as he was named the NFL's Defensive Rookie of the Year and a Pro Bowl selection. By 1972 the Steelers were division champs.

Greene was born on September 24, 1946. He picked cotton as a child growing up in Temple, Texas. At North Texas State, he was All-America his senior year, top lineman on the Senior Bowl's South team, and a College All-Star Game selection. He was nicknamed "Mean Joe" Greene after his varsity team, "the Mean Green Machine." Greene hated that name, and off the field he was a gentle man. On the field, he earned his reputation. He was nasty and intimidating. Sometimes reckless, he got into fights and was taken out of plays. But he was one of those few defensive players who could single-handedly turn a game around.

Greene demonstrated that ability in the 1972 AFC Central game against Houston. Fighting for their first-ever championship, the Steelers offense was racked with injuries. When the score was 3–3 Greene turned to linebacker Andy Russell and told him that the defense would have to win the game. Greene sacked Houston's quarterback 5 times, made 6 unassisted tackles, and blocked a field goal attempt. On one play he fought off three blockers, forced a fumble, and then recovered it to set up the winning field goal. Pittsburgh won 9–3.

The 1972 season was perhaps Greene's best. He won Defensive Player of the Year honors and he totaled 11 quarterback sacks—a team and career high. In 1974 he was named Defensive Player of the Year again.

KNOWING HIS LIMITS

In his 1975 season Joe Greene suffered neck, back, and groin injuries. By the fall of 1976, his eighth year with the Steelers, a pinched nerve in his neck had caused his left arm to wither and lose strength. Pittsburgh lost four of its first five games that season before Greene regained strength in his arm.

"Up to that time, I had no respect for any other person's ability because I had so much respect for my own," Greene said. "I figured that no matter what the other guy did, I'd take care of him. Suddenly that all changed."

After his injuries healed, Greene wasn't the same player. "I never was completely healthy again," he admitted. "I never got back to the confidence level I once had. I changed my game, I started playing very conservatively. I didn't do things to get myself in trouble. If I couldn't make the play, I'd funnel it to someone else. That gave me my worth."

Tell that to the opposing players he tackled. Even after his injuries, Greene achieved Pro Bowl and All-AFC his five remaining seasons.

For his career, Greene was named All-Pro five times and played in ten Pro Bowls. He finished with 66 sacks and 16 fumble recoveries. When he retired, Greene said, "I want to be remembered for playing thirteen years and contributing to four championship teams. I would like to be remembered for maybe setting a standard for others to achieve." His induction into the Pro Football Hall of Fame the first year he was eligible proved he had succeeded in gaining his wish.

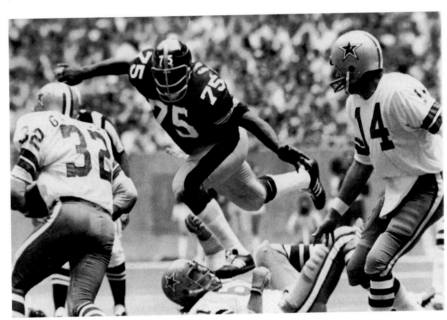

"Mean" Joe Greene (75), left tackle for the Pittsburgh Steelers, takes a shortcut across a Dallas Cowboys guard to stop a runner.

FREDERICK BILETNIKOFF

1943–
Position: wide receiver
Team: Oakland Raiders
Inducted: 1988

PASS THE ANTACID, PLEASE

Fred Biletnikoff was an intense player and a worrier. This combination of traits gave him an ulcer when he was in college. During his pro career he kept a case of antacid in his locker. In spite of gulping down the stuff in the locker room, Biletnikoff often threw up before going on the field. Before a game he paced the dressing room, and after the game it took him six to eight hours to calm down.

In more than 20 years of football—in high school, in college, and in the pros—Fred Biletnikoff played one position: wide receiver. "I like catching passes," he said. "I would be lost if I were ever told to do anything on a football field except catch passes."

The 6-foot 1-inch, 190-pound Biletnikoff spent his fourteen-year pro career with the Oakland Raiders. During that time he caught more than 40 passes a season for ten straight years, and his 76 touchdowns were the most scored by a Raider. The Raiders never had a losing season while Biletnikoff played for them.

Biletnikoff played high school football, basketball, and baseball, and ran track in Erie, Pennsylvania, where he was born on February 23, 1943. He credits his pass catching abilities to his high school coaches, who taught their teams to play a passing game. "We probably threw 25 times a game in high school," Biletnikoff remembered, "really just as much as we did in Oakland."

A football scholarship took Biletnikoff to Florida State University, where he continued the passing game. An All-America selection his senior year, Biletnikoff finished fourth in the nation with 57 receptions for 11 touchdowns. He was drafted by the NFL's Detroit Lions and by the Raiders, who belonged to the rival American Football League.

Biletnikoff chose the Raiders for two reasons. First, he didn't want to play too much in the cold weather, remembering the winters of his childhood in Erie. Second, he thought he'd have a better chance to play with the Raiders, since the Lions already had several star receivers. During the Gator Bowl—his last college game—Biletnikoff caught 4 touchdown passes to carry Florida State to victory over Oklahoma. Right after the game, in front of a national television audience, he stood under the goalposts and signed with the Raiders.

In his rookie year Biletnikoff dropped more passes than he caught and was assigned to the special teams. His first year totals were 24 receptions for 331 yards but no touchdowns. In the ninth

FRED BILETNIKOFF			
Pass Receptions	589	**Total Points**	456 (76 touchdowns)
Pass Receiving Yards	8,974		
Average Gain	15.2		
Touchdowns	76		

HARD WORK AND GREEN GOO

Fred Biletnikoff had just one deficiency as a wide receiver: His lack of breakaway speed kept him from making spectacular long gains. Still, it was never a major problem. "I can run the 40 [yard dash] in 4.7, and that's fast enough," he pointed out. "I know how to beat those speed burners. The secret is to get the jump on the defensive back."

To help get that jump, Biletnikoff did a lot of hard work. After studying opponents on film, he practiced his patterns hour after hour. He also worked out on a light punching bag. "Pass catching is reflexes, the hands and eyes working together," he explained. "The bag comes back at different angles, and that helps the coordination between my hands and my eyes."

In spite of his "slowness," Biletnikoff often got double coverage from the opposition because he caught such a high percentage of passes. "He can catch anything he can touch," said Raiders coach John Madden. "That's no accident. Some receivers might catch 15 or 20 passes in practice. Fred will catch 100."

Biletnikoff also had a secret weapon in his battles for the ball. Before games, he smeared a green gooey substance on his hands to improve his grip.

week of his second year, he injured his knee and was out for the rest of the year. After playing his first four games as a reserve in his third season, he was put into the starting lineup. He never left.

From 1967 through 1972 Biletnikoff teamed up with quarterback Daryle Lamonica to make an unbeatable pass catching duo. Their first year together Biletnikoff caught 40 passes for 895 yards and 5 touchdowns, and the Raiders won the AFL championship. After that season he was picked for the AFL All-Star Game. The Raiders lost Super Bowl II to the Packers that year, and Biletnikoff only made 2 catches in that game.

From 1973 until he retired in 1978, quarterback Ken Stabler was Biletnikoff's passer. Together they took the Raiders to a 32–14 victory over the Minnesota Vikings in Super Bowl XI. Biletnikoff caught 4 passes for 79 yards that day, and was named the game's MVP.

Biletnikoff was picked for three AFL All-Star Games and four AFC-NFC Pro Bowls. He was All-AFL in 1969 and All-AFC in 1970, 1972, and 1973. When he retired in 1978, his total of 589 receptions was the fourth-best career total at that time. Biletnikoff also added 70 receptions for 1,167 yards and 10 touchdowns in nineteen postseason games, which still ranks among the all-time leaders in each category.

Wide receiver Fred Biletnikoff (25) gets ready to catch a pass for the Oakland Raiders.

JACK RAPHAEL HAM

1948–
Position: linebacker
Team: Pittsburgh Steelers
Inducted: 1988

JACK NEVER HAMMED IT UP

A quiet, modest guy, Jack Ham saw himself as simply one member of a great defensive lineup. "If I had been with another team, I might not have been thought of in the same light," he said. "We have a unique type of defense, and it is honed around the kind of talent we have."

But during the 1970s, when the Steelers ruled the NFL, football ruled in Pittsburgh, and Ham was the crown prince. The fans even formed a fan club for their *Dobre Shunka*, which is Slovak for "Great Ham."

During an evening mass in Pittsburgh, the monsignor suddenly proclaimed, "How about those Steelers?" Then he asked if Steelers vice president Dan Rooney was there. Rooney wasn't, but a church member announced that Jack Ham was.

"They gave me a big ovation just like we were out at the stadium," Ham recalled. "I even stayed after mass and signed autographs."

An anchor on Pittsburgh's "Steel Curtain" defense, Jack Ham set a new standard for outside linebackers in modern-day pro football. At 6 feet 1 inch and 220 pounds, Ham was small, but he had speed and the ability to read a play and act quickly to thwart it. Ham could track down any running back who got through the defensive line. At the same time, Ham often acted as a fifth member of the secondary line.

Defending receivers suited Ham just fine. "I love playing pass coverage," he said. "Some people think of a linebacker only as a guy who can get to the right hole in a hurry and hit hard. To me, that's less than half of being a linebacker. You've got to do your job on pass coverage, or else you're a liability."

A liability is something Ham never was. During his twelve-year career with the Steelers he totaled 32 interceptions, 19 fumble recoveries, and 25.5 sacks. He was All-NFL for seven straight years (1973–79) and All-Pro for six (1974–79). He was also selected for eight straight Pro Bowls—a record at the time. In 1975 he was the NFL Defensive Player of the Year and the only unanimous choice for the NFL Team of the 1970s Decade.

Ham joined the Steelers in 1971 after winning All-America honors at Penn State. Ham impressed Coach Chuck Noll in training, and the rookie assured himself a starting job when he picked off 3 passes in the final preseason game against the New York Giants. In a 21–17 regular-season win over the San Diego Chargers, he intercepted a pass at the Steelers 17. Then, on the last play of the game, he deflected a 2-yard pass that probably would have put San Diego on top.

His second season, Ham intercepted 7 passes and recovered 4 opponents' fumbles, helping the Steelers win their first AFC championship title. The team began an eight-year streak that put them first in all but one division finish. During that streak the Steelers won four Super Bowls.

A defender who could hit an opponent as well as outsmart him, Ham was at his best in the biggest games. His 2 interceptions helped

JACK HAM			
Interceptions	32	Average Gain	6.8
Yards	218	Touchdowns	1

As a teenager in Johnstown, Pennsylvania, where he was born on December 23, 1948, Jack Ham didn't look like a future Hall of Fame linebacker. He didn't play that position until his senior year in high school, and then he weighed only 185 pounds. He decided to attend Pennsylvania State, and just before he left for college, he was awarded the last available scholarship.

By his senior year in college, Ham had grown into a 220-pound All-America eager for the pros. However, when he was drafted by the Steelers in 1971, he wasn't thrilled. Founded in 1933, the Steelers had never won even a division championship. "I never had experienced a 5–9 season, and I didn't want to start in the pros," he complained. He didn't have to.

As part of the Steel Curtain defense, Ham took Pittsburgh to its first AFC Central championship in 1972. It was the first of eight straight playoff seasons. The Steelers won four AFC titles and four Super Bowls from 1974 to 1978. "Goal-wise, I didn't come into the league to be an All-Pro, but I do like to play on a winning team," he said.

win the 1974 AFC championship title that put the Steelers in their first Super Bowl. In three 1978 playoff games, he had 18 unassisted tackles. But Ham wasn't comfortable with his big-play reputation. "I prefer to play consistent, error-free football. If you're doing your job well and defending your area, you might not get tested that often, or get a chance to make big plays."

Ham missed only two games in his first ten years, but in 1979 a dislocated toe on his left foot forced him to miss Super Bowl XIV. For the next three seasons Ham played in pain and struggled to regain his old style, but he could no longer drive off his foot from his left to his right. Opponents were able to get outside him, trapping him in the mass of blockers. In 1982 he decided to quit. In 1988, the first year he was eligible, he became a member of the Pro Football Hall of Fame.

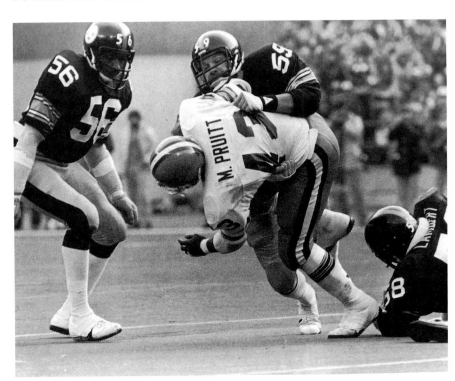

Pittsburgh Steelers linebacker Jack Ham (59)
does his job of bringing down the opposition.

ALAN CEDRIC PAGE

1945–
Position: defensive tackle
Teams: Minnesota Vikings, Chicago Bears
Inducted: 1988

HE DID IT HIS WAY

Alan Page had his own philosophy about defensive football. He wanted to pull off a quick opening thrust to get past the offensive line to the ballcarrier. "A defensive player should think of himself more as an aggressor, not as a defender," he maintained. "I've got a job to do, and my job is not to sit back and wait and then react to what the offense does. My job is to go after them. If you are going to make a mistake, make it aggressively."

Page also liked to go all over the field, within the guidelines of his team's defensive system. "The coaches basically left me alone," he said. "They told me their defensive plan and the job I was expected to do, and then I was allowed to go my way to get the necessary and expected results."

Minnesota Vikings coach Bud Grant once described the kind of player he hoped to acquire. "Whatever position he plays, [he must be] someone who can turn a game around, maybe even on one play.... Of course, someone like that comes along infrequently and sometimes never." Grant was lucky–he found that kind of player in Alan Page.

Page spent his career at defensive tackle. As part of Minnesota's deadly defensive front line known as "the Purple People Eaters," Page was a consistent star. Through the 1970s he racked up at least 125 tackles every year, with sack totals in the double figures.

Few linemen had more impressive career numbers. Page totaled 173 quarterback sacks, 28 blocked punts or place kicks, and 23 opponents' fumbles recovered. Records for tackles were not kept until 1970, but for his last twelve seasons, Page is credited with 1,423 tackles–1,071 unassisted. In 1971 he became the first interior lineman and the first defensive player to win the NFL MVP Award.

Given his hometown, Page seemed destined to play football. He was born in Canton, Ohio–the birthplace of the NFL and the Pro Football Hall of Fame–on August 7, 1945. An All-America defensive end at Notre Dame, Page was Minnesota's first-round pick in the 1967 draft.

With the Vikings, Page had to adjust to defensive tackle, a job with completely different responsibilities. He learned quickly and moved into the starting lineup in his fourth week. He never missed a start again or sat out a game with an injury. Altogether he played 238 games–218 in the regular season, sixteen in the postseason, and four Super Bowls.

With Page starting, the Vikings' pass rush improved dramatically. Page helped set up tackles for the two ends, while still getting his own tackles and sacks. No defensive star seemed to play quite like him. Some depended on pure strength and a savage attack to bring down an opponent–Page relied on his incredible quickness to control the scrimmage line.

Page made a point of getting off the line the instant the ball was snapped. Then, using the shortest possible line of attack, he'd get past the guard to the ballcarrier. He preferred to play at a light weight for his position, making tackles from all over the field. He

A LOSING BATTLE

His experience in the 1967 College All-Star Game made Alan Page rethink his playing philosophy. The College All-Stars faced the NFL champions, the Green Bay Packers. Page was surprised to see that the huge Packers didn't use their size and strength. He realized that weight was not the only consideration for a pro football player. "Nobody tried to overpower me," he recalled. "They didn't hit me that hard. They just got in my way and handled me like I was nothing."

At 6 feet 4 inches and 278 pounds, Page carried a normal weight for a defensive tackle, yet he was always incredibly quick and light on his feet. However, after his experience in the game against Green Bay, he became almost obsessed with losing weight. Page's strenuous weight-loss programs annoyed his coach so much that it eventually led to the Vikings' letting him go. The Chicago Bears then signed him. In Chicago Page continued to lose weight *and* pick up sacks—which might have made the Vikings the real losers.

made plays no other defensive tackle seemed able to duplicate.

But Coach Grant was irritated with Page's obsession with losing weight. Page, who stood 6 feet 4 inches, weighed 278 pounds when he joined the Vikings. He gradually got down to 220 pounds during his career. Even at his heaviest, he played as if he were an acrobat, but he was convinced he should be lighter. Grant felt Page's weight-loss program, which included running marathons, was hurting his performances.

Midway through the 1978 season, Page was placed on waivers, and Chicago snapped him up. In four seasons with the Bears he had 40 sacks and 12 blocked kicks. Page retired in 1981 to practice law.

Chicago Bears tackle Alan Page (in back) sacks the opposition's quarterback.

TERRY PAXTON BRADSHAW

1948–
Position: quarterback
Team: Pittsburgh Steelers
Inducted: 1989

THE IMMACULATE RECEPTION

Terry Bradshaw is partly responsible for perhaps the most famous play in football history, "the Immaculate Reception." It happened on the final play of the 1972 AFC playoff between the Steelers and the Oakland Raiders. The Steelers were trailing 7–6 with 22 seconds left in the game.

On fourth down at the Steelers 40-yard line, Bradshaw dropped back and passed to receiver Frenchy Fuqua. Just as the ball reached Fuqua, it bounced off Raiders defensive back Jack Tatum and flew toward Steelers running back Franco Harris. Harris caught the ball just before it touched his shoe tops, then raced into the end zone. What was the perhaps the most bizarre reception on the gridiron gave the Steelers a 13–7 victory.

Terry Bradshaw's pro football career began on the highest possible note when he was the first player selected in the 1970 college draft. It ended on a high note when he was inducted into the Pro Football Hall of Fame in 1989. But in between those events, Bradshaw's career went up and down like a roller coaster.

Bradshaw was born on September 2, 1948, in Shreveport, Louisiana. He led his high school to the state finals his senior year. At Louisiana Tech he wound up with 7,149 yards and 42 touchdown passes and was named the Most Valuable Player in the Senior Bowl, his last college game. But the hottest pro prospect had a lukewarm rookie year.

With the 6-foot 3-inch, 210-pound quarterback starting eight games, the Steelers' record went from 1–13 to 5–9. But Bradshaw completed just 38.1 percent of his passes and led the NFL in interceptions with 24. "I was totally unprepared for pro ball," Bradshaw said. "I had had no schooling on reading defenses. I had never studied the game films the way a quarterback should."

In 1972 Bradshaw led the Steelers to their first division championship in 40 years, but the next year his playing time was reduced by a separated shoulder. In 1974 Joe Gilliam became the number one quarterback, and a sulking Bradshaw sat on the bench for six games. In the seventh game, injuries sidelined Gilliam and second-string quarterback Terry Hanratty, and Bradshaw stepped in.

That year Coach Chuck Noll decided to use the forward pass more. Bradshaw had a sensational throwing arm, and this was his kind of game. Noll told Bradshaw to call his own signals and to take charge of the offense. With his coach's backing, Bradshaw began to blossom. "When I got the confidence from [Noll] was when I became a pro quarterback," he said. An NFL rule change helped too.

TERRY BRADSHAW			
Passing Attempts	3,901	Rushing Attempts	444
Passing Completions	2,025	Rushing Yards	2,255
Passing Percentage	51.9	Average Gain	5.1
Passing Yards	22,989	Touchdowns	32
Average Pass Gain	7.17		
Touchdown Passes	212		
Passes Intercepted	210		

A SUPER BOWL SUPERSTAR

With Terry Bradshaw leading the offense, the Pittsburgh Steelers became the first team to win four Super Bowls. In Super Bowl IX, Bradshaw's pass to Larry Brown in the fourth quarter clinched the Steelers' first Super Bowl win, a 16–6 victory over the Minnesota Vikings.

In Super Bowl X, a touchdown pass to Randy Grossman tied the score against the Dallas Cowboys. Then Bradshaw's 64-yard pass to Lynn Swann won the game. But Bradshaw didn't know that until after the game. Just as he released the ball, he was knocked cold by a blitzing Cliff Harris.

When the Steelers and Cowboys met again in Super Bowl XIII, Bradshaw beat Dallas almost single-handedly, with a 318-yard, 4-touchdown passing explosion. In Super Bowl XIV, he passed the Steelers to their fourth championship victory with 309 aerial yards, a 47-yard scoring pass to Swann and a 73-yard bomb to John Stallworth.

Bradshaw's Super Bowl career marks included most yards passing (932) and most touchdown passes (9), records since surpassed by Joe Montana. Bradshaw's 3,833 passing yards and 30 touchdown passes were also records for all postseason games, until Montana beat those as well.

The "bump and run" tactics used by defensive backs on receivers were prohibited more than 5 yards past the scrimmage line. Those rules were put into place specifically to increase scoring. With two superior receivers–Lynn Swann and John Stallworth–for Bradshaw to pass to, the Steelers did exactly that.

Bradshaw led Pittsburgh to two straight victories in Super Bowls IX and X. He became the youngest quarterback since Johnny Unitas to win back-to-back championships. In 1977 Bradshaw broke his left wrist in a game against Houston and played his final eleven games with his hand in a hard cast, starting in every game. His team voted him MVP for the first of two straight years.

Pittsburgh's star quarterback pulled out all the stops in 1978. Bradshaw was AFC Player of the Year, and his Super Bowl MVP performance took the Steelers to their third championship–his 318 passing yards and 4 touchdown passes were Super Bowl records at the time.

In 1979 Bradshaw set team records with 472 attempts, 259 completions, and 3,724 yards. He had three 300-yard games–a career first–and threw 26 touchdown passes. The Steelers won Super Bowl XIV, and Bradshaw won his second straight Super Bowl MVP Award.

In the early 1980s Pittsburgh lost many of its finest players, and the team's record suffered. Bradshaw, however, passed for 3,339 and 2,887 yards in 1980 and 1981, respectively. Then in 1983, he had elbow surgery. After the surgery, his passing arm was gone, and he was forced to retire in 1984.

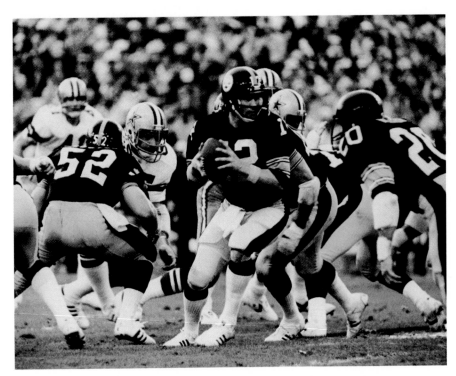

Pittsburgh Steelers quarterback Terry Bradshaw (12) gets ready to pass.

ARTHUR SHELL

1946–
Position: tackle
Teams: Oakland Raiders, Los Angeles Raiders
Inducted: 1989

THE WEIGHING GAME

Everyone knew Art Shell was big, but during his pro football career, no one knew exactly how big. For some reason, he kept his weight a secret. "When everybody else got on the scales, I would walk by," Shell said. Early on, the Raiders listed his weight at 255 pounds, then 265. By 1981 it was 285. Some people were convinced it was nearer 300 pounds—maybe even 320.

"I will tell you honestly the day when I weighed the most," he confessed once. "It was the day of Super Bowl XI. I went into the locker room alone and weighed myself just before the game. I weighed 310 pounds…. [Coach] John Madden told me as long as I performed, it didn't matter to him how much I weighed."

Considering the Hall of Famer's remarkable career, who could argue with the weight of that logic?

For fifteen years, from 1968 to 1982, Art Shell played left offensive tackle for the Oakland—then Los Angeles—Raiders. The club boasted awesome forward lines for years, and Shell was considered the most outstanding among those linemen. At 6 feet 5 inches and an estimated 285 pounds, Shell was an ideal size for an offensive tackle. He combined that size with brains, speed, and agility.

Shell was born on November 26, 1946, in Charleston, South Carolina. In high school he was an All-State star in football and basketball. He was considering Grambling State University for college when the Maryland State–Eastern Shore football coach showed up at his house. "I'm not leaving without you," the coach insisted. Shell chose Maryland partly to ease his father's financial burden of paying for his school.

At Maryland Shell played center and defensive tackle his first two years and two-way tackle his last two. He made All-Conference three years and All-America two years. He also continued to play basketball in college, and those skills were considered a plus by the Raiders scouts.

In 1968 the Raiders picked Shell as their third-round draft choice. "The primary thing we saw in Art was his great size," said Coach John Madden. "But we also were excited that he was an accomplished basketball player. With that size, combined with his ability to move his feet and the agility he showed on the basketball court, we knew we had a quality prospect."

Shell once described his rookie year: "Coming to the pros was an eye-opening experience. The toughest adjustment was pass blocking. In college, we ran more than we passed. When we did pass block, it was like taking the guy right there on the line in what you called a short set. In the pros, you can't do it that way every time. Sometimes you have to change up…drop deep, medium, and short."

His first two seasons, Shell was a reserve tackle and played on the special teams. He won the starting job in the 1970 preseason and never lost it. For most of his career Shell was teamed with left guard Gene Upshaw. One opponent described the blocking duo: "The two of them block out the sun!"

Shell was equally effective as a pass protector or as a blocker on running plays. "I'd rather play a strong guy, because the finesse guy

A PERFECT GAME

Art Shell's peak game was Super Bowl XI, when the Oakland Raiders whipped the Minnesota Vikings 32–14. Neutralizing the Vikings defense with crushing blocks, Shell and left guard Gene Upshaw paved the way for a record-breaking total of 429 yards, including 266 yards rushing.

Alan Page and Jim Marshall were the Vikings' premier performers on the right side of Minnesota's defensive front. In the first half the Raiders offense aimed 27 of 33 running plays at them. When the final stats were totaled, Marshall—Shell's primary blocking target—had no tackles and no assists. He may as well not have been on the field. Art Shell had played a perfect game!

"I was shocked, because I had no idea Marshall had not been in on even one play," Shell said. "I was too busy to keep track. Play by play, quarter by quarter, I was totally involved in doing the best job I could."

who runs real fast is hard to stay with," he said. "That's why quickness is important at my position. My job takes place within an area of 5 yards, so it's not how fast I run a 40, but how quick I get off the ball."

Shell's playing style was never mean—unless an opponent took a cheap shot. When that happened, Shell might wait a few plays to retaliate. When he did, he usually shot both hands up under the opponent's chin. He'd bend the player's neck back just hard enough to let him know that the move was on purpose.

After twelve injury-free years Shell was carried off the field with a damaged knee in the 1979 preseason. Most players would have been out for the season, but Shell worked out four times a day on his own and was back on the field in just seven weeks.

Shell was an All-AFC selection six times, from 1973 to 1978, and an All-Pro three times. He played in eight Pro Bowls and 24 postseason contests, including eight AFL or AFC championship games and Raiders victories in Super Bowls XI and XV. When he retired in 1982, he became an assistant coach for the Raiders. In 1990 he took over as the Raiders head coach, a position he held through 1994. Shell finished with a regular-season coaching record of 47–33.

Oakland Raiders tackle Art Shell (78) protects his running back.

LEONARD RAY DAWSON

1935–
Position: quarterback
Teams: Pittsburgh Steelers, Cleveland Browns, Dallas Texans, Kansas City Chiefs
Inducted: 1987

The first five years of Len Dawson's fabulous pro football career were spent mostly on the bench. His first two coaches, Buddy Parker of the Pittsburgh Steelers and Paul Brown of the Cleveland Browns, believed that a coach should pick the best quarterback on the team and use only him. Unfortunately for Dawson, these two coaches already had their star passers picked out.

In 1962 Dawson signed with the Dallas Texans (changed to the Kansas City Chiefs one year later). His coach, Hank Stram, also believed in the "one quarterback" theory. But this time, the quarterback was Dawson. Dawson had worked with Stram while attending Purdue University during the late 1950s.

Dawson had been a multisport high school star in Alliance, Ohio, where he was born on June 20, 1935. As a Boilermaker he won All-America honors under Stram. Now that Dawson was teamed with his old coach again, his career took off.

When Dawson joined the Texans, he moved from the established National Football League to the American Football League, a second pro league formed in 1960. With his new team, Dawson finally had a chance to prove his talents. During his rookie season in the AFL, Dawson won his first individual passing championship, played in the AFL All-Star Game, and was named the AFL's Player of the Year. The 6-foot, 190-pound quarterback won AFL individual passing titles again in 1964, 1966, and 1968. For years he was the number one forward passer.

Under Dawson's leadership the Chiefs won AFL championships in 1962, 1966, and 1969. Dawson played in a total of five AFL All-Star Games. Besides being an extremely accurate passer, he was a great team leader who was noted for his calm, intelligent approach to every situation. He understood his own shortcomings, as well as those of his teammates, and called his plays accordingly.

Perhaps Dawson's greatest achievement came in Super Bowl IV. Facing the Minnesota Vikings, the Chiefs were underdogs. The morning of the game, Dawson woke up with leg cramps and nausea, but he found the strength to take the field and lead the Chiefs to a 23–7 victory. Dawson was named the game's MVP.

Dawson had another great year in 1971, completing 167 passes for 2,504 yards and 15 touchdowns. In 1973 injuries kept him on the bench, and in 1975 he called it quits for a television sportscasting career.

LEN DAWSON			
Passing Attempts	3,741	Rushing Attempts	294
Passing Completions	2,136	Rushing Yards	1,293
Passing Percentage	57.1	Average Gain	4.4
Passing Yards	28,711	Touchdowns	9
Average Pass Gain	7.67		
Touchdown Passes	239		
Passes Intercepted	183		

JOHN HENRY JOHNSON

1929–
Position: fullback
Teams: San Francisco 49ers, Detroit Lions, Pittsburgh Steelers, Houston Oilers
Inducted: 1987

Big John Henry Johnson has been called the most underrated fullback in the NFL. During his thirteen-season career Johnson played under seven different coaches. Each of them had a different idea of what his abilities were. As a result, his rushing and receiving stats were never as spectacular as they might have been. Nevertheless, when he retired after the 1966 season his 6,803 career rushing yards ranked as the fourth-best mark in history.

Johnson had an unusual running style. Getting down in a half-crouch, he'd twist and turn and pour on a burst of speed. An extremely competitive player, he had a killer instinct on the field and was often accused of playing dirty. As a result he was often the target of extra-high pileups and stray elbows.

Johnson was born in Waterproof, Louisiana, on November 24, 1929. His family moved to the San Francisco Bay area when he was a youngster. He starred in high school football and basketball, but his best sport was track. In 1952 a sprained ankle forced him to drop out of the Olympic decathlon trials.

After attending St. Mary's College, then Arizona State, Johnson was picked by the Pittsburgh Steelers in the 1953 draft. Instead, he went with Canada's Calgary Stampeders, where there was more money. After being voted the Canadian Football League's MVP, the San Francisco 49ers realized his talent and were willing to pay Johnson what he was worth. He joined the 49ers in 1954.

In San Francisco Johnson became the fourth man in "the Million Dollar Backfield," which included Y.A. Tittle, Joe Perry, and Hugh McElhenny. Although he was considered the blocking specialist, Johnson gained 681 yards, rushing for a 5.1-yard average and 9 touchdowns.

After the 1956 season Johnson was traded to Detroit. The next year he was considered the major reason for the Lions' march to the NFL title. Johnson helped the Lions beat his old 49ers teammates in the Western Division playoff. The Lions then whipped the Cleveland Browns 59–14 for the championship title. Two years later Detroit traded Johnson to Pittsburgh.

There were fewer quality runners in the Steelers lineup, so Johnson got to handle the ball more. He led the Steelers in rushing for four straight years (1961–64). In 1962 he became the first Steeler to run for 1,000 yards in a season, racking up 1,141 yards. He added 226 yards on 32 pass receptions and was named

to his first Pro Bowl. He played in two more Pro Bowls and broke the 1,000-yard mark again in 1964, with 1,048.

After a knee injury forced Johnson to sit out the 1965 season, the Steelers released him. He played his final season in 1966 with the Houston Oilers.

JOHN HENRY JOHNSON

Rushing Attempts	1,571	Pass Receptions	186
Rushing Yards	6,803	Pass Receiving Yards	1,478
Average Gain	4.3	Average Gain	7.9
Touchdowns	48	Touchdowns	7

JAMES JOHN LANGER

1948–
Position: center
Teams: Miami Dolphins, Minnesota Vikings
Inducted: 1987

Jim Langer's first two years with the Miami Dolphins were spent on the special teams, serving as a little-used backup for guard and offensive center. In 1972 he won a duel for starting center, where he stayed for the next eight years. That same year the Dolphins won the AFC championship and Super Bowl VII, winding up with a perfect 17–0 season. The 6-foot 2-inch, 253-pound Langer played every offensive down but received little attention. When the Dolphins coaches reviewed the films of the games at the end of the season, they were amazed. In more than 500 blocking assignments, Langer had handled all but three plays without any help.

The Dolphins offensive line coach, Monte Clark, felt that Langer's playing guard on the special teams helped make him a good pass blocker. Langer's own hard work paid off too. Snapping caused Langer some trouble when he first switched to center. It was difficult to pass block with his arm between his legs in snap position. But Langer practiced endlessly at center, both on the field and in his backyard with his wife or a neighborhood teenager. Eventually he could snap for everything–including kicks– then be ready to block.

For six seasons Langer was one of the top centers in the NFL. He was named to both the All-Pro and Pro Bowl teams. After surgery on a chipped bone in his knee in 1979, he decided he wanted to be closer to home, so the Dolphins traded him to the Minnesota Vikings, where he played for two more years.

Langer was born in Little Falls, Minnesota, on May 16, 1948. He originally wanted to play pro baseball. He attended South Dakota State so he could play baseball, but he also played football and wrestled. A calcium deposit in his pitching arm narrowed his career choice to football. It proved to be a good choice; Langer ended up being inducted into the Pro Football Hall of Fame in 1987.

DONALD MAYNARD

1937–

Position: wide receiver

Teams: New York Giants, New York Titans, New York Jets, St. Louis Cardinals

Inducted: 1987

During his fifteen-year pro football career, Don Maynard received very little recognition. He had a low-key personality, and for many years he was overshadowed by his flamboyant New York Jets teammate, Joe Namath. Maynard did his job quietly, and along the way he compiled some very impressive stats.

Maynard caught 50 or more passes for 1,000 or more yards in each of five different seasons. He also had 100 or more yards receiving in 50 games, which was a record that stood for more than 20 years. When he retired Maynard held many major receiving records, including 633 career catches. His record of 11,834 reception yards stood for thirteen seasons, and his 88

touchdown catches ranked him second to the legendary Don Hutson. In spite of those records, Maynard played on an All-League team just once, in 1969, and was selected for American Football League All-Star Games only three times. His one major honor came in 1969, when he was chosen for the AFL's All-Time Team.

Maynard was born on January 25, 1935, in Crosbyton, Texas. During his junior and senior years in high school, he lettered as a halfback in football, as a guard in basketball, and as a hurdler in track. In college at Texas Western, he was an All-Conference halfback and was drafted by the NFL's New York Giants.

In his rookie year, 1958, Maynard made the Giants as a running back. When a new coach cut him the next season, Vince Lombardi offered him a spot with the Green Bay Packers. As an assistant coach in New York, Lombardi had seen Maynard's skills. But Maynard went to Canada instead, where he played for the Hamilton TigerCats. He knew the American Football League was opening shop soon to rival the established National Football League, and he wanted to join it.

In 1960, when the AFL formed, Maynard returned to New York. From 1960 to 1970 the 6-foot 1-inch, 185-pound pass receiver played for the AFL Titans (in 1963 they became the Jets). His first season with the team, Maynard caught 72 passes. At the end of ten years with the Jets, his 546 receptions were the second-best AFL mark.

In Maynard's first five years in the AFL, the Titans and Jets had a total of 25 quarterbacks. Maynard never had time to develop the close connection necessary to make a good pass-catch duo with any of them. Then Joe Namath came on board in 1965 and all that changed. For the rest of Maynard's eight seasons, he and Namath were one of the best pass-catch duos around. An independent thinker, Maynard often improvised on running patterns in order to get himself open.

After playing briefly for the St. Louis Cardinals in 1973, Maynard left the playing field. After his retirement, his reputation began to grow until he finally received the ultimate recognition for a pro player. To many, his induction into the Pro Football Hall of Fame in 1987 was long overdue.

DON MAYNARD			
Pass Receptions	633	Average Gain	18.7
Pass Receiving Yards	11,834	Touchdowns	88

EUGENE UPSHAW

1945–
Position: guard
Team: Oakland Raiders
Inducted: 1987

Gene Upshaw was a fixture at left offensive guard for Oakland for fifteen seasons. Guards don't often attract much attention, but Upshaw's bruising blocks for the Raiders won him a niche in the Pro Football Hall of Fame in 1987. He played in six Pro Bowls and was named an All-Pro eight times. A key member of some great Raiders teams, he is the only player to appear in Super Bowls in three different decades. And Upshaw was the first player to make it into the Hall who spent his entire career exclusively at guard.

Before Upshaw hit the field, most NFL guards were "fireplug" types—strong and stocky, standing only an inch or two above 6 feet. Upshaw was 6 feet 5 inches and weighed 255 pounds, and as big as he was, he could still run like the wind.

Upshaw's speed made him a high school track star in his hometown of Robstown, Texas. (He was born there on August 15, 1945.) He also starred in baseball but didn't make the football team until his senior year. After receiving no scholarship offers, he visited Texas A&I. There he ran into the football coach, who was surprised that Upshaw wasn't on the field practicing. "No one asked me," Upshaw responded. Within three days, he had a full scholarship and a spot on the team.

At Texas A&I, Upshaw played center, tackle, and end, making NAIA All-America, All-Texas, and All-Conference his senior year. Not surprisingly, he also received three letters in track.

The Raiders drafted Upshaw in 1967. His rookie year, the Raiders had a 13–1 record and beat Houston 40–7 in the AFL championship game to play in Super Bowl II. During Upshaw's first fourteen seasons, Oakland won 75 percent of its games, tied for or won nine division titles, and finished second in four others. The Raiders won two AFC championships, in 1976 and 1980, and two of the three Super Bowls they played in, XI and XV.

As left guard, Upshaw's job was leading the sweep left, getting out in front to lead the rushing line and clear away any opposing defensive backs in his ballcarrier's path. He believed a quick getaway was the key to a successful sweep, and Upshaw was quick—he could run the 40-yard dash in 4.6 seconds.

Upshaw started in all but one game of his 218-game career and was a team leader. Named offensive captain by the head coach in his third year, his teammates voted him that honor every year afterward. He had a close relationship with manager Al Davis and with his teammates, particularly the younger ones, who looked to him for advice. After he retired in 1982, Upshaw put his leadership skills to work as executive director of the NFL Players Association.

MICHAEL KELLER DITKA

1939–
Position: tight end
Teams: Chicago Bears, Philadelphia Eagles, Dallas Cowboys
Inducted: 1988

Mike Ditka was the first tight end inducted into the Pro Football Hall of Fame. When he was drafted by the Chicago Bears in 1961, tight end was a fairly new position. The player had to be big and tough enough to block and fast enough to catch and carry the ball on a forward pass play. Ditka was. He fit in perfectly with his fellow Bears, who were known for their physical approach to playing. At 6 feet 3 inches and 230 pounds, Ditka had a bull neck and broad, muscled shoulders. He became one of the most feared players in the league, both as a blocker and as a pass receiver. After he got the ball, he used an amazing straight-arm move to knock down any defender in his way

Ditka was born on October 18, 1939, in Carnegie, Pennsylvania. He weighed only 130 pounds when he went out for high school football. In time he beefed up. He played end on offense and outside linebacker on defense, then played fullback his senior year. At the University of Pittsburgh he made All-America playing both defensive end and linebacker, in addition to blocking and receiving on offense.

When Ditka joined the Bears, a tight end usually played close to the tackle, blocking most of the time. Occasionally he would catch a short pass. Ditka changed that his rookie season by making 56 catches for 1,076 yards and 12 touchdowns. He was voted Rookie of the Year and named to the Pro Bowl squad.

In 1963 the Bears won their first NFL championship in seventeen years. They could not have won without Ditka, who snared 59 passes that season. Although a severe shoulder injury forced him to wear a protective harness throughout the 1964 season, Ditka had his best year ever.

He made 75 receptions and finished second for the NFL pass catching title. But in 1966 his catch totals declined, and he was traded to the Philadelphia Eagles in 1967.

Ditka's two years with the Eagles were plagued with injuries, and the Eagles traded him to the Dallas Cowboys. By 1971 he was almost back to his old form. He had 30 regular-season receptions—his best total since 1966. What's more, he wound up the season with a 7-yard reception in Super Bowl VI, helping the Cowboys beat Miami 24–3.

After twelve seasons in the pros, Mike Ditka retired in 1973 to become an assistant coach with the Cowboys. He became head coach of his beloved Bears in 1982, and in 1985 he guided them to victory in Super Bowl XX. Ditka will be most remembered for his fiercely competitive spirit, as well as for his many accomplishments on the field.

MIKE DITKA			
Pass Receptions	427	Average Gain	13.6
Pass Receiving Yards	5,812	Touchdowns	43

MELVIN CORNELL BLOUNT

1948–
Position: cornerback
Team: Pittsburgh Steelers
Inducted: 1989

Cornerback Mel Blount was a major reason the Pittsburgh Steelers were the dominant NFL team of the 1970s. Using his size, speed, quickness, and toughness, the 6-foot 3-inch, 205-pounder had a rugged, aggressive style of play. Cornerbacks usually try to intimidate their opposition. All Blount had to do was run side by side with a player to scare him.

When Blount first began playing pro football in 1970, a defensive back could maintain contact with the opposition receiver until the pass was thrown. The NFL's Competition Committee decided this kind of defense was shutting down the offense, thus making the game less interesting. In order to increase scoring, the committee changed the rules, outlawing contact more than 5 yards beyond the scrimmage line.

Blount adjusted quickly. Instead of running alongside the receiver and using a "bump-and-run" tactic, he simply followed behind. When the pass was thrown he swooped in to deflect or intercept it. With at least 1 interception in each of his fourteen seasons, Blount wound up with 57 steals, a Steelers career record. He played in six American Football Conference championships and was on winning teams in Super Bowls IX, X, XIII, and XIV.

In spite of his success, Blount had a difficult time in his first couple of pro years. Forced into the regular lineup his first two years, he wasn't ready, and his playing suffered. When the fans started booing him, he thought about quitting. After the 1971 season he returned to his family's farm near Vidalia, Georgia, where he was born on April 10, 1948.

Blount thought about his college years at Southern University in Baton Rouge, Louisiana, where he starred as a safety and a cornerback. Voted team MVP his junior and senior years, he was named to three All-America teams. He realized that college football was a less complex and more physical game, played mostly on natural ability. Once he understood the cause of his slow start in the pros, his attitude changed. He began to see every mistake as a lesson to be learned.

Blount's next season, 1972, saw a complete turnaround in his playing. He didn't let a single receiver beat him for a touchdown. He went on to develop into one of the top cornerbacks in the NFL. In 1975 he was named the NFL's Most Valuable Defensive Player. Between 1975 and 1981 he played in five Pro Bowls, earning MVP honors in the 1977 game, and he was

voted All-AFC four times. He retired in 1983 and was inducted into the Pro Football Hall of Fame in 1989, the first year he was eligible.

MEL BLOUNT			
Interceptions	57	Average Gain	12.9
Yards	736	Touchdowns	3

WILLIAM VERNELL WOOD

1936–
Position: safety
Team: Green Bay Packers
Inducted: 1989

During his twelve-year career with the Green Bay Packers, Willie Wood set the style for the Packers' type of defense. When he sensed a play coming, he was able to interpret a defensive call and do something to break the play up.

Wood was born in Washington, D. C., two days before Christmas in 1936. After playing quarterback and defensive back for the University of Southern California, Wood was determined to make the pros. When he was skipped over in the draft, he sent letters to several NFL teams asking for a tryout. The Packers agreed, liked what they saw, and signed him as free agent. (Wood is one of just six free agents inducted into the Hall.)

The 5-foot 10-inch, 185-pounder spent his rookie year doing special teams duty on the punt return squad. The next season Wood replaced Emlen Tunnell as free safety, or roving "center fielder." Wood's assignment was to fill the "interception zone," the area to which the oppositions' right-handed quarterbacks normally threw.

In 1961, his first full season, Wood intercepted 5 passes and returned 2 punts for touchdowns—one a 72-yarder. He won the NFL individual punt return title, and the next year he was the league's leader in interceptions, with 9.

Wood went on to win All-NFL honors seven times in eight years between 1964 and his final season of 1971. A Pro Bowl selection eight times, Wood also played in six NFL championship games. He helped the Packers win five titles, including Super Bowls I and II. In the first Super Bowl he intercepted a pass and ran for a 50 yard touchdown.

In addition to his 48 interceptions, Wood finished his career with 1,391 yards and 2 touchdowns on 187 punt returns. In 1989 he was given football's highest honor—he was inducted into the Pro Football Hall of Fame.

WILLIE WOOD			
Interceptions	48	**Average Gain**	14.6
Yards	699	**Touchdowns**	2

Inductees
1990–1992

FRANCO HARRIS

1950–
Position: running back
Teams: Pittsburgh Steelers, Seattle Seahawks
Inducted: 1990

EVERY MOVE COUNTS

Franco Harris never seemed to move unless it counted. For example, imagine he was running a 40-yard sprint toward the goal. If he knew no one was going to catch him, he would pour on the heat for the first 30 yards, then coast. "Who cares what time he ran?" exclaimed Coach Dick Hoak. "I don't recall ever seeing him get caught from behind. He was a 225-pounder who ran like he weighed 195."

Harris also avoided contact in practice, whenever possible. He was convinced that most injuries occurred unnecessarily and in practice. If there was no way to gain extra yardage by making contact, he would run out of bounds rather than blast into a tackler. This way, Harris figured, he was saving himself for the heavy pounding he took during games.

Franco Harris was one of the last building blocks Coach Chuck Noll signed when he was putting together a winning Pittsburgh team. With Mean Joe Greene, Jack Ham, and Mel Blount on defense, plus Terry Bradshaw as quarterback, Noll needed a big-play running back. When the 6-foot 2-inch, 225-pounder from Penn State came on board in 1972, the Steelers were almost magically transformed into a championship team.

During Harris's twelve years with Pittsburgh, the Steelers never had a losing record. They won eight AFC Central Division championships, four AFC titles, and Super Bowls IX, X, XIII, and XIV. Year after year, Harris's ground attack was a consistent factor the team could count on. "What Joe Greene meant to our defense—setting the tone—that's what Franco did for our offense," Jack Ham said. "The constant factor became our running game."

Drafted in 1972, Harris had a sensational rookie season, becoming only the fourth rookie ever to rush for 1,000 yards. He had a streak of six straight 100-yard games, winding up with 1,055 yards rushing, another 180 yards on receptions, and Rookie of the Year honors.

That year the Steelers won the AFC Central Division—their first title of any kind in their 40-year history. In 1974 they won their first AFC title and Super Bowl IX. With a 1,006-yard season, Harris rushed for a then-record 158 yards in the Super Bowl, winning Super Bowl MVP.

By 1980 Harris was approaching Jim Brown's all-time rushing record of 12,312 yards. If the NFL players' strike hadn't cut the 1982 season to nine games, he probably would have established a new record in 1983. Even with 1,007 yards in 1983, he was 363 yards short.

At the time of his retirement, Harris held or shared 24 NFL records. He currently ranks number five in career rushing, with 12,120 yards, and his 91 rushing touchdowns are sixth-best. He had

FRANCO HARRIS			
Rushing Attempts	2,949	**Pass Receptions**	307
Rushing Yards	12,120	**Pass Receiving Yards**	2,267
Average Gain	4.1	**Average Gain**	7.4
Touchdowns	91	**Touchdowns**	9
		Total Points	600 (100 touchdowns)

NOT JUST A FLASHY STAR

Franco Harris was born on March 7, 1950, in Fort Dix, New Jersey. One of nine children, Harris worked to help pay family bills whenever he could. Being a star didn't change him much. During his rookie season he wouldn't even buy a car. Instead, he rode the bus everywhere.

"The reason is that kids will ask what kind of a car or what kind of jewelry I have," he explained. "I just want kids to know that it takes hard work to make something of yourself, and you don't have to be flashy and show it off. Material things are not the important things. People relating to people is what is important."

Little wonder that Harris was named 1976 NFL Man of the Year as outstanding citizen-athlete. In 1982 he was given the Byron "Whizzer" White Humanitarian Service Award by the NFL Players Association.

eight 1,000-yard seasons and 47 games over 100 yards.

In nineteen postseason games, Harris was lead rusher thirteen times. He had a total of 400 rushes for 1,556 yards and 16 touchdowns in postseason play. In four Super Bowls he carried 101 times for 354 yards—both still records—and scored 4 rushing touchdowns.

Harris's honors are as impressive as his stats: A three-time All-AFC pick and an unanimous All-Pro choice in 1977, he was selected for nine straight Pro Bowls from 1972 to 1980.

In 1984 Harris was released from Pittsburgh when a contract dispute could not be resolved. He signed with Seattle. Everyone regretted the move: Harris, the Steelers, and Steelers owner Art Rooney. After gaining just 170 yards in eight games for the Seahawks, Harris retired. But as Harris said, "A player should not be measured by statistics alone. He should be measured by something more special, such as the sharing of teammates and fans. Both the city of Pittsburgh and the Steelers team were building at the same time. It was a good feeling to be a part of it."

During Super Bowl IX, Franco Harris (32) sets a record for most yardage gained in a Super Bowl game.

JOHN HAROLD LAMBERT

1952–
Position: linebacker
Team: Pittsburgh Steelers
Inducted: 1990

The Pittsburgh Steelers almost didn't choose Jack Lambert in the 1974 draft. At 6 feet 4 inches and 218 pounds, Lambert (born in Mantua, Ohio, on July 8, 1952) was taller and skinnier than most middle linebackers, but that had been his position at Kent State University. Then in his rookie year, Lambert got a chance to play his preferred position, and he stayed there for his entire career. The Steelers put him in the lineup after their regular middle linebacker went out with an injury. For the next ten years Lambert was a starter and a central player on Pittsburgh's famous Steel Curtain defense.

Before Lambert joined the team, the Steelers had some great players, but not a great defense. In 1973 they lost a chance to win the AFC Central title after their defense gave up 30 points in a game against Miami. Then the defense surrendered 33 points to Oakland, who ousted the Steelers from the playoffs. But with Lambert roaming the field, the Steelers offense clicked into high gear. In his first six years with the Steelers, Pittsburgh won four Super Bowls.

The very beginning of Lambert's career was rocky for the rookie. After a good start in the 1974 season, the Steelers allowed 52 points over a two-week period. The media began to say opposing teams could win by running their big backs at "the undersized [Pittsburgh] middle linebacker." The next week Lambert proved them wrong. He made a team-leading 8 tackles against Houston, sparking a five-game winning streak. That year Pittsburgh was first in the league in total defense, scoring defense, sacks, and takeaways. The team also won the AFC title and Super Bowl IX. Lambert averaged 11 tackles per game the last five weeks of his rookie season and was named NFL Defensive Rookie of the Year.

The Steelers defensive captain for his last eight seasons, Lambert was lean and mean. In spite of his small size, he was a punishing, nasty player who loved to hit. As he barked out defensive signals, his toothless snarl gave the impression that he had been in many brutal fights. He pumped his arms and legs before each play until the second he hurled himself onto his poor opponent.

NO INTIMIDATING PERMITTED

In only his second season, Jack Lambert displayed the mettle that made him the Steelers defensive captain for eight years. It was Super Bowl X. The Steelers trailed the Cowboys 10–7 at the half. Roy Gerela had just missed a 36-yard field goal attempt that would have tied the score.

As the teams jogged off the field, Lambert saw Dallas safety Cliff Harris pat Gerela on the helmet, then put his arm around the kicker's shoulder and thank him for missing. Enraged, Lambert grabbed Harris and flipped him to the ground.

"I couldn't permit anyone to intimidate our team," Lambert recalled. He carried his fury into the locker room, and when the Steelers emerged, they fought back to a 21–17 victory.

"Jack didn't have to psych himself to play," said teammate Joe Greene. "He lived to play."

JACK LAMBERT			
Interceptions	28	Average Gain	8.7
Yards	243	Touchdowns	0

FINDING HIS JOB

When the Steelers drafted Jack Lambert in 1974, they didn't know where to play him. But it didn't take long for the Steelers to learn that Lambert was no ordinary player.

When he heard that he was drafted, Lambert told linebacker coach Woody Widenhofer he wanted to come to Pittsburgh immediately. He wanted to study the films to learn Pittsburgh's defense. Pleasantly stunned, Widenhofer didn't believe the rookie would do it, but Lambert drove to Pittsburgh every weekend until summer camp. Even though he had learned quickly, Lambert and the coaches still hadn't figured out his job.

"I didn't feel I was big enough for the middle," Lambert admitted. "And from watching films, I knew I couldn't beat out Jack Ham or Andy Russell on the outside. But after watching the middle linebacker [Harry Davis] on film, I felt I could play just as well as he did."

As fate would have it, Harry Davis was injured in a preseason game, and Lambert took his place. From then on, there was never any doubt which position Jack Lambert would play.

"I play the way that suits me best," Lambert said. "Most of your middle linebackers are 20 to 30 pounds heavier. Because of my size, I have to be active and aggressive."

Aside from his vicious tackling, the secret of Lambert's success was his quickness, his ability to get to the ballcarrier. "I try to get to the football as opposed to the Butkus and Nitschke types who stood in the middle and dared you to knock them down," he explained. "If I can run around a blocker and make the tackle, I'll do it." Unlike most middle linebackers, Lambert was able to keep up with the running backs and tight ends, and he developed into an exceptional pass defender. In his eleven years, he intercepted 28 passes, returning them for a total of 243 yards.

During ten years of being battered on the field, Lambert missed only six games because of injuries. Then in 1984, he dislocated a toe. He played eight games that season in great pain, then reluctantly called it quits.

During his eleven-year career, Lambert played in nine straight Pro Bowls (1976–84)—more than any other player of his era. Twice, in 1976 and 1979, he was named NFL Defensive Player of the Year. A perfect career ended with his election to the Pro Football Hall of Fame in 1990, the first year he was eligible.

Pittsburgh Steelers linebacker Jack Lambert (58) grits his teeth and digs in to stop Miami Dolphins fullback Larry Csonka.

EARL CHRISTIAN CAMPBELL

1955–
Position: running back
Teams: Houston Oilers, New Orleans Saints
Inducted: 1991

WHAT A RUNNER!

Earl Campbell burst on the scene with the Houston Oilers, compiling some fantastic numbers. Following are some of his NFL high marks in rushing.

- Most yards rushing in a season: 1,934 (1980), third-best of all time

- Most games in a season with 200 or more yards rushing: 4 (1980), an NFL record

- Most consecutive games with 200 or more yards rushing: 2 (1980), an NFL record shared with O.J. Simpson

- Most games in a season with 100 or more yards rushing: 11 (1979), second-best of all time

- Most consecutive games with 100 or more yards rushing: 7 (1979), third-best of all time

Earl Campbell was the first person in the 20th century to be named a Texas legend by the state legislature. To Texas football fans, the multitalented Campbell was a homestate hero. For six and a half years, the 5-foot 11-inch, 233-pound superstar anchored the Houston Oilers offense and made them championship contenders.

The Oilers paid a high price to sign Campbell. They traded a tight end and four high-round draft picks to the Tampa Bay Buccaneers to make sure they drafted first in 1978. After using that draft pick to get Campbell, the Oilers gave him a $1.4 million, multiyear contract. He proved he was worth that large investment.

His rookie year, Campbell was the NFL's Most Outstanding Offensive Player, All-NFL, and Rookie of the Year. With 1,450 yards on the ground, he was the first rookie to lead the NFL in rushing since Jim Brown in 1957. He was also named to the AFC Pro Bowl team and he led the Oilers to their first postseason appearance since 1969. With this performance, Campbell more than lived up to his promise as the 1977 Heisman Trophy winner. He came to Houston after rushing for 4,443 yards in his four seasons at the University of Texas and playing on the All–Southwest Conference team four times. But Campbell could do more than run. As a rookie he surprised the Oilers with his blocking, faking, and pass protection abilities as well.

The next year, 1979, Campbell won his second straight rushing title, with 1,697 yards, and led the league with 19 rushing touchdowns. In his third season, his best, he rushed for more than 200 yards for four games and racked up a 1,934-yard season record—the third-highest behind O.J. Simpson and Eric Dickerson. In both 1979 and 1980 he was All-Pro, NFL Player of the Year, and a Pro Bowl selection. During his first three years, he twice led the Oilers to the AFC championship game.

EARL CAMPBELL

Rushing Attempts	2,187		**Pass Receptions**	121
Rushing Yards	9,407		**Pass Receiving Yards**	806
Average Gain	4.3		**Average Gain**	6.7
Touchdowns	74		**Touchdowns**	0
			Total Points	444 (74 touchdowns)

A GENTLEMAN AND A SCHOLAR

Earl Campbell's years as a pro football star were quite different from his early, humble years. Campbell was born on March 29, 1955, in Tyler, Texas. He grew up in a shack that stood beside a blacktop country road. When he was in the sixth grade, Campbell's father died. To keep her eleven children together, his mother worked as a maid and tended her employer's 100-acre rose field.

By the time Campbell was in high school, he was hustling pool. He was suspended for skipping school in his junior year and couldn't play in the final football game of the season.

Campbell's mother put it to him bluntly: If he straightened up, he could have a lucrative career in pro football. He straightened up, leading the undefeated Tyler Lions to the Texas State 4A championship his senior year.

Campbell was recruited by two colleges, but he chose the University of Texas. Majoring in speech communications, he became the first member of his family to earn a college degree. After he signed with the Oilers, he fulfilled a promise he had made to his mother when he first entered college. He built her a house—a four-bedroom, brick, ranch house with a two-car garage.

In 1981 new Oilers coach Ed Biles decided to have Campbell try other things such as receiving. That year Campbell caught 36 passes and rushed for 1,376 yards and 10 touchdowns. He went to a fourth Pro Bowl, but for the first time did not make the All-NFL team. In 1983 he rushed for 1,301 yards and 12 touchdowns and went to his fifth and last Pro Bowl. After a knee injury benched him halfway through the 1984 season, he was traded to the New Orleans Saints. He retired one year later.

During his eight seasons Campbell averaged 1,175 rushing yards a year—the fourth-best record in football history. From 1978 to 1981 he averaged 22.6 carries and 104 yards rushing per game. His production dropped during his last four seasons, to 14.8 rushes and 56 yards per game.

After retirement the three-time NFL MVP operated a football camp for youngsters and became a counselor at the University of Texas. Campbell was voted into the Pro Football Hall of Fame in 1991, the first year he was eligible.

Running back Earl Campbell (34) carries the ball for the Houston Oilers.

BORN TO BE BIG

John Hannah was born to be a football player. He weighed 11 pounds when he was born, on April 4, 1951, in Canton, Georgia. He weighed 35 pounds when he was a year old and 210 pounds when he was in the eighth grade. No wonder his nickname in college was "Ham Hocks." During his pro years with the Patriots, he was called "Hog"—respectfully.

JOHN ALLEN HANNAH

1951–
Position: guard
Team: New England Patriots
Inducted: 1991

John Hannah played guard with the New England Patriots for thirteen seasons. During that time he earned practically every honor an offensive lineman can win. In 1991, the first year he was eligible, he received the honor he most coveted—membership into the Pro Football Hall of Fame.

By 1991 few guards had been elected to the Hall, partly because playing guard is a low profile job. What's more, it's done in the middle of the pack, where it's hard to see what each player is doing. However, it was hard to ignore John Hannah.

Sometimes called a "blocking machine," Hannah was a bulldozer going full speed at defensive ends or linebackers in pulling situations. One of the outstanding run blockers of his era, Hannah was the major thrust behind the Patriots' power running attack.

His first season, 1973, Hannah showed his potential and was named to the All-Rookie team. The next year he made All-AFC. From 1973 through 1982, he was an All-Pro pick for ten straight seasons and an AFC Pro Bowl selection nine times. He won the NFL Players Association Offensive Lineman of the Year Award for four straight seasons, from 1978 to 1981.

Hannah was a two-time All-America under famous coach Bear Bryant at the University of Alabama. Hannah was also an undefeated freshman wrestler and was accomplished at discus and shot put in track. Altogether he won eight letters and was rated second-best collegiate athlete in the country his senior year.

However, when he entered the pros, Hannah had to adjust to a blocking technique that called for dropping back rather than charging out, which Bryant had taught him. And at 6 feet 3 inches and 265 pounds, Hannah was not the biggest man on field.

Hannah not only had the ability to learn quickly, he also had the quickness, intensity, and intelligence that put him a cut above. He had exceptional speed for his size, as well as balance and agility, and he was willing to work hard and long. "Bear Bryant taught us how to win," Hannah said. "He inspired you to give your maximum effort on every play. He told us that usually a game is decided by only four or five plays. You never know when those plays are coming, so you have to be ready on every play."

Winning wasn't always easy with the Patriots. They had winning

IT RUNS IN THE FAMILY

A sportswriter once wrote that John Hannah's father, Herb, must have had a contract to produce talented football players for the University of Alabama. After playing offensive tackle for Alabama, then for the New York Giants in the early 1950s, Herb Hannah turned out three sons who followed in his footsteps. John was an All-America guard, and Charley and David earned All-Conference honors as defensive tackles for the Crimson Tide.

Like their father, John and Charley went on to pro careers. Charley spent twelve seasons in the NFL with the Tampa Bay Buccaneers and the Los Angeles Raiders. After thirteen seasons with the Patriots, John wound up in the Hall of Fame.

records in eight of Hannah's thirteen seasons, but they made the playoffs only four times. Still, with Hannah leading the charge, New England rushed for an NFL record of 3,165 yards in 1978. In 1985, Hannah's last season, the Patriots won the AFC championship but lost Super Bowl XX.

For most of his career Hannah played with pain, something he considered a by-product of football. Of 188 games, he missed only five. A nagging neck problem required him to wear a special neck brace for much of 1984 and 1985. He played in the Super Bowl in spite of torn rotator cuffs in both shoulders and a knee that wouldn't work. Injuries forced him to retire in 1986.

Big John Hannah (73), guard for the New England Patriots, protects his runner.

JOHN MACKEY

1941–
Position: tight end
Teams: Baltimore Colts, San Diego Chargers
Inducted: 1992

John Mackey was considered the "walking textbook" of the modern-day tight end. A bull of a man, he was big and strong enough to block defensive linemen. His sure-fingered hands helped him make impossible catches. And with breakaway speed, Mackey could go deep for big yardage like no tight end before him.

Mackey was born on September 24, 1941, in Queens, New York. He grew up in Roosevelt, a quiet Long Island community. When he was a high school senior, Mackey decided to attend Syracuse University. Why? Because Jim Brown—a football star who had also grown up on Long Island—went there.

At Syracuse Mackey made both the dean's list with a degree in political science and the College All-Star squad. If he didn't make the pros, he could always go to law school, where he'd already been accepted. His rookie season left no doubt which career path he'd take.

When the Baltimore Colts picked Mackey in the 1963 draft, rookie head coach Don Shula placed Mackey at tight end. Mackey started all fourteen games and caught 35 passes to lead the team with 726 yards, a 20.7-yard average, and 7 touchdowns. He also averaged 30.1 yards on 9 kickoff returns. That year he was the only rookie named to the Pro Bowl.

Although the fans loved his long-distance touchdowns, Mackey had more fun clearing a path for the Colts runners. "My job was to wipe out the defensive end and go get the linebacker," he said. "Man, that's what I loved. I ran over a lot of those guys."

Even when he didn't have the ball, Mackey was lethal. He blocked the defensive end or outside linebacker on the sweeps. He pulverized the middle linebacker on rushes up the middle. He acted as a decoy when the wide receivers went out on passing patterns. His only fault was dropping passes occasionally. Not surprisingly, Mackey was often double-teamed.

ABOUT THAT MACKEY...

John Mackey was often double-teamed. His attitude toward that was this: "The only time a double-team bothers me is when no one gets open. I don't care if I don't catch a pass, just as long as I can take two men with me on my patterns."

"There aren't many safetymen around who can handle Mackey," Colts end coach Dick Bielski once said. "Once he catches the ball, the great adventure begins. Those people on defense climb all over him. The lucky defenders fall off, the others may get trampled. They attack as though he is a giant redwood. But he's also moving in high gear. And he can dig out. You know he does 40 yards in 4.7 seconds."

JOHN MACKEY			
Pass Receptions	331	Rushing Attempts	19
Pass Receiving Yards	5,236	Rushing Yards	127
Average Gain	15.8	Average Gain	6.7
Touchdowns	38	Touchdowns	0
		Total Points	228 (38 touchdowns)

1970: A LANDMARK YEAR

For John Mackey, 1970 was an eventful year. He was chosen as tight end for the NFL All-Time Team and was elected president of the NFL Players Association. As leader of the association, Mackey became a national figure when the NFLPA began an unprecedented strike before the 1970 preseason.

The NFLPA wanted the league's team owners to contribute more money to the players' retirement fund and introduce other benefits. When the owners said no, almost 1,300 pro players refused to report to training camp. In August Mackey led a team of player representatives in a marathon bargaining session with owners. After 22 straight hours, the owners and the players reached a compromise.

"There wasn't any winner," Mackey said. "We have an agreement, that's the important thing." Millions of football fans definitely agreed.

The dedicated rookie studied game films for hours. He learned to constantly vary the number of steps he took before cutting so that his patterns wouldn't be predictable. Mackey also learned to use his forearm to fend off tacklers. "It's very hard to make a tackle when I use the chop," he said. "If I let them get in the first blow, I'm more likely to get hurt, and I don't like getting hurt."

His third season, 1965, Mackey scored 7 touchdowns and went to his second Pro Bowl. For the next three years he had a spot on the All-NFL and Pro Bowl teams. He achieved a lifetime-high 829 yards and 9 touchdowns in 1966. Six of those touchdown receptions came on plays of over 50 yards. In 1967 Mackey had a career-high 55 catches.

When the NFL chose an all-time team to celebrate its 50th anniversary in 1970, Mackey was picked at tight end. In Baltimore's Super Bowl V victory over Dallas that year, Mackey caught a pass by Unitas that produced a 75-yard game-tying touchdown.

In 1971 a knee injury kept Mackey's season to three games and 11 catches. When he was replaced as starting tight end in 1972, he demanded a trade. He spent his final year with the San Diego Chargers, retiring in 1973. Some 25 years later, John Mackey is still remembered as the best of all tight ends.

Tight end John Mackey (18) finds a hole in the offensive line to "run for daylight."

HAIR TODAY, HAWK TOMORROW

Early in his career, John Riggins shocked his fans and his coaches with his unconventional hairstyles. One year he had an Afro, and the next he had a Mohawk, with a neat arrow down the middle of his scalp. "I actually grew the Mohawk…to show everybody I was my own boss," he explained. "I always wanted one as a kid, but my folks wouldn't let me have it."

JOHN RIGGINS

1949–
Position: running back
Teams: New York Jets, Washington Redskins
Inducted: 1992

Even though he was the number one pick of the New York Jets and the sixth player chosen in the 1971 draft, John Riggins didn't believe he would make it in the pros. But 6-foot 2-inch, 240-pound "Riggo" played fourteen years and got better with age. In 1984, at age 35, he became the oldest player to rush for 1,000 yards in a season.

When his teams needed to grind out tough yards up the middle, Riggins got the call. Said his Washington Redskins teammate Joe Theismann, "John…felt he was just a guard who happened to carry the football." Riggins bowled over countless tacklers on his way to 11,352 career yards, the sixth-highest at the time of his retirement in 1985. And Riggins knew how to find the end zone—his 104 rushing touchdowns put him third of all time in that category when he finally hung up his cleats.

Riggins was born on August 4, 1949, in Seneca, Kansas. He was All-America at the University of Kansas. He rushed for 2,706 yards, including a record 1,131 yards as a senior, and the Jets rated him the best collegiate back in the nation in 1970. His rookie year, 1971, he became the first Jet to lead the team in both yards rushing and receptions. After three injury-plagued years, he had his finest season in New York in 1975. Playing all fourteen games, he rushed 1,005 yards, caught 30 passes for 363 yards, and was selected for the Pro Bowl.

Declaring he was tired of playing for a losing team, Riggins moved to the Redskins in 1976. A knee injury benched him for most of 1977; then he had two 1,000-yard seasons. He rushed for 1,014 yards in 1978 and 1,153 yards in 1979.

In 1980 Riggins walked out of training camp and announced he was retiring. Frustrated by the Redskins' losing record, their failure to negotiate his contract, and his injuries, he spent a year on his farm in Kansas. After Coach Joe Gibbs went to see him, Riggins returned

JOHN RIGGINS				
Rushing Attempts	2,916		Pass Receptions	250
Rushing Yards	11,352		Pass Receiving Yards	2,090
Average Gain	3.9		Average Gain	8.4
Touchdowns	104		Touchdowns	12
			Total Points	696 (116 touchdowns)

ONE, TWO, THREE, YOU'RE OUT!

Controversy surrounded all three of Riggins's departures from football. With his first departure from the Jets, he wanted off a losing team, so he asked for a contract that matched Joe Namath's, knowing the Jets wouldn't agree. Then he played without a contract in 1975 so that he could sign with the team of his choice the following year.

Riggins swore the Redskins' winning record won him over, though a $300,000 contract probably didn't hurt. Then on the last day of the 1979 season, the Redskins lost to the Dallas Cowboys 35–34. The loss killed their chance of going to the playoffs. "I played as well that day as I ever played, and we still lost," Riggins complained bitterly. After stewing over that loss for the rest of the year, he stormed out of next season's training camp.

Riggins spent a year on his Kansas farm, then returned to Washington. He gave the Redskins two back-to-back 1,000-yard years and helped them to a Super Bowl win, Then they abruptly asked him to retire. Their reason? He wasn't averaging 30 carries a game. Stunned, Riggins wasn't ready for a third departure from football, but when he refused to retire, the Redskins released him. This time he left football for good.

with another announcement: "I'm bored, I'm broke, and I'm back!"

Riggins's football career then took a dramatic turn. Consistency, endurance, and prodding had finally turned him into a great runner. And since he was carrying the ball more—375 rushes in 1983 and 327 in 1984—he was able to pile up the big yardage. For the next three years, he got the attention most big-yardage runners receive early in their careers.

Riggins's most memorable performance was in 1982, against the Miami Dolphins in Super Bowl XVII. He rushed 38 times for a then-record 166 yards. In the fourth quarter the Redskins were behind 17–13 when Riggins raced 43 yards for the winning touchdown. He was named game MVP.

The 1983 season was Riggins's finest. He rushed for a career-high 1,347 yards and an NFL record 24 touchdowns. He scored at least 1 touchdown in thirteen straight games. Every All-NFL team claimed him, and the Maxwell Club named him NFL Player of the Year.

The next year Riggins had his fifth 1,000-yard rushing season. The Redskins fans' "Diesel of Desire" gained 1,239 yards and led the NFC with 14 rushing touchdowns. However, the Redskins released Riggins in 1985. "If John can't average 30 carries per game, I don't think we can use him as just a short-yardage man," Coach Gibbs said. Reluctantly, Riggins left. After about a year, he found a new profession—acting. "I often thought I played football just to please my father," he said. "But now I feel acting is for me, and me alone."

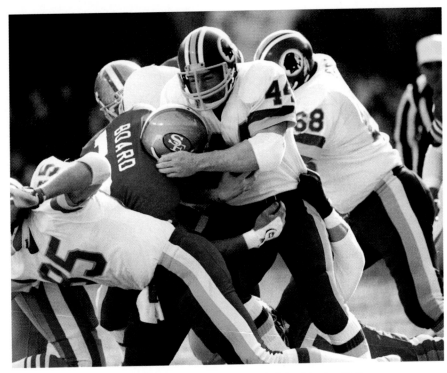

Washington Redskins running back John Riggins (44) battles for yardage against the San Francisco 49ers.

JUNIOUS "BUCK" BUCHANAN

1940–
Position: defensive tackle
Team: Kansas City Chiefs
Inducted: 1990

In 1963 Buck Buchanan became the first player from a small black school to be drafted in the first round. The Kansas City Chiefs—then the American Football League's Dallas Texans—chose the unknown player over the 1962 Heisman Trophy winner. Why? To Coach Hank Stram, Buchanan had it all—size, speed, and strength. At 6 feet 7 inches, Buchanan usually weighed in at 274 pounds, yet he could run the 100-yard dash in 10.2 seconds.

Buchanan was born in Gainesville, Alabama, on September 10, 1940. He began his football career as the captain of his high school team. At Grambling State University, he played defense as well as left tackle on offense and made the College All-Star team in 1963.

As a Chiefs rookie Buchanan played both end and tackle, then moved to a permanent role as right defensive tackle in 1964. That year he was named to his first AFL All-Star Game. For the next seven seasons he played in either the AFL All-Star Game or the AFC-NFC Pro Bowl. From 1966 to 1970 he was a unanimous choice for the All-AFL, then All-AFC teams. In 1965 and 1967 he was picked as team MVP.

Buchanan was an intimidating pass rusher. In 1967 alone he batted down 16 opposition passes at or behind the line of scrimmage. His great speed allowed him to run quickly from one sideline to the other to make tackles.

But it wasn't strength or speed alone that made Buchanan such an outstanding defensive tackle. His success was also dependent on what he called "thinking with your opponent," by which he meant constantly moving toward the passer wherever he went. Buchanan was always learning new strategies, and he studied films of his opponents to figure out how to make them change their moves.

In 1970 Buchanan played a important role in the Chiefs' Super Bowl IV win over the favored Minnesota Vikings. Using a new defensive strategy, Buchanan lined up over the Vikings center instead of in front of the left guard, his normal position. Doing this, he was able to disrupt the Vikings' normal blocking patterns so that their offense couldn't score. As a result, Minnesota lost in a 23–7 upset.

Buchanan retired in 1975 because of injuries. During his thirteen-year career, he played in 181 games, including 166 in a row. After coaching awhile, he became a businessman. In 1990 he was enshrined in the Pro Football Hall of Fame.

ROBERT ALLEN GRIESE

1945–
Position: quarterback
Team: Miami Dolphins
Inducted: 1990

From 1971 to 1974 Bob Griese led the Miami Dolphins to a 47–7–1 record. When the Dolphins went undefeated in 1972—the only undefeated season ever for an NFL team—Griese was at the helm of the offense. Joe Robbie, owner and founder of the Dolphins, once called Griese "the cornerstone of the franchise." Blessed with graceful feet and a quick arm, Griese was also alert and always listened attentively to his coaches. Eventually his intelligence and determination to learn everything about defense made him an all-time great quarterback.

Football had always been very important to Griese. He was born on February 3, 1945, in Evansville, Indiana. His father died when Griese was only ten. Early on Griese realized that an athletic scholarship was the only way he would get a college education. He was captain of his high school baseball, basketball, and football teams. His senior year, dozens of offers for football scholarships came in, and Griese chose Purdue University.

At Purdue, Griese was a two-time All-America pick and held several Purdue offensive records. His senior year, he was the 1966 Big Ten Player of the Year. Still, at 6 feet 1 inch and 190 pounds, he was considered small by many pro teams—but not by the Miami Dolphins, who drafted him in 1967. Griese unselfishly gave some of his contract money to an older brother and a younger sister for their college tuitions.

Griese was considered unselfish on the field as well. Whereas most quarterbacks preferred to pass, he willingly carried the ball if it helped the team. And he wasn't afraid to block either. In his rookie season Griese was named Dolphins MVP. He completed more than half of his 331 passes and wound up with 2,005 yards and 15 touchdowns. He threw 122 straight passes without an interception, setting a team record.

In Griese's first three seasons with the Dolphins, from 1967 through 1969, the Dolphins favored the forward pass. Then in the 1970s, the team switched to a running attack and had its greatest success. Later in the decade, the Dolphins again went to a passing game. Griese adjusted easily, but the shifts in playing strategy kept him from compiling overwhelming passing statistics. The team however, always did well, and in the 1970s it won five AFC East championships, three AFC titles, and Super Bowls VII and VIII.

During his career Griese was plagued with numerous injuries and 20-200 vision in his right eye, which made him legally blind. Despite these setbacks, he racked up honors his entire career. He was named NFL Player of the Year in 1971 and 1977, and All-Pro or All-AFC four times. He also played in two AFL All-Star

Games and six AFC-NFC Pro Bowls. In 1990, ten years after he retired, Bob Griese was inducted into the Pro Football Hall of Fame.

BOB GRIESE			
Passing Attempts	3,429	Average Pass Gain	7.32
Passing Completions	1,926	Touchdown Passes	192
Passing Percentage	56.2	Passes Intercepted	172
Passing Yards	25,092		

THEODORE PAUL HENDRICKS

1947–
Position: linebacker
Teams: Baltimore Colts, Green Bay Packers, Oakland Raiders, Los Angeles Raiders
Inducted: 1990

A three-time All-America at the University of Miami, Ted Hendricks almost didn't get picked for the pros. The 6-foot 7-inch, 215-pounder was considered too skinny and too tall. But the lanky linebacker proved to be a punishing tackler for the Baltimore Colts, who picked him in the 1969 draft.

When contract talks began, the Colts wanted to weigh Hendricks. Fully clothed, he tipped the scale at just 218 pounds. Later his agent lamented, "If he'd eaten before the meeting, it would have been worth at least $1,000 a pound. Ted would have been about $5,000 ahead [salary-wise]." When he retired, Hendricks weighed only 235.

Hendricks's slender appearance was deceiving, however. His tall, lean frame didn't show how well-muscled his long arms were and how powerful his wrists were. He would wrap his arms around a quarterback like a python wraps around its prey. Hendricks was able to make some uncommon plays too, such as the "leaping interception." He could reverse his direction and go straight up to intercept a pass with one hand. A quarterback trying to throw a pass over him was not expecting such a move from a linebacker.

Hendricks was born on November 1, 1947, in Guatemala City, Guatemala, his mother's home. The family later moved to Miami, where Hendricks was a two-way end in high school and All-America at the University of Miami. At Miami he took an honors curriculum in mathematics with a minor in psychology.

From 1969 through 1973 Hendricks played for the Colts, then for the Green Bay Packers for a season in 1974. He joined the Raiders in 1975 and was with them until he retired in 1983. During his fifteen-year career he blocked 25 field goals or extra points. He racked up a huge number of sacks and blocked passes. He also recovered 16 opponents' fumbles and intercepted 26 passes, which he returned for 332 yards. Additionally, he scored a record-tying 4 safeties. As testimony to Hendricks's ability to make big plays, he also had 1 touchdown each on an interception, a fumble return, and a blocked punt return.

Hendricks was All-AFC three times as a Colt, and four times as a Raider. He was a 1974 All-NFC pick as a Packer. He was selected as an All-Pro seven times in his career and played in eight Pro Bowl Games between 1971 and 1983. He also played on Super Bowl winners in 1971, with Baltimore, and in 1977 and 1981 with the Raiders. In 1990 he was inducted into the Pro Football Hall of Fame.

TED HENDRICKS			
Interceptions	26	Average Gain	12.8
Yards	332	Touchdowns	1

THOMAS WADE LANDRY

1924–
Coach
Team: Dallas Cowboys
Inducted: 1990

The Dallas Cowboys have been called "America's Team." And one man played a great role in shaping the Cowboys' reputation and winning tradition: Tom Landry. From their first game in 1960 through the 1988 season, Landry was the Cowboys' only head coach. Just one other coach, Curly Lambeau, has coached one team for more consecutive years. With his steely stare and trademark hat, Landry became one of the most recognizable people in football. He guided the Cowboys to thirteen division titles and five Super Bowl appearances, winning Super Bowls XI and XII.

Landry began his pro football career as a player. A fullback and defensive back at the University of Texas, Landry joined the New York Yankees of the All-America Football Conference in 1949. When the AAFC folded, he moved to the NFL's New York Giants, where he played defensive back, kick returner, and punter from 1950 to 1955.

During his seven playing seasons, Landry intercepted 32 passes–3 for touchdowns. He punted 389 times for a 40.9-yard average and was selected for the Pro Bowl in 1954. But Landry wasn't very fast, so to get where he wanted without having to outrun anyone, he began to analyze his opponent's offensive tactics. Soon he began telling his teammates what the offense was going to do on every play. "I got the idea of a coordinated system of defense in which everybody read certain keys the offense provided and then controlled a specific area," he explained.

Landry was so good at his analyzing that he was made a player-coach in 1954, then assistant coach when he retired from playing in 1955. In 1960, when Dallas got its franchise, Landry was offered the head coaching job. He accepted. Landry was born in Texas on September 11, 1924, in the town of Mission. He wanted to return to Texas.

The brand-new Dallas team lost eleven games and tied one in its first season. Landry began building the Cowboys into a class team, but after the fourth season the Cowboys record was 13–38–3. In 1965 the Cowboys broke even, then won the NFL Eastern Conference championships the next two years. The 1966 season started a string of 20 straight winning seasons, until 1985–a record that has never been equaled.

In addition to being a great defensive coach, Landry favored a multiple offense that taught his players to adjust to a situation in order to take advantage of it. In the 1980s the "situation substitution" concept was introduced. Immediately Landry took up this practice of inserting players on certain downs for specific assignments.

Landry's regular-season career record was 250–162–6. Including playoffs, his record is 270–178–6. The only coaches to top Landry's 270 career wins are the legendary George Halas of the Chicago Bears and former Colts and Dolphins coach Don Shula.

In 1986 Landry's winning streak ended. Three seasons later, his career also ended when a new Cowboys owner let him go. Football fans everywhere were stunned and angry. For nearly 30 years Landry had quietly paced the Dallas sidelines. He never shouted at an official, belittled a player, or threw down a clipboard. All he did was build winning teams. After an emotional farewell to his players, the city of Dallas honored Landry with a parade. Tens of thousands of cheering fans lined the streets to pay him tribute.

TOM LANDRY			
Wins	270	**Ties**	6
Losses	178	**Win Percentage**	.601

ROBERT BRUCE ST. CLAIR

1931–
Position: tackle
Team: San Francisco 49ers
Inducted: 1990

At 6 feet 9 inches and 265 pounds, Bob St. Clair was the biggest player in the NFL during his time. His biceps measured 2 1/2 inches larger than the champion heavyweight boxer Sonny Liston's, and his chest was 4 inches bigger than Liston's. For eleven seasons St. Clair used that great size to protect his quarterback and blast open holes in the opposition's defensive line

St. Clair was born on February 18, 1931, in San Francisco, California. He was an average-sized youngster. As a teenager, he joined a gang of hoodlums. He was headed for jail until he found football. When St. Clair was a sophomore in high school, he happened to watch the school football team practice. Fascinated by the rough-and-tumble activity, he tried to join, but at 5 feet 9 inches and 150 pounds, he was too small. He went to work bodybuilding, and the next year he had grown to an amazing 6 feet 4 inches and 210 pounds. He made the team, won a scholarship to the University of San Francisco, and became a third-round draft choice of the 49ers in 1953.

With the 49ers, St. Clair blocked for the team's famous "Million Dollar Backfield," which featured quarterback Y.A. Tittle, and running backs Joe Perry, John Henry Johnson, and Hugh McElhenny. St. Clair was fast enough to overtake 180-pound halfbacks, and he loved to hit. His brute power and blocking ability allowed him to crush even the largest and strongest opponents.

St. Clair also played on the 49ers goal-line defense and defended against punts and field goal attempts. In 1956 he blocked 10 field goals—an amazing accomplishment. What's more, he enjoyed intimidating his opponents and got a thrill out of the violence of football. He once lost five teeth blocking a punt.

Not only was St. Clair known for his brutal tactics on the field, he was also known for his flamboyant lifestyle off the field. He ate many foods raw, including meat. One of his favorite pastimes was sitting down at the rookies' table and gnawing on raw liver to gross them out. He also served as councilman, then mayor, of Daly City, California, while still playing football.

St. Clair played on three All-NFL teams and started in five Pro Bowl Games. Injuries cut short his career, which ended in 1963. In 1990 his contributions were honored when he was inducted into the Pro Football Hall of Fame.

STANLEY PAUL JONES

1931–
Positions: guard, defensive tackle
Teams: Chicago Bears, Washington Redskins
Inducted: 1991

The Chicago Bears wanted Stan Jones so badly that they used one of their draft picks to sign him even though he would still be in college for another year. The investment paid off. The 6-foot 1-inch, 250-pounder turned out to be an All-America tackle in his senior year and went on to have a long, successful career with the Bears.

Jones was born on November 24, 1931, in Altoona, Pennsylvania. He developed a weight-lifting program in high school that helped him succeed in football. The 140-pound high school freshman weighed 220 pounds by the time he entered the University of Maryland. By his senior year Smith was one of the top players in the country, and he received the Knute Rockne Memorial Trophy as the nation's outstanding college lineman.

When Jones joined the Bears in 1954, he was immediately put in the lineup as an offensive tackle. The following season he was moved to left guard, where he stayed for the next eight

seasons. He easily adapted to his new position and became a top offensive lineman. Jones was named to seven straight Pro Bowls, from 1955 through 1961.

In 1963 Jones became a full-time defensive tackle. The switch from offense to defense was difficult, but that year the Bears won the conference title as Jones and the rest of the Bears defense allowed an average of only 10 points per game. During the NFL championship game, the Bears defense forced 6 turnovers and shut down the potent Giants offense in a 14–10 victory.

Jones was traded to the Washington Redskins in 1966, where he played one season. In 1977 he was named to the Atlantic Coast Conference 25-year all-star team. He was inducted into the Pro Football Hall of Fame fourteen years later.

TEXAS E. SCHRAMM

1920–
Team President, General Manager
Team: Dallas Cowboys
Inducted: 1991

Businessman, promoter, football innovator–Tex Schramm was all of these. Schramm played a key role in bringing about the merger of the AFL and the NFL in 1966. He suggested that the new league be divided into two conferences, with a championship playoff at the end of the season. As general manager of the Dallas Cowboys, Schramm's shrewd moves turned the Cowboys into winners with national appeal, so much so that they became known as "America's Team."

Schramm joined the Cowboys in 1959, before their first NFL season. He believed that the team should be built by signing players from the college draft and free agents, rather than by trading for veterans. Schramm's philosophy worked; the Cowboys had 20 straight winning seasons. During that period the team appeared in the playoffs eighteen times. They won thirteen division titles, five NFC championships, and two of the five Super Bowls they played in.

Schramm was born on June 2, 1920, in San Gabriel, California. He received a journalism degree from the University of Texas. In 1947 he became publicity director for the Los Angeles Rams. Ten years later he left the Rams to join CBS Sports. In 1960, while covering the Winter Olympics, he came up with the idea of using a sports anchor for major sporting events.

Once in Dallas, Schramm's background in publicity helped him come up with many clever ways to promote his team. He set up the *Dallas Cowboys Newsweekly* and the largest radio network of any sports team. By 1979 Dallas games were broadcast on 225 stations, including Spanish-speaking stations, in nineteen states. Schramm produced Cowboys souvenirs, using the logo *America's Team.* He introduced the Dallas Cowboys cheerleaders and made them famous by featuring them at Super Bowls and on international tours. He built the 65,000-seat Texas Stadium, which sold out as soon as it was completed.

A smart businessman, Schramm was named NFL Executive of the Year in 1977. A year later he received the Bert Bell Award for outstanding NFL executive leadership. He was also made chair of the NFL's Competition Committee, where he introduced new rules to make the game more exciting.

Schramm did everything from using computers to scout players to lobbying for instant replay. Some of his innovations include the referee's microphone, multicolor striping on the 20- and 50-yard lines, and the 30-second clock between plays.

In 1989, after 30 years with the Cowboys, Schramm served a brief term as president of the new World League of American Football. In 1991 Schramm was voted into the Pro Football Hall of Fame.

JAN STENERUD

1942–
Position: placekicker
Teams: Kansas City Chiefs, Green Bay Packers, Minnesota Vikings
Inducted: 1991

When Jan Stenerud was inducted into the Pro Football Hall of Fame in 1991, he was the first player whose only job had been placekicking. For years the Hall's Selection Committee felt that someone who only kicked the ball wasn't a legitimate candidate for football's highest honor. A kicker is used sparingly and doesn't get pounded every game the way most football players do. Even practices for kickers aren't as demanding as those of scrimmage-line regulars.

However, the Hall of Fame selectors eventually decided that a placekicker's job *is* demanding. Kickers have become more important; they're specialists who often face incredible pressure to pull out victories in the last seconds of games. And everyone agreed that Jan Stenerud was outstanding in this position.

When he was inducted into the Hall, Stenerud's career record of 373 successful field goals beat the legendary George Blanda's record by 38. (Stenerud's record was surpassed by Nick Lowery in 1996.) He ranked second in all-time total points, with 1,699, second in field goals over 50 yards, with 17, and third in career extra points, with 580. He also scored over 100 points per seasons in his first five seasons with the Cheifs.

Stenerud played in two AFL All-Star Games and four AFC-NFC Pro Bowls. His 4 field goals and 2 extra points won him Offensive MVP honors in the 1972 Pro Bowl. From 1967 to 1970, Stenerud's success rate for field goal attempts was 71 percent. The AFL norm at the time was around 50 percent.

Stenerud was born on November 26, 1942, in Fetsund, Norway. He played soccer and hockey as a youngster, and earned a scholarship as a ski jumper to Montana State University.

During his sophomore year, he held the ball for MSU's kicker when he practiced. After a while Stenerud tried kicking the ball himself. When the football coach heard about Stenerud's long, booming kicks, Stenerud was put on the football team. He kicked 18 of 33 field goals in two years. In 1967 he signed with Kansas City, whose coach, Hank Stram, had been a kicker at Purdue.

Stenerud kicked 16 straight field goals in 1969. Then in Super Bowl IV, Stenerud scored a record-long 48-yard field goal, followed by a 32-yarder, then a 25-yarder, as the Chiefs beat the Minnesota Vikings 23–7.

In 1980 the Chiefs wanted a younger kicker and released Stenerud. A few months later, the 6-foot 2-inch, 190-pounder signed with the Green Bay Packers. In 1981 he converted 22 of 24 attempts—the best success ratio of his career.

Stenerud was traded to the Minnesota Vikings in 1984, one of his finest seasons. That year, at age 42, he was the oldest player to play in the Pro Bowl. A bad back forced him to retire in 1985.

JAN STENERUD			
Extra Point Attempts	601	Field Goal Attempts	558
Extra Points	580	Field Goals	373

LEMUEL JACKSON BARNEY

1945–
Position: cornerback
Team: Detroit Lions
Inducted: 1992

Lem Barney was one of football's finest cornerbacks ever and he excelled as a punter and kickoff return specialist as well. In 1992 he became only the fifth cornerback to enter the Pro Football Hall of Fame. Known as Detroit's "offense on defense," Barney scored 11 touchdowns during his ten years with the Lions. Of those 11 touchdowns, 7 were made on interceptions, 2 on punt returns, 1 on a kickoff return, and 1 on a blocked field goal return. His excellent defensive skills and great speed helped Barney win All-Pro honors three times, and he played in seven Pro Bowls.

Barney played quarterback on his high school football team in Gulfport, Mississippi, where he was born on September 8, 1945. When he wasn't recruited for college, he almost didn't go. But his mother urged him to try one year at Jackson State. At Jackson State Barney realized "there was no demand for black quarterbacks in the pros back then." So he asked his coach to switch him to defensive back. He played that position so well that he became Detroit's second-round choice in the 1967 college draft.

Still, Lions coach Joe Schmidt was certain his rookie cornerback wouldn't play much his first year. The cornerback position is one of the most difficult in football, even for a seasoned veteran. However, in the very first scrimmage of training camp, Barney impressed Schmidt with his interception skills, catching a pass with just one arm. At the end of camp, the 6-foot, 190-pound rookie was the Lions' starting left cornerback.

His rookie season, Barney shared the league lead in interceptions with 10. The entire year he allowed only 1 touchdown, and he quickly proved he could do more on defense than just guard against passes. Using his amazing speed, he routinely tackled star running backs such as Gayle Sayers. Not a violent player, Barney preferred to bring down an opponent with a leg tackle instead of the vicious shoulder-high "clothesline" stop. Then he always offered a hand to help the player up.

During his first three years in pro football, Barney could do no wrong. Then in 1970, he signed a $42,000 contract that made him the highest-paid cornerback in the NFL. After that his gambling style of defense didn't seem to work anymore. He let the opposition score touchdowns and failed to make easy tackles. During a game against the Minnesota Vikings, he fumbled a punt return. The Vikings recovered it, then kicked a winning field goal. After an injury benched him for five games, the fans began to boo him.

However, Barney bounced back in 1972, making it to the Pro Bowl. He played in three more Pro Bowls before retiring in 1977. In addition to his 56 career interceptions, Barney finished with 143 punt returns for 1,312 yards and 2 touchdowns, as well as 50 kickoff returns for 1,274 yards and a touchdown.

LEM BARNEY			
Interceptions	56	Average Gain	18.8
Yards	1,051	Touchdowns	7

AL DAVIS

1929–
American Football League Commissioner, Coach, Team Owner
Teams: Oakland Raiders, Los Angeles Raiders
Inducted: 1992

Al Davis never played a pro football game, but his determination to win at any cost helped create the AFL-NFL merger, and his fierce independence led to a historic lawsuit against the NFL. When Davis, as the Oakland Raiders owner, wanted to move the team to Los Angeles, the NFL said no. Davis felt he could move his team to any city he wanted, and the courts agreed. People learned it didn't pay to say no to Al Davis.

Appropriately enough, Davis was born on Independence Day of 1929, in Brockton, Massachusetts, and grew up in Brooklyn, New York. He began coaching in 1950, after college. In 1960 he was hired as the offensive coach for the Los Angeles Chargers; then in 1963 he became head coach and general manager of the Oakland Raiders. (He later bought the team as well.) Both teams belonged to the American Football League, formed in 1960 to compete with the National Football League.

Before Davis joined the Raiders, Oakland had won nine of its last 33 games. His first year, the Raiders went 10–4 and Davis was named AFL Coach of the Year. He finished his tenure as Raiders coach with a 23–16–3 record. From 1963 to 1991, the year before Davis entered the Hall of Fame, the Raiders compiled a .670 win percentage—the best record of any pro sports team in that period. From 1965 to 1985 the team had only one losing season: 1981. They won three of the four Super Bowls they played in.

Davis used every method available to recruit the finest players for his AFL team. He used the college draft and trades, but he was famous for taking other teams' castoffs and turning them into All-Pros. As proof, seven of his Raiders are Hall of Famers.

There are many stories about the sly tricks Davis used to get his players. One story tells about a meeting Davis had with Dallas Cowboys scout Gil Brandt in a hotel. When Davis discovered they were both there to sign the same player, he left the meeting and called the front desk. Pretending to be Brandt, he asked the desk clerk to hold his calls until the next morning.

In April 1966, Davis was made AFL commissioner, partly because of his reputation as a schemer. He began a ruthless campaign to bring many of the NFL's top players to the AFL when their NFL contracts ran out. The league war was killing both leagues financially, and they had already begun talks for a merger. However, Davis's raiding of its players gave the NFL even more incentive for a quick merger.

Davis instilled his competitive, "win at all cost" attitude in his players, and he did everything to make them happy, providing them with special meals and comfortable jets for traveling. Davis's tactics worked well—the Raiders were one of the most powerful teams of the 1960s and 1970s. In 1992, after nearly 30 years in pro football, Al Davis was inducted into the Pro Football Hall of Fame.

Inductees
1993–1996

CHARLES HENRY NOLL

1932–
Coach
Team: Pittsburgh Steelers
Inducted: 1993

A SUPERSTAR STRATEGY

Coach Chuck Noll's strategy for building a winning team was to use the college draft. Every year he picked a potential superstar: L.C. Greenwood and Mean Joe Greene in 1969; Terry Bradshaw and Mel Blount in 1970; Jack Ham, Dwight White, and Mike Wagner in 1971; Franco Harris in 1972; Lynn Swann, Jack Lambert, John Stallworth, and Mike Webster in 1974. Greene, Bradshaw, Blount, Ham, Harris, and Lambert became Hall of Famers. In the Steelers' first Super Bowl, seven of the eleven defensive starters had been acquired through the draft.

When Chuck Noll became Pittsburgh's head coach in 1969, the Steelers hadn't won any kind of championship in almost 40 years. Ten years later the Steelers were the Team of the Decade.

Noll's strategy was to build a winning team through the college draft, rather than through trades for what were often "other team's problems." Every year he picked a potential superstar. Every year the team got better.

In his fourth season, 1972, Noll brought Pittsburgh to its first-ever championship, the AFC Central Division crown. Two years later the team won its first of four Super Bowls in six years. Noll had a 209–156–1 record in his 23 years with the Steelers. In addition to the four Super Bowls, Noll guided the Steelers to nine Central Division titles and sixteen winning seasons.

Noll's career in Pittsburgh got off to a rocky start. He won his first game with the Steelers, but then lost the next thirteen. His next season, the Steelers won five, then six in 1971. In 1972 the Steelers did better than expected, ending the season with an 11–3 record, the AFC Central title, and a 13–7 AFC division playoff victory.

In 1973 the Steelers landed a wild card playoff berth, but in 1974 they went straight to the top. The Steelers won their first of six straight AFC Central crowns, the AFC championship title, and Super Bowl IX. In 1975 they took Super Bowl X. Then in 1978 and 1979 they grabbed unprecedented third and fourth Super Bowl triumphs.

Noll was born in Cleveland, Ohio, on January 5, 1932. He was captain of his football team at the University of Dayton. In 1953 he signed with the Cleveland Browns. He played linebacker and offensive guard. At the young age of 27, he quit playing to coach, first under Sid Gillman of the Los Angeles–and later San Diego–Chargers, then under Don Shula with the Baltimore Colts.

Noll's coaching techniques weren't too different from those of other successful coaches. He stressed gaining at least 4 yards on first down. Good yardage on first down gave his team more flexibility for

CHUCK NOLL			
Wins	209	**Ties**	1
Losses	156	**Win Percentage**	.572

SOME COACHING

Chuck Noll worked under three coaches who greatly influenced him: he was a player for Paul Brown, and an assistant coach under Sid Gillman of the Chargers and Don Shula in Baltimore.

"Sid was one of the game's prime researchers and offensive specialists," Noll said. "For six years, I had more exposure to football than I normally would have received in twelve years." From Shula, Noll gained "organization and attitudes."

But Noll had talent of his own. "After a while, Chuck could have called the plays himself, without any help from the bench," said Paul Brown. "He was that kind of a football student."

the next few plays. He preferred a running game rather than a passing game "because football is a game of contact." However, when the passing game became the trend in football, he moved that way also.

Noll coached players individually whenever he could, mostly on basic techniques. "One-on-one after practice is best for me," he said. Just as important, he patiently gave his players whatever time they needed to develop. Sometimes that took years.

"[Noll] was very stern, very strict," said linebacker Andy Russell. "On the other hand, he was very realistic about what the players could or could not do. He didn't wear us out at practice. Sundays were our hard days. To that extent, he was a player's coach."

Noll's coaching reign lasted until 1991. After the sensational 1970s, the Steelers produced four more playoff appearances but no more Super Bowls. In 1989 Noll was named AFC Coach of the Year, an honor long overdue. But Noll never cared about fame or fortune. He only cared about winning, and he gladly gave his players credit.

When linebacker Jack Ham heard his coach was elected to the Hall of Fame in 1993, he said, "I think [that] of all the people who were involved in the Steelers organization during our Super Bowl years, Chuck Noll is by far the most deserving to be inducted."

Pittsburgh Steelers head coach Chuck Noll is presented the game ball by his team after winning Super Bowl IX.

WALTER JERRY PAYTON

1954–
Position: running back
Team: Chicago Bears
Inducted: 1993

RUNNING BEAR

Walter Payton had a very unusual running style—he rarely bent his knees. Instead, he swung his straight legs from the hips. Swinging the leg from the hip took the burden of running off the knees, the most vulnerable joints. By putting that burden on the thighs, Payton gave himself more power and extra leverage.

Running straight-legged also made it easier for Payton to run on his toes. This would have been impossible for many players, but Payton was able to do this because he had extremely strong thighs, hamstrings, and buttocks. Physically he was more of a power runner than a breakaway speedster, which is what most high-yardage ballcarriers are.

In his thirteen seasons with the Chicago Bears, from 1975 to 1987, Walter Payton rewrote the NFL record book with his ballcarrying feats. When he retired he held 27 team records and eight NFL marks. His 16,726 yards rushing are the all-time record, as are his 21,803 combined net yards. His total of 125 touchdowns is the second-most ever and he carried the ball a record 3,838 times. Payton rushed for more than 1,000 yards in ten of his thirteen seasons, and he had an NFL record three consecutive seasons with 2,000 total yards from scrimmage. He rushed for an all-time game high of 275 yards, and during his career he rushed for more than 100 yards in a record 77 games.

The amazing rushing stats can hide the fact that Payton was a great all-around player. "He is a complete football player," said Jim Finks, who drafted Payton for the Bears. "He is better than Jim Brown. He is better than O.J. Simpson."

"As far as blocking, tackling, running, durability, intelligence, throwing—he does it all," said Bill Tobin, former Bears executive.

In Payton's prime years, scouts considered him the best blocking back in the league. His teammate, Brian Baschnagel, believed Payton could play any position, but "his size," Baschnagel joked, "might limit him at defensive tackle."

The fact is, Payton could do whatever he was asked. He could run the ball, outsprint speedy linebackers, and dish out punishing hits to tacklers. He even served as backup punter and placekicker. But he was best at running with the ball.

At 5 feet 10 inches and 202 pounds, Payton was relatively small, but not defenseless. He relished contact and would rather hit a tackler than run out of bounds to avoid him. "What people didn't know was how rough he was," said Raiders linebacker Matt Millen. "He didn't give straight-arms, he'd punch you. Or he would lower his

WALTER PAYTON				
Rushing Attempts	3,838	**Pass Receptions**	492
Rushing Yards	16,726	**Pass Receiving Yards**	4,538
Average Gain	4.4	**Average Gain**	9.2
Touchdowns	110	**Touchdowns**	15
		Total Points	750 (125 touchdowns)

AN OBSESSION WITH ONE

Walter Payton sometimes went to obsessive lengths to be the best. He was always the last to take the Bears' strength and running tests. He wanted to know what the highest score was so he'd know what he'd have to achieve to beat it. Payton was frustrated that his perfect attendance record was marred by one game he had missed in his rookie season. "I could have played, but my coach wouldn't let me. I don't count that as a miss," he insisted.

In 1984 both Payton and Franco Harris were approaching Jim Brown's all-time record of 12,312 rushing yards. "I want to get it before Franco," Payton announced. Even after he beat out Harris in the season's fourth game, he still wasn't satisfied. "Brown set his record in nine seasons," he complained. "I could have too, if the strike hadn't shortened the 1982 season."

shoulder and kind of jump into you. He was one of the few who got personal fouls running with the ball."

Payton was born on July 25, 1954, in Columbia, Mississippi. He enrolled at Jackson State University so he could play in the same backfield as his older brother, Edward. In college Payton rushed for 3,563 yards in four seasons and scored a Division I-AA record 464 points on 66 touchdowns, 5 field goals, and 534 extra points. He also picked up his nickname, "Sweetness," because of the smooth way he ran.

The Bears made Payton their first-choice draft pick in 1975. In his rookie season Payton led the NFL in kickoff returns. His 679 rushing yards were the most for a Bears running back since Gale Sayers ran for 1,032 in 1969. The next year Payton had four 100-yard games and led the league with 1,390 yards and 13 touchdowns. In 1977 he had his career-high 1,852 yards and led the league with 16 touchdowns for 96 points.

Payton won one NFL and five NFC rushing titles. He was named All-Pro nine times, from 1976 through 1980 and from 1983 through 1986. He was NFL Most Valuable Player in 1977 and 1985 and NFC Player of the Year three times. He retired in 1987, at the top of the heap.

Chicago Bears running back Walter Payton (34) carries the ball through the opposition's lineup.

WILLIAM ERNEST WALSH

1931–
Coach
Team: San Francisco 49ers
Inducted: 1993

Bill Walsh took over as head coach of the San Francisco 49ers in January 1979. The 49ers were coming off a dismal 2–14 season in 1978, and in Walsh's first year the team did no better. But as the 49ers entered a new decade, Walsh began to turn the club around. By the time the 1980s were over, Walsh had shaped the Niners into one of the greatest pro football teams ever.

By 1981 San Francisco had improved its record to 13–3 and won its first NFC title. In Super Bowl XVI the 49ers pulled out a tight 26–21 win over the Cincinnati Bengals. Walsh later guided his team to victories in Super Bowls XIX and XXIII.

When Walsh came on board, the 49ers ship was full of holes. With the exception of the offensive line, the entire team had to be rebuilt. Walsh was ready. He had worked under the legendary Paul Brown, as well as Oakland's Al Davis, and had studied other coaches' techniques.

Walsh used every means available to get the players he wanted. He had three rules for the college draft. The first was to have several people to discuss a draft choice but have only one man to decide yea or nay. That one man was Bill Walsh, of course. His second rule was to target the players he wanted and make trade deals for them. He didn't agree with the philosophy of taking the best players available regardless of their position. His third rule was to refrain from watching a candidate over and over. If he saw a player give an exceptional performance during a game, Walsh figured the player could do it again.

The 49er's coach signed veterans from other teams, as well as free agents. However, Walsh was more partial to trading draft choices. He might trade eight in exchange for two, if those two were what he wanted. In his search for the right players to build a top team, Walsh considered everyone—even players who didn't play football in college.

Walsh patterned his team-building and coaching techniques after some of the coaches he had worked with and others he had studied. He took many of his organizational procedures from Paul

TWO WAYS TO BUILD A FOOTBALL TEAM

When he took over as head coach for the San Francisco 49ers, Bill Walsh began adding players to rebuild his team. His building efforts erected a tower of a team that dominated the 1980s, with players such as Jerry Rice, Joe Montana, Ronnie Lott, and Roger Craig. Still, every year Walsh brought in new players to add to his core of stars. As a result, in his ten years with the 49ers, the team won three Super Bowls with three different teams.

Ten years before Walsh joined the 49ers, Pittsburgh Steelers coach Chuck Noll also had to rebuild a losing team. Like Walsh, Noll carefully chose from the college draft. But unlike Walsh, Noll acquired the backbone of his team early in his tenure, then patiently allowed his players to develop into the premier team of the decade. During the 1970s the Steelers' four Super Bowl victories were won by basically the same roster of superstars.

BILL WALSH			
Wins	102	**Ties**	1
Losses	63	**Win Percentage**	.617

FOOTBALL IS MY GAME

Bill Walsh was always some-how involved with football—particularly coaching. Walsh was born in Los Angeles on November 30, 1931. He played quarterback in high school. Walsh attended San Jose State on a scholarship and played end, but injuries cut his playing time to five games in his senior year. After graduation his coach offered him an assistant coach job. While Walsh worked with the players, he worked on his master's degree in education. Even his master's thesis, *Defensing the Spread-T Offense,* was related to football.

In 1957, after one year as an assistant at San Jose, Walsh began coaching a high school team. After another stint as an assistant coach in the college ranks, Walsh took his first NFL coaching job in 1966. Walsh served ten years in the pros, then took over as head coach at Stanford University for two seasons. After his ten-year stint as head coach with the San Francisco 49ers, he retired to take a job with NBC as an NFL game analyst to—what else?—talk about football! Walsh then returned to coaching in 1992, taking the helm at Stanford again for three more seasons.

Brown. Walsh had worked eight years under Brown when the famous coach was head of the Cincinnati Bengals. Walsh got much of his offensive approach from studying Sid Gillman, the coach for San Diego and Houston.

Walsh felt it took three qualities to be an effective leader as head coach and offensive coordinator. He had to have supreme confidence in himself. He also had to be able to think clearly. And finally, he had to be innovative, creative, and flexible.

A workaholic, Walsh wasted no time putting his ideas into action to get the 49ers up and going. He was named NFL Coach of the Year in 1981 and NFC Coach of the Year in 1984. But in between those years, he was often ready to quit. He was particularly low during 1982. A players' strike had shortened the season, which had left the champion 49ers with a 3–6 record.

The pressures of coaching evnetually got to Walsh. After his third Super Bowl victory in 1989, he decided to retire. But he had established a tradition of excellence in San Francisco that remained after he left.

San Francisco 49ers coach Bill Walsh is carried on the shoulders of his team after winning Super Bowl XIX.

ANTHONY DREW DORSETT

1954–
Position: running back
Teams: Dallas Cowboys, Denver Broncos
Inducted: 1994

One of the great running backs in pro football, Tony Dorsett was the NFL's second all-time rusher when he retired. Dorsett had all the tools a great ballcarrier needs: speed, strength, and smarts. "Dorsett had great ability to pick a hole," one opposing coach said. "Then he would just explode."

Drafted in 1977 by the Dallas Cowboys, Dorsett gained more than 1,000 yards each of his first five seasons. His streak of five 1,000-yard pro seasons was broken in 1982, when a players' strike shortened the season. When he retired in 1989, his 16,326 combined net yards passed Jim Brown's career total and were second only to Walter Payton's.

His first season, Dorsett was named Rookie of the Year after rushing for 1,007 yards and 12 touchdowns and adding 273 yards and a touchdown on 29 receptions. In Super Bowl XII Dorsett rushed 15 times for 66 yards and scored the game's first touchdown to spark a 27–10 victory over the Denver Broncos. The next year, 1978, Dorsett gained 1,325 yards rushing and 378 yards receiving. Dallas lost the Super Bowl to Pittsburgh, but Dorsett carried the ball 16 times for 96 yards and added 44 more yards on 5 receptions.

Dorsett's fifth season, 1981, was the first season he put forth a real effort in training camp. As a result, he was in the best shape of his career, and that outstanding season was the peak of his career. He rushed for a team record of 1,646 yards and caught 32 passes for 325 yards. Rushing for 100 yards or more in nine games, he led the Cowboys to a 12–4 record and another NFC Eastern Division championship.

Capable of making game-breaking, long-distance gains, Dorsett had runs of 75 or more yards five times in his twelve-year career. His record came in January 1983 during a game against the Minnesota Vikings. Dorsett took a handoff at his own 1-yard line and ran 99

FITTING IN

Tony Dorsett always thought that if he could run the ball as many times as Walter Payton or Earl Campbell did, he could match or top their yardage. Jim Brown, the Hall of Fame running back, agreed.

"Anytime you talk about a running back, you have to take his situation into consideration," Brown said, "When you're talking about Earl Campbell, for instance, you are talking about a great back who is with a team [that] clearly looks to him as The Man. They know it, and he knows it. In Dallas, Dorsett has not gotten the ball as if he was The Man. So what you have is a great back working under a strict system. It's illogical to expect Dallas to abandon its system, so what Dorsett has to do is fit in."

However, Dallas coach Tom Landry refused to use Dorsett more for fear that he would get hurt. If he had, Dorsett might have held the rushing record today.

TONY DORSETT				
Rushing Attempts	2,936		**Pass Receptions**	398
Rushing Yards	12,739		**Pass Receiving Yards**	3,554
Average Gain	4.3		**Average Gain**	8.9
Touchdowns	77		**Touchdowns**	13
			Total Points	546 (91 touchdowns)

AN ELEVEN-YEAR RUN

Tony Dorsett was born on April 7, 1954, in Rochester, Pennsylvania. When he was young, his family moved to be near the steel mills in Aliquippa. The thought of spending his life in the mills gave Dorsett nightmares. Then his high school football coach helped him achieve a dream of something better. He switched the youngster from linebacker to running back.

That switch started Dorsett on eleven straight 1,000-yard seasons, beginning in his junior year of high school, when he gained 1,034, and continuing his senior year. Then Dorsett had four 1,000-yard seasons at the University of Pittsburgh. Named to the All-America team three of those years, he established an all-time NCAA record of 6,082 career rushing yards. His senior year at Pittsburgh he ran for 1,948 yards and 21 touchdowns to win the 1976 Heisman Trophy.

Dorsett's 1,000-plus-yard streak continued in his first five years with the Dallas Cowboys. The 1982 player strike finally ended his incredible run.

yards for a touchdown. It was the longest run from scrimmage in NFL history.

In spite of his spectacular achievements, Dorsett was named All-NFL only once, in 1981. He received All-NFC honors in 1978, 1981, and 1982, but he played in only four Pro Bowls. And oddly enough, for all his spectacular yardage, he never won an NFC rushing title. His 1981 total of 1,646 yards was 28 yards shy of the conference leader, George Rogers.

At 5 feet 11 inches and 185 pounds, Dorsett was small, but despite his size and the pounding he took, he missed only three games due to injury in his first nine years with Dallas. His incredible balance enabled him to suddenly change direction to avoid tacklers. In 1986 and 1987, however, injuries were partly responsible for a drop in yardage. The other factor was the addition of another great running back, Herschel Walker.

After surgery on both his ankles, Dorsett was outdistanced by Walker 891 yards to 456 yards in 1987. The next year, Dorsett was traded to the Broncos. In Denver, Dorsett had one goal: to beat Jim Brown's rushing record. He did it that year, in a September game against the L.A. Raiders. During a preseason practice the next year, Dorsett's knee "crumbled like a piece of spaghetti." His career was over. In 1994, the first year he was eligible, he was voted into the Pro Football Hall of Fame.

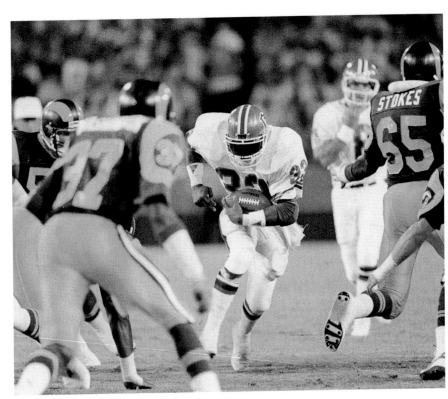

*Denver Broncos running back Tony Dorsett (33)
charges through the L.A. Rams line to pick up some yardage.*

A BLUE-COLLAR WORKER

Randy White was once called a "blue-collar worker" on a "country-club" team. His willingness to work hard was what set him apart as a consistent player, and his drive was focused on bettering his team, rather than himself. When his coach told him to lift weights, he would have to be told to stop. When he was told to practice, everyone on the team would have trouble keeping up with him.

When injuries told White it was time for him to retire, he wouldn't listen, because the team needed him. The only way he would leave was after helping to train his successor.

RANDY LEE WHITE

1953–
Position: defensive tackle
Team: Dallas Cowboys
Inducted: 1994

In 1980 a national magazine took a poll of NFL personnel directors. The magazine asked the experts which player they would select first if they were starting a team. Randy White got twice as many votes as any other player.

White fits the description of a perfect candidate for the Pro Football Hall of Fame. All-America player in college. Winner of both the Lombardi Award and the Outland Trophy, the defense's version of the Heisman Trophy. First-round draft pick. All-Pro almost every year of his NFL career. Randy White was all of the above.

White began his fourteen-year career in Dallas in 1975 as a middle linebacker. He struggled with the position for two years with no success. "I just didn't have the natural reactions it takes to play middle linebacker," he admitted. "At first I was confused by the position, and then I was embarrassed." It was the first and only time he ever failed at anything on the football field.

When White was moved to right defensive tackle in 1978, he said, "It was just like somebody took the handcuffs off and I could go play." The move was the best thing that could have happened to White and Dallas. As soon as Coach Tom Landry put White in the trenches, he blossomed into a totally effective player. He quickly learned the Cowboys' complicated "flex" defense, although he was allowed to play outside that strategy—the only Cowboy to do so. "You've got to let a man like that go with his ability," said defensive linemate John Dutton. "You can't hold him down with different techniques."

White was so good and so tough that it didn't take the opposition long to start double- and triple-teaming him. But 6-foot 4-inch, 265-pound White had the incredible strength to handle it. His huge arms felt like clubs to blockers. He could throw 300-pound linemen to the ground. And he could chase down running backs with the speed of a track star. With White attracting double teams, his defensive end teammate, Harvey Martin, became a demon pass rusher. White and Martin shared sacks and MVP honors in the Cowboys' 27–10 Super Bowl XII victory over the Denver Broncos.

In 1977 White had 12 sacks, and he had 16 sacks the next season, his single-season high mark. In 1977 he was selected for the first

THE NAME GAME

"Hunk." That's what Randy White's parents called him from the time he was a baby. This large baby boy was born on January 15, 1953, in Pittsburgh, Pennsylvania, and he never changed. One of the strongest Cowboys, White routinely bench-pressed 475 pounds. He once bench-pressed 450 pounds ten times in a team contest.

"Monster" is the moniker Charlie Waters, a Dallas safety, gave White because "the way Randy plays, he has to be part-man, part-monster."

"Mean" is how White's long-time defensive partner Harvey Martin described him. "He's mean. That's all you can say. He just gets up for games. Off the field, he's a nice guy… But he's mean otherwise."

"Jekyll and Hyde," said one sportswriter. Shy and soft-spoken off the field, White's personality changed as soon as he put on a uniform. Dallas tackle Dave Stalls said he could actually see White change on the field from nice guy to nasty.

"Intense" is the way everyone referred to White. Driven to succeed, not for himself, but for his team. "You very seldom have the opportunity to coach a player with the intensity he had," said Coach Ernie Stautner.

of nine consecutive Pro Bowls, and 1978 was his first of eight straight All-Pro seasons. During his career White made 1,104 tackles—701 of which were unassisted—and 111 sacks. He helped the Cowboys to six NFC championship games and three Super Bowls.

Often playing with injuries, White ignored the pain, missing just one game in 1979. However, during his last two seasons, a pinched nerve in his neck prevented him from lifting weights. The pain was so bad that he couldn't lift his head when he took his stance on the line of scrimmage. But White was so driven to help his team win that he couldn't admit he was failing to do just that.

Then defensive line coach Ernie Stautner asked White to help Danny Noonan, who was White's replacement. White was proud do something useful for his team by helping Noonan, rather than sitting uselessly on the bench. When White retired at the end of the 1988 season, Stautner said, "You very seldom have the opportunity to coach a player with the intensity he had."

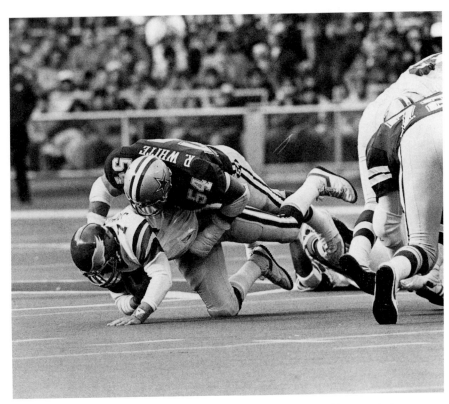

Dallas Cowboys tackle Randy White (54) sacks the opposition quarterback.

STEVE M. LARGENT

1954–
Position: wide receiver
Team: Seattle Seahawks
Inducted: 1995

HIS SUCCESS IS CATCHING

In his final season of 1989, on December 10, Steve Largent scored his 100th touchdown. In that moment, he broke Don Hutson's record of 99 touchdown catches—a mark that had stood since 1945.

During his fourteen-year career with the Seahawks, Largent broke six major NFL receiving records. He caught 819 passes for 13,089 yards and 100 touchdowns. He also had ten seasons with 50 or more receptions, 177 straight games with at least 1 pass reception, and eight seasons with 1,000 or more yards on receptions.

By the time he was elected to the Hall of Fame, most of Largent's record had been tied or broken. "I didn't play football to set records," Largent said modestly. "Setting records was just part of the process of playing."

When Steve Largent retired from pro football in 1989, he took six major receiving records with him. And he achieved his incredible statistics while playing for a mostly mediocre team. At the beginning of his career, Largent didn't seem like superstar or even pro material. He had no gazellelike speed, no track-meet leaping ability, no All-America honors. He didn't get picked until the fourth round of the 1976 draft. Then, after he caught only 2 passes during the preseason, the Houston Oilers traded him to the Seattle Seahawks.

Training camp with the Seahawks was a disaster too. Largent dropped every ball thrown to him. But he calmed down, and by the regular-season opener, he came off the bench to catch 5 passes and do some great blocking. His rookie year, Largent caught a respectable 54 passes for 705 yards.

In the tenth game of his second season, Largent caught 2 passes. That began a record string of 177 games with at least one reception—a streak that ended only with his retirement. This record has since been broken, by Art Monk in 1995. He was named Seahawks MVP in 1977. The next year he took the AFC receiving title with 71 catches and became Seattle's first Pro Bowl player. In the nine seasons from 1978 to 1986, Largent averaged 67 catches per year.

In spite of Largent's accomplishments, the media ignored him because his team rarely made the headlines. Then, beginning in 1983, Seattle finished at .500 or better for six straight seasons under new coach Chuck Knox. Largent continued his strong play. In 1985 he led the league with 1,287 receiving yards and made a career-high 79 receptions. He made the All-Pro and All-AFC teams that year and again in 1987. During his career Largent was selected for seven Pro Bowls, missing one because of injuries.

At 5 feet 11 inches and 191 pounds, Steve Largent was considered too small, as well as too slow, for pro football. However, what he lacked in speed or athletic strength, he made up for with a wily

STEVE LARGENT			
Pass Receptions	819	**Total Points**	608 (101 touchdowns,
Pass Receiving Yards	13,089		2 extra points)
Average Gain	16.0		
Touchdowns	100		

PRACTICE MAKES PERFECT

Some people called Steve Largent an overachiever. Others called him a hard worker. For Largent, working hard in football began in high school.

Largent was born on September 28, 1954, in Tulsa, Oklahoma. His family moved several times, ending up in Oklahoma City, where he attended high school.

Largent almost didn't go out for football because there were 140 other boys trying out—all bigger and faster. But assistant coach Gene Abney took him in hand. Abney drilled him in the wide receiver's spot every hot Oklahoma day until the boy was exhausted. But Largent thrived on the hard work, and he made the team.

Even after he turned pro, Largent continued to work hard. He spent hours on the practice field, catching as many as 200 machine-propelled passes every day.

cleverness he used to baffle the enemy. Seahawks president and general manager Mike McCormack thought Largent kept up the myth that he wasn't a fast receiver on purpose. That way he could fool opposing defenders into underestimating him.

Largent was recognized as a textbook case on how to run pass routes. If a coach wanted a rookie to study one wide receiver, Largent was the one. His teammate, Ken Easley, a defensive back who often guarded Largent in practice, knew what set Largent apart from other receivers. "He has a phenomenal ability to 'sight adjust' on a pass route, meaning when a defensive back isn't right where he is supposed to be, Steve will make a spur-of-the moment adjustment in his route to get open."

Four years after he retired in 1989, Largent ran for Congress and won. In January 1995 he was sworn in for his first term as a U.S. congressman from Oklahoma. The same month, he was inducted into the Football Hall of Fame.

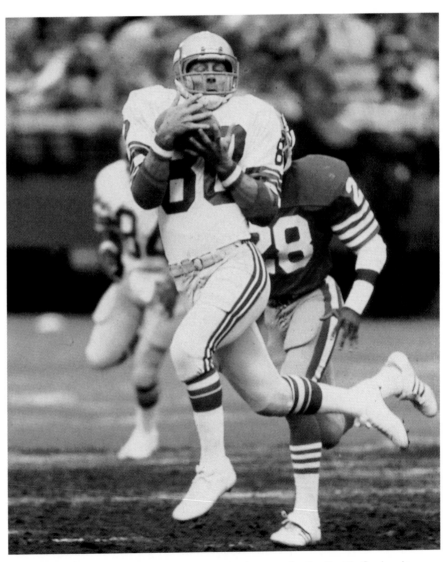

Wide receiver Steve Largent leaps to catch a pass for the Seattle Seahawks.

KELLEN BOSWELL WINSLOW

1957–
Position: tight end
Team: San Diego Chargers
Inducted: 1995

SURVIVAL OF THE HAND-IEST

In the early 1980s it became trendy for pass receivers to wear gloves. But not Kellen Winslow. "I don't like gloves," he said. "I think you drop more balls than you catch with them."

Winslow did wear gloves twice, however. Once was in the 1981 AFC championship game, when the wind chill factor was 59 degrees below zero. "I had two pairs of gloves on that day and still got a touch of frostbite in my right thumb. I used them [gloves] that day just out of a basic survival instinct. The only other time I wore gloves was in a season-ending blizzard in Denver."

Kellen Winslow and the San Diego Chargers offense were a perfect match. The Chargers played an aerial offensive game in which they relied heavily on the forward pass. They called this wide-open passing attack "Air-Coryell," in honor of their coach, Don Coryell. With his size, speed, and "hands like glue," 6-foot 5-inch, 250-pound Winslow (born on November 5, 1957, in St. Louis, Missouri) was a key part of Coryell's offense. That Chargers lineup included quarterback Dan Fouts, who passed for more than 40,000 yards in his career. At tight end, Winslow joined wide receivers Charlie Joiner, John Jefferson, and Wes Chandler to turn Fouts's passes into yardage and touchdowns.

Coryell used his superstar tight end for more than just blocking and occasional receiving. The coach also slotted Winslow as a wide receiver, and occasionally as halfback or fullback. As a result, the opposition never knew what Winslow was going to do on the field on any given play.

At first the opposition tended to give Winslow single coverage and double-team Joiner, Jefferson, and Chandler. "We really took advantage of that," Winslow said. "Then it got to the point they [opponents] were trying to decide who to double. Those were the headaches we gave our opponents in the early 1980s."

Headaches is right. In 1980 Winslow, Joiner, and Jefferson became the first trio from one team in NFL history to each catch passes for more than 100 yards in a game and more than 1,000 yards in a season. That year Winslow led the league with 89 catches, which was a record for a tight end at that time. His 88 receptions led the league again in 1981, and in 1983 he had another 88 catches.

The Chargers were the top passing team for seven seasons between 1978 and 1985 and led the NFL in total offense five times. With their awesome firepower, the Chargers won the AFC Western Division title in 1979, 1980, and 1981, and tallied a 33–15 win-loss record for those three years. However, they never made it to the

KELLEN WINSLOW			
Average Gain	12.5	Pass Receptions	541
Touchdowns	45	Pass Receiving Yards	6,741
		Total Points 270 (45 touchdowns)	

HOT HEROICS

Kellen Winslow gave one of his most heroic performances in the Chargers' 41–38 overtime victory over the Miami Dolphins in a 1981 division playoff. The Chargers had blown a 24-point lead. Winslow made a 25-yard touchdown catch to put San Diego back on top, but the Dolphins again tied the game. In the last seconds, with the score 38–38, Winslow blocked a Dolphins field goal attempt, sending the game into overtime. Eventually the Chargers kicked a field goal and won.

But here's where the heroics came in. Winslow was already getting his usual punishment on the scrimmage line every time he had the ball. Then he began dehydrating in the humid, ovenlike heat of Florida. By the third quarter, he needed oxygen.

Winslow was helped off the field three times, but each time he came back, he caught a pass. Although he blocked for the Chargers' winning field goal, he didn't see it. He had fallen to the ground, unable to move. He assumed San Diego had won because the stands, full of Dolphins fans, were quiet. That day the NBC television broadcast team declared Winslow "the all-universe tight end."

Super Bowl, twice losing in the AFC championship game.

In the five years between 1980 and 1984, Winslow made 374 catches—the best record of any NFL receiver during that period. He began 1984 with 55 receptions in his first seven games—an average of nearly 8 catches per week. He was heading for a 100-reception season when Raiders linebacker Jeff Barnes hit him with a devastating tackle. It was a clean hit, but it resulted in knee surgery.

Getting himself back in shape was very hard—mentally, emotionally, and physically. "Learning how to play the game over completely is basically what I had to do," Winslow said. Over his last three seasons, he caught 142 more passes, but his playing was never the same. After the 1987 season he retired.

Winslow was a consensus All-Pro choice from 1980 to 1982 and he was selected as AFC tight end for five Pro Bowls. His 1981 Pro Bowl performance—6 receptions for 86 yards—earned him Offensive Player of the Game. Winslow's ultimate awards came when he was picked for the NFL's 75th Anniversary Team in 1994, then voted into the Pro Football Hall of Fame a few months later.

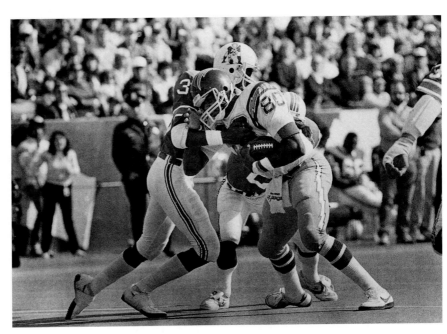

San Diego Chargers tight end Kellen Winslow (80) runs into a human wall while trying to score.

CHARLES JOINER JR.

1947–
Position: wide receiver
Teams: Houston Oilers, Cincinnati Bengals, San Diego Chargers
Inducted: 1996

NUMBER ONE FOR A WHILE

In 1984, his sixteenth pro season, Charlie Joiner caught his 650th pass. In that moment, he became pro football's leading lifetime receiver, passing Charley Taylor. Two years later, Joiner became the all-time leader in reception yardage, passing Don Maynard's mark of 12,146 yards.

But Joiner knew his records would soon belong to the Seattle Seahawks' Steve Largent. "I'm just glad my name is up there for two or three years," he said modestly. When he retired in 1986 he said, "The receiving records are the ones I am most proud of, even though Steve Largent broke them. But the one I still have that he doesn't is the most games, 239 overall, by a wide receiver."

Ten years later, as Joiner entered the Hall of Fame, Steve Largent's records had been passed too. However, Joiner's 239 games played as a wide receiver still stands and probably will for a long time.

At 5 feet 11 inches and 180 pounds, Charlie Joiner was small physically, but as a pro football legend, he was a giant. He was obsessed with practicing until his patterns were perfectly precise, and underneath his quiet, unassuming manner was a fierce, competitive nature on the field. Joiner played wide receiver for eighteen seasons—longer than any other player in pro football at his position. When he retired in 1986, he had caught more passes (750) for more yards (12,146) than any other player up to that time.

The Houston Oilers selected the Grambling State University star as a defensive back in the 1969 draft. Joiner was switched to wide receiver in his rookie year. After a broken arm benched him for part of his first and second seasons, he started in all but one game his third year, 1971. His 681 yards and 7 touchdowns on 31 receptions led the Oilers receivers, but in 1972 he was traded to Cincinnati.

Joiner didn't see much action in Cincinnati. The Bengals already had excellent veteran receivers. In three full years with Cincinnati, he caught just 74 passes. The good news was that he worked with Bill Walsh, a superior offensive coach. It was a mutual admiration. When Walsh went to San Diego, he recommended that the team trade for Joiner, and in 1976 the Chargers did. That year, with Walsh's game plan and quarterback Dan Fouts throwing precision balls, Joiner finally hit the big numbers. His 20.1-yard average on 50 receptions netted 1,056 yards and 7 touchdowns. He was selected for the Pro Bowl and named team MVP.

Joiner's biggest years were from 1979 to 1981, when the Chargers won three straight AFC West titles. He caught 70 or more passes for more than 1,000 yards each year. He grabbed a career-high 72 catches in 1979, and his 1,188 yards receiving in 1981 were also a career high. He was selected for the Pro Bowl twice more, in 1979 and 1980.

The 1980 AFC championship game was one of Joiner's finest, even though San Diego lost to Oakland 34–27. He scored 2 touch-

CHARLIE JOINER			
Pass Receptions	750	**Total Points**	390 (65 touchdowns)
Pass Receiving Yards	12,146		
Average Gain	16.2		
Touchdowns	65		

WITH A LITTLE HELP FROM MY COACH

Charlie Joiner owes much of his success, both on and off the football field, to his coaches. Born in Many, Louisiana, on October 14, 1947, Joiner later moved to Lake Charles, where he joined the football team in his junior year of high school. His high school coaches instilled a strong work ethic in the young receiver. They also got him a scholarship to Grambling State University, where he met Coach Eddie Robinson.

"Playing for Coach Robinson was one of the finest experiences I ever had," Joiner said. "He taught you how to be a responsible person in the real world. … If you listened to Coach Robinson, it was hard not to be successful."Under Robinson Joiner became a three-time All-Southwestern Athletic Conference selection and was named Outstanding Offensive Player in the 1968 Little Rose Bowl. That year the Houston Oilers drafted him.

In 1972 Joiner was traded to the Cincinnati Bengals. With Cincinnati, he got to work with Coach Bill Walsh. When Walsh moved to San Diego, he convinced the team to acquire Joiner in 1976. It was the all-important boost Joiner needed at the time. In San Diego Joiner worked for Joe Gibbs and Don Coryell as well as Walsh. "When Coryell became head coach in 1978, that's when my career took off," said Joiner. "I caught fire when they started throwing me passes."

downs on passes of 48 yards and 8 yards, winding up with 6 receptions for a game-leading 130 yards.

Joiner's favorite game was San Diego's AFC West championship-clinching win over Denver in 1979. Joiner was taken to the dressing room twice with injuries, but he returned to catch a 32-yard touchdown pass that gave the Chargers their first of three straight division titles.

Obsessed with precision, Joiner ran his routes over and over in practice. His patterns, his bursts, and his concentration had to be exact. "I know where he will be on any given play," Fouts said. "I know what he will do. He will do the right thing."

For three years, Joiner led the Chargers in receptions. He caught 50 or more passes in a season seven times. Counting the postseason, he had more than 100 yards in receptions 28 times during his career. He was team MVP again in 1983, Most Inspirational Player from 1980 to 1986, and team captain from 1984 until he retired.

In Joiner's last year, 1986, worn-out knees pushed his decision to retire. A job as the Chargers receiver coach was waiting for him. When he was inducted into the Pro Football Hall of Fame in 1996, one of his records still stood: most games played by a wide receiver (239).

San Diego wide receiver Charlie Joiner makes an amazing twisting turn to catch a pass before running 20 yards.

DANIEL FRANCIS FOUTS

1951–
Position: quarterback
Team: San Diego Chargers
Inducted: 1993

When Dan Fouts signed with the San Diego Chargers in 1973, he was the backup quarterback for the great Johnny Unitas, who had just finished seventeen sensational years with the Baltimore Colts. In the third game of the 1973 season, Unitas became the first player in football history to pass for 40,000 yards. When his knee injuries forced Unitas to retire in midseason, Fouts took his place. Fourteen years later, Fouts broke the passing yardage record he had watched Unitas set. Besides Fouts and Unitas, only Fran Tarkenton and Dan Marino have passed for 40,000 or more yards.

For three straight seasons, beginning in 1979, Fouts passed for more than 4,000 yards. He had 51 games with more than 300 yards passing and six seasons with more than 3,000 yards. Even though he rarely ran with the ball, he scored 13 touchdowns rushing. In 1982 he was named NFL Player of the Year, and he was AFC Player of the Year in 1979 and 1982. Three times he was chosen as an All-Pro, and he played in six Pro Bowls.

Fouts was born on June 10, 1951, in San Francisco, California. His father was a sportscaster for the 49ers. For many years, young Dan was the team's ball boy and statistician for his father. He wanted to play end when he joined the Pop Warner League, but his father insisted he learn the quarterback position. After quarterbacking his high school team to a city championship, Fouts attended the University of Oregon. There he broke school records by passing for 5,995 yards and 37 touchdowns in three years.

During Fouts's first three pro seasons, the Chargers had a combined 9–32–1 record, and during his third season, they lost eleven straight games. Still, Fouts kept improving, hitting individual high marks in 1976 by passing for 2,535 yards and 14 touchdowns.

When the Chargers acquired an older, highly paid quarterback in 1977, an angry Fouts said he would retire if he wasn't traded. He joined eighteen other players in a lawsuit to overturn the agreement that tied him to the Chargers. In court, he claimed he wouldn't have a chance of reaching the Super Bowl with the Chargers.

When the suit failed, Fouts returned in the eleventh game of the 1977 season. Even without having practiced, he completed 19 of 24 passes for 279 yards and 2 touchdowns. The following year he led the Chargers to their first winning season since 1969, with a 9–7 record.

From 1979 through 1981, Fouts took the Chargers to three straight AFC Western Division titles. The 1981 season was his best statistically, with a career-high 4,802 yards and 33 touchdown passes. However, in his fifteen-year career, he never fulfilled his dream of winning a Super Bowl ring. Injury after injury caused him to miss eighteen games in his last five seasons until he retired in 1987.

DAN FOUTS			
Passing Attempts	5,604	Average Pass Gain	7.68
Passing Completions	3,297	Touchdown Passes	254
Passing Percentage	58.8	Passes Intercepted	242
Passing Yards	43,040		

LARRY CHATMON LITTLE

1945–
Position: guard
Teams: San Diego Chargers, Miami Dolphins
Inducted: 1993

When he was a small boy, Larry Little dreamed of being a pro football player. Little was born on November 2, 1945, in Groveland, Georgia, and grew up in Miami, Florida. His house was within walking distance of the Orange Bowl, where he would someday play. Until then,

Little played tackle football in the street with no equipment.

In high school the 190-pound lineman didn't attract any big college scouts, so he settled for tiny Bethune-Cookman College. When he graduated, he was a 6-foot 1-inch, 255-pound team captain and MVP. He was All-Conference and All-America, but he wasn't drafted because he was considered too short for a lineman. In 1967 he signed as a free agent with the San Diego Chargers for $750 and no guarantee he would play. Little started just four games with the Chargers, who shifted him from fullback to offensive lineman, and finally to guard. But his weight was a problem; he now weighed 285 pounds.

In 1968 Little ballooned to 300 pounds and picked up the nickname "Chicken Little" because he could eat a lot of chicken at one sitting. Frustrated because Little couldn't lose weight, San Diego traded him in 1969 to the Miami Dolphins. A starter in his first season with Miami, Little played in the final AFL All-Star Game.

The following season Miami hired Don Shula as head coach. Shula took one look at Little's bulk and gave him an ultimatum: Get down to 265 pounds by the time training camp opened or pay $10 a day for each pound over 265. Little made the deadline, but he had lost so much weight so quickly that he collapsed during one practice.

Once he got into condition, Little joined an offensive line that featured Bob Kuechenberg and future Hall of Famer Jim Langer. Blessed with great speed for a big man, Little was the classic "pulling guard" who led the team's sweeps. The Dolphins won ten games in 1970, their first AFC East title in 1971, and Super Bowl championships in 1972 and 1973. In 1972 they won 17 straight games. During that perfect season, they racked up a record 2,960 rushing yards.

A hero off the field too, Little organized the Gold Coast Summer Camp for underprivileged boys in 1970. The football-oriented camp was designed to teach the boys discipline and to give them constructive activities during the summer. With the Dolphins' backing, it became a model program, allowing several hundred boys to spend time with pro football stars during the summer.

Little once said he came in the back door of football when he signed as a free agent. But he left through the front door as a superstar. A six-time All-Pro, he played in one AFL All-Star Game and four AFC-NFC Pro Bowls, and started in three Super Bowls. The NFL Players Association selected him as the AFC Outstanding Offensive Lineman in 1970, 1971, and 1972.

In 1978 Little was elected to the Florida Sports Hall of Fame. After suffering a knee injury, he retired in 1980. In 1993 all his pro football dreams came true when the Pro Football Hall of Fame inducted him.

HAROLD PETER "BUD" GRANT

1927–
Coach
Team: Minnesota Vikings
Inducted: 1994

Bud Grant had a unique coaching style. He didn't start training camp until the week before the first preseason game. During the cold Minnesota winters he never allowed the players to have a heater on the sidelines. He never arrived at a game any earlier than one hour before kickoff. He rarely called a full staff meeting of his assistant coaches. He went over game films only a couple of times. He had only a two-hour practice session on a Saturday before a Sunday game.

But Grant's style worked. During his eighteen seasons with the Vikings, he won 158 regular-season games and ten playoff games to become the eighth-winningest coach of all time. His Vikings won the NFL championship in 1969 and NFC titles in 1973, 1974, and 1976, as well as eleven Central Division championships.

From 1968 to 1978 the Vikings had a .500 or better record. Minnesota won ten or more regular-season games seven times. The only thing they didn't do was win a Super Bowl. But they made it to the big game four times.

Grant was born on May 20, 1927, in Superior, Wisconsin. He had polio when he was five. Exercise was prescribed for his shorter, thinner left leg, so Grant turned to athletics. After playing baseball, basketball, and football in high school, he spent a year at the Great Lakes Naval Training Station playing football under legendary coach Paul Brown. Brown's approach to football impressed Grant, and he returned to college in order to secure a future in coaching. He won a total of nine varsity letters in basketball, baseball, and football.

After two years playing with the Minneapolis Lakers basketball team, Grant signed with the Philadelphia Eagles in 1951. Two years later he joined the Winnipeg Blue Bombers of the Canadian Football League. In 1957 he became the team's head coach, leading the Blue Bombers to a 102–56–2 record and four Grey Cup victories. (The Grey Cup is awarded to the CFL champions.)

In 1967 Grant replaced Norm Van Brocklin as coach of the Vikings. In addition to having had ten years' experience as a CFL coach, Grant had played offensive and defensive end, defensive halfback, linebacker, and running back—more positions than any other major coach.

With the Vikings, Grant built an "all-weather team" that could adapt to various field conditions without domes and sideline heaters. He avoided smaller, faster players, who he felt would be useless on a muddy or icy field. Grant brought the Vikings to the dressing room only one hour before a game in an effort to reduce the players' pregame jitters. He selected his assistant coaches carefully, then let them do the

weekly planning and teaching. He felt that six weeks of training camp was an awful way to live, so he cut it to nine days and expected the players to come to camp in shape.

After seventeen seasons Grant retired in 1983, but the Vikings' next season was a disaster, so he returned to help. After the team improved from 3–11 to 7–9 in 1985, Grant quit for good.

BUD GRANT			
Wins	168	**Ties**	5
Losses	108	**Win Percentage**	.598

JAMES EARL JOHNSON

1938–
Position: cornerback
Team: San Francisco 49ers
Inducted: 1994

Jimmy Johnson was often ignored because he did his job so well. Opposing quarterbacks knew all about Johnson's skills as a pass defender, and they finally stopped throwing into his defensive area. During his sixteen-year career with the San Francisco 49ers, Johnson intercepted 47 passes, which he returned for 615 yards. If the opposing quarterbacks had thrown toward Johnson more often, his interception totals would have soared. As it was, twice he was the 49ers' top interceptor. Many of the players of his era recognized his skills, calling him one of the top cornerbacks of all time.

Johnson was born in Dallas, Texas, on March 31, 1938. His family moved to Kingsburg, California, when he was young. He was captain of his high school's football, basketball, and baseball teams. An honor student at UCLA, he earned three varsity football letters and was named UCLA's best blocker and tackler.

Because of an injured hand, Johnson played safety for his NFL debut in 1961. His rookie season saw 5 interceptions for 116 yards.

He was moved back and forth from safety to wide receiver until 1964, when he was shifted to his permanent position of left cornerback.

"The lonesome cornerback," as he was sometimes called, had a "little nonagressive" style. This 6-foot 2-inch, 187-pounder didn't do any elbow smashes or judo chops. Instead, he was a very calculating defender who rarely made a mistake. Opposing teams tried to trick him with different patterns or decoys, but it didn't work.

The soft-spoken premier cornerback was named All-Pro for the first time in his ninth season, 1969. He was an All-Pro choice again in 1971 and 1972, and an All-NFC pick three times. He was picked for the Pro Bowl team from 1969 through 1975. His latest honor, election into the Pro Football Hall of Fame, came in 1994.

JIMMY JOHNSON			
Interceptions	47	Average Gain	13.1
Yards	615	Touchdowns	2

LEROY KELLY

1942–

Position: running back
Team: Cleveland Browns
Inducted: 1994

When the legendary Jim Brown retired in 1966, Leroy Kelly had the impossible job of replacing him. At the time Kelly was a third-year running back with limited playing experience, and at 6 feet and 205 pounds, he weighed nearly 30 pounds less than Brown. Still, the Cleveland Browns' new yardage-maker averaged 5.5 yards on 209 rushes in his first season as a regular. He wound up with 1,141 yards and led the league with 15 touchdowns. The next two seasons, 1967 and 1968, Kelly was NFL rushing champ, with more than 1,200 yards in each season. In 1968 he also led the NFL in scoring, with 120 points on 20 touchdowns.

Kelly was born on May 20, 1942, in Philadelphia, Pennsylvania. He won three letters each in football, basketball, and baseball in high school. At Morgan State in Baltimore, he played offense and defense and was named team co-captain and MVP. The Browns chose him in the eighth round of the 1964 draft.

In spite of the fact that he played primarily on the special teams in his first two years, Kelly's ten-year career stats are impressive. In addition to his 7,274 rushing yards and 2,281 receiving yards, as a kickoff returner he totaled 76 returns for 1,784 yards. Kelly also returned 94 punts a total of 990 yards for 3 touchdowns; he won the NFL punt return championship in 1965, and the AFC punt return title in 1971. His combined net yard total was 12,329 yards. When he retired he ranked number four in rushing and combined net yards. In addition, Kelly won All-NFL honors five times from 1966 to 1970, and played in six straight Pro Bowl Games from 1967 to 1972.

Knee problems slowed Kelly down until he retired in 1974. In 1994 he was inducted into the Pro Football Hall of Fame.

LEROY KELLY			
Rushing Attempts	1,727	Pass Receptions	190
Rushing Yards	7,274	Pass Receiving Yards	2,281
Average Gain	4.2	Average Gain	12.0
Touchdowns	74	Touchdowns	13

JACKIE LARUE SMITH

1940–

Position: tight end
Teams: St. Louis Cardinals, Dallas Cowboys
Inducted: 1994

In 1994 Jackie Smith became only the third tight end to be inducted into the Pro Football Hall of Fame. When he began his sixteen-year pro career in 1963, the position was relatively new. A tight end handles both a lineman's and a receiver's duties. When Smith started, the position was used mostly for blocking. After several years it evolved into an offensive weapon as an extra receiver who was fast enough to get away from linebackers.

Smith was born on February 23, 1940, in Columbia, Mississippi. His family moved to Louisiana when he was a youngster. He liked football but injuries prevented him from playing all four years of high school. His outstanding ability at track won him a partial scholarship to Northwestern State University of Louisiana. Agreeing to play football there earned him another scholarship that paid the rest of his expenses.

The St. Louis Cardinals signed Smith in 1963. They first used him at flanker, then moved him to tight end. During his first landmark game as a rookie, he caught 9 passes for 212 yards. Smith was given patterns much like those for a wide receiver. When he got the ball, nothing could stop him from trying to reach the end zone–he possessed a 232-pound body on a 6-foot 4-inch frame, and he could run the 40-yard dash in 4.7 seconds. Smith didn't avoid tacklers–he ran through them and over them.

Smith was a talented receiver; he was also a punishing blocker. And he was the Cardinals' regular punter from 1964 to 1966. During the mid-1970s, he also filled in as a kickoff returner.

After playing fifteen years with the Cardinals, from 1963 to 1977, Smith finished his career in 1978, after one season with the Dallas Cowboys. The one Super Bowl he played in was with Dallas. During the third quarter, Roger Staubach passed to Smith and he dropped the ball in the end zone. A touchdown would have tied the game. The Cowboys eventually lost by 4 points. Unfortunately Smith's great career is sometimes overshadowed by that one drop.

Usually sure-handed, Smith caught 40 or more passes in each of seven different seasons and was selected to play in the Pro Bowl after five of those seasons. He was named to the All-NFL team in 1967 after making 56 receptions

for 1,205 yards and 9 touchdowns. When he retired, Smith was the leading tight end receiver in NFL history.

JACKIE SMITH			
Pass Receptions	480	Rushing Attempts	38
Pass Receiving Yards	7,918	Rushing Yards	327
Average Gain	16.5	Average Gain	8.6
Touchdowns	40	Touchdowns	3

JAMES E. FINKS

1927–1994
General Manager
Teams: Minnesota Vikings, Chicago Bears, New Orleans Saints
Inducted: 1995

Jim Finks was born on August 31, 1927. He was a native of St. Louis, Missouri. He began his 45-year career in football as a player with the Pittsburgh Steelers in 1949. Finks first played defensive back, then starting quarterback for the Steelers. In his seven years with Pittsburgh, he completed 661 passes for 8,622 yards and 55 touchdowns. However, it was his off-the-field activities that put him in the Pro Football Hall of Fame. Finks took three struggling NFL teams—the Minnesota Vikings, the Chicago Bears, and the New Orleans Saints—and turned them into serious competitors or Super Bowl champs.

When Finks took over the Vikings in 1964, the team had only won ten games the previous three seasons. In ten years under Finks, Minnesota won five NFC Central Division crowns and made two Super Bowl appearances; the club added six more division titles after his departure. In 1974 Finks joined the Chicago Bears. Under his management, the Bears reached the playoffs in 1977 for the first time in fourteen years. And one year after Finks took over New Orleans in 1986, the Saints had their first winning season in their 20-year history.

Finks's formula for building a well-organized team was the same each time: he made shrewd trades. One example of Finks's savvy was his trading of Vikings quarterback Fran Tarkenton. Tarkenton had a feud with Coach Norm Van Brocklin in 1966; Finks traded him to the New York Giants the next year. In return the Vikings received two first-round and two second-round draft picks, which Finks used to add young, quality talent to the team. Then in 1972, Finks traded with the Giants again to bring Tarkenton back.

In between managing teams, Finks served as special consultant to the NFL Management Council in its dealing with the NFL Players Association. In 1989, when Pete Rozelle retired as NFL commissioner, Finks was expected to replace him. Paul Tagliabue was chosen instead, but he named Finks to the key position of chair of the league's Competition Committee. The committee served as an advisory board for all competitive matters, including playing rules, officiating, and player personnel.

Jim Finks's successful career ended abruptly when he was diagnosed with lung cancer. He died on May 8, 1994.

HENRY WENDELL JORDAN

1935–1977

Position: defensive tackle
Teams: Cleveland Browns, Green Bay Packers
Inducted: 1995

Henry Jordan's father wouldn't let him play high school football because Jordan still had "baby bones." But at thirteen, Henry's "baby bones" were already 6 feet 2 inches tall, and he weighed 230 pounds—just 10 pounds less than his pro football playing weight.

Jordan finally played high school football, and he was also on the wrestling and track teams in Emporia, Virginia, where he was born on January 26, 1935. He was president of his class for all four years. He earned a football scholarship to the University of Virginia, where he received a B.S. in commerce. In 1957 he was signed by the Browns.

During his two years with Cleveland, Jordan wasn't a regular player. In spite of that, he played many positions. He was offensive tackle, offensive guard, defensive tackle, and defensive end and played on the kickoff team, the kickoff return team, and the punt return team. A trade in 1959 sent him to Green Bay, where he played defensive tackle for the rest of his career.

Vince Lombardi joined the Packers the same year as Jordan, and Green Bay's record went from 1–10 to 7–5, giving the Packers their first .500 plus season since 1944. The next year, in 1960, the Packers finished first in the NFL Western Conference, winning their first title of any kind since 1944.

With Jordan, the Packers won both the 1961 and 1962 championships, beating the Giants each year. The defense took the Packers to league championships again in 1965, 1966, and 1967. During those winning years, Jordan was 1 of Green Bay's most honored defensive stars. He was named All-NFL six times. He also played in the 1960, 1961, 1963, and 1966 Pro Bowls and was named the 1962 Pro Bowl Most Valuable Lineman.

When Jordan first joined Green Bay, the defensive ends did the pass rushing and the defensive tackles stayed in the middle to protect against the run. However, in 1960 Lombardi made Jordan a pass rusher too. Even though he only made 1 interception, Jordan's rushing tactics enabled other players to make countless more.

Jordan once explained his position. "Football has developed into a game of playing 'keys,' which means watching what a certain man does and reacting a certain way. In the case of the defensive tackle, the key is the offensive guard facing him. If I have an idea of what the guard is going to do, it will be harder for the tackle or center to block effectively."

In 1969 Jordan played only five games because of acute back pain. He retired that season after thirteen years in the NFL. Then on February 21, 1977, Jordan suffered a heart attack and died an untimely death at age 42. In 1995 his son, Henry Jordan Jr., represented Jordan when he was inducted into the Pro Football Hall of Fame.

LEE ROY SELMON

1954–

Position: defensive end
Team: Tampa Bay Buccaneers
Inducted: 1995

Lee Roy Selmon was the first player drafted by the Tampa Bay Buccaneers. Both Tampa Bay and Selmon made their NFL debut in 1976. For the next nine years, 6-foot 3-inch, 250-pound Selmon was the backbone of the team. The defensive end became the first Buccaneer to be elected to the Pro Football Hall of Fame.

Selmon was born on October 20, 1954, in Eufaula, Oklahoma. He wasn't the only Selmon to play pro football. He and his older brothers, Lucius and Dewey, played together in high school, then at the University of Oklahoma, where all three were All-America players. Selmon won the Lombardi Award as well as the Outland Trophy for most outstanding college lineman. Leading with 132 tackles, he helped the Sooners win all but two of 45 games during his four years there. After a brief stint in the World Football League, Lucius became defensive line coach for the Sooners. Dewey, eleven months and one day older than Lee Roy, was also drafted by Tampa Bay in 1976.

The new Buccaneers team lost all fourteen games its first season, but Lee Roy did well. Even though he missed six games due to injuries, he was named Rookie of the Year and team MVP. In 1977 the Buccaneers lost their first twelve games but were becoming competitive, especially on defense. Offensively, however, they were shut out six times and held to 10 points or fewer in eleven of their first twelve games that season. Their first win was over the New Orleans Saints 33–14 in their thirteenth game of the season. Selmon had 12 tackles and 3 sacks. That year he racked up 110 tackles, forced 5 fumbles for a team-high mark, and led Tampa Bay with 13 sacks.

Tampa Bay improved to 5–11 in 1978, and Selmon became the first Buccaneer to play in a Pro bowl. In 1979, only their fourth season, the Bucs won the NFC Central Division championship. With a 10–6 regular-season record, their stingy defense led the way, allowing only 14.8 points per game. They also won their first playoff game 24–17 over the Philadelphia Eagles.

That year Selmon made 117 tackles and 11 sacks, forced 3 fumbles and recovered 2 (1 for a 29-yard touchdown), and pressured the quarterback 60 times. He won every honor a defensive lineman can win. In addition to being a consensus All-Pro, he was the NFL Defensive Player of the Year.

During his nine-year career Selmon received six straight Pro Bowl invites. He won All-Pro honors three years and All-NFC recognition four years. In 1980 he was named NFL Man of the Year so honored for his contributions to the community. After suffering a herniated disk in 1984, he retired the next year.

LOUIS CREEKMUR

1927–

Positions: tackle, guard
Team: Detroit Lions
Inducted: 1996

Thirty-seven years passed between Lou Creekmur's last season and his induction into the Pro Football Hall of Fame. The colorful 6-foot 4-

inch, 255-pound lineman played both guard and tackle for the Detroit Lions during the 1950s. Whatever position he played, Creekmur was extremely effective. "The Smiling Assassin" was a master of holding and also knew how to use his elbows, as did many players of that "no-holds-barred" era.

Creekmur was born on January 22, 1927, in Hopelawn, New Jersey. His family moved to Woodridge, where Creekmur played tackle in high school. He entered the College of William and Mary in 1944. Two years in the Army interrupted his studies, but when he returned from the Army, he went on to earn a master's degree. As a senior he won the Jacobs Blocking Trophy and played in both the Senior Bowl and College All-Star Game.

When the Lions signed Creekmur in 1950, they used him in every way possible–tackle, guard, even defensive lineman in short-yardage situations. An outstanding blocker on both passing and rushing plays, Creekmur began his career as a guard. He was shifted to offensive left tackle in 1953. He finished out his career in that spot except for 1955, when he filled in at defensive middle guard for most of the season.

Creekmur's only complaint about being switched back and forth was regarding his weight. "If I am going to play offensive tackle, I'd like to weigh about 255 pounds," he said. "But if I'm to play guard, I should get down to 240 pounds to increase my speed. I sure wish Coach [Buddy] Parker would tell me in advance so I'll know how much to eat the week before a game."

The talented and versatile lineman won All-League honors at guard in 1951 and 1952, then made All-NFL at tackle in 1953, 1954, 1956, and 1957. He was also a starter in the Pro Bowl from 1950 through 1958. After ten years with the Lions, he retired in 1959.

DANIEL LEE DIERDORF

1949–
Position: tackle
Team: St. Louis Cardinals
Inducted: 1996

Playing for the St. Louis Cardinals, Dan Dierdorf was the heart of the team's offensive line, nicknamed "the Mean Machine." From 1975 through 1980 the Mean Machine led the NFC in fewest sacks allowed five times. During that stretch Dierdorf was singled out three times for his blocking skills, as the NFL Players Association named him the NFL's best offensive lineman in 1976, 1977, and 1978.

Dierdorf was born in Canton, Ohio, the home of the Pro Football Hall of Fame, on June 29, 1949. By the time he was a sophomore in high school, he was 6 feet 3 inches and weighed 250 pounds. At the University of Michigan, he was named All-America offensive tackle. The Cardinals thought Dierdorf's size, strength, mobility, and aggressiveness would make an ideal tackle, if he could just beef up another 40 pounds, which he did. His playing weight in the pros was 290.

Dierdorf was drafted by the St. Louis Cardinals in 1971 and reached his peak as part of the Mean Machine. The line was famous for its strong pass protection, but it could also spring Cardinals runners for consistent gains. From 1974 through 1976 the offense produced 950 points, helping the Cardinals to NFC East titles in 1974 and 1975. Dierdorf was a unanimous All-NFL selection from 1975 to 1978 and in 1980. He played in six Pro Bowls, and after the 1979 season he was named to the NFL's Team of the 1970s Decade.

When injuries forced Dierdorf to retire in 1983, he said, "Ninety-five percent of me is very sad. But the other five percent—my knees—

are very happy." He continued his second career as a sports broadcaster, which he had started in his fourth pro season. Eventually, he became a member of the Monday Night Football broadcast team.

JOE JACKSON GIBBS

1940–
Coach
Team: Washington Redskins
Inducted: 1996

Joe Gibbs spent his entire pro football head coaching career with the Washington Redskins. During his twelve-year term he led the Redskins to a 124–60–0 regular-season record and a 16–5 record in 21 postseason games. His combined .683 win percentage is surpassed only by Vince Lombardi's .740 and John Madden's .731. Under Gibbs, the Redskins made seven playoff appearances. Five NFC East titles led to four NFC championships. Of the four Super Bowls the Redskins played, they won three.

When he was a child, Gibbs's family moved from Mocksville, North Carolina (where he was born on November 25, 1940), to the West Coast. He played tight end, linebacker, and guard at San Diego State, where he majored in physical education. After graduation, he was named offensive line coach at San Diego State, and in three seasons the college won 27 of 30 games. Gibbs spent seventeen seasons as a college and pro football assistant coach before joining Washington in 1981.

In Gibbs's first season with the Redskins, the team went from an 0–5 to an 8–8 record. In strike-shortened 1982 his team's 8–1 season record carried them to Super Bowl XVII, and they beat the Miami Dolphins 27–17 for the championship. The next year, 1983, Gibbs's offense set an NFL record for points scored in a season (541) on their way to winning the NFC championship. That year the Redskins

made it to Super Bowl XVIII but lost to the Los Angeles Raiders 38–9. In both 1982 and 1983 Gibbs was named Coach of the Year. He was the first coach in 20 years to receive that honor two seasons in a row.

In 1987 the Redskins won Super Bowl XXII, beating Denver 42–10. Then in 1991, they beat Buffalo 37–24 in Super Bowl XXVI. It was Gibbs's third Super Bowl win and the third time he was named Coach of the Year. Three coaches have won three Super Bowls in NFL history, but only Joe Gibbs did it with three different quarterbacks.

When Gibbs retired for health reasons after the 1992 season, the Redskins had won at least ten games in each of eight seasons. Out of twelve years, Gibbs had only one losing season, in 1988, when the Redskins finished 7–9. His brilliant coaching career put him into the Pro Football Hall of Fame in 1996.

JOE GIBBS			
Wins	140	**Ties**	0
Losses	65	**Win Percentage**	.683

MELVIN LACY RENFRO

1941–
Positions: cornerback, safety
Team: Dallas Cowboys
Inducted: 1996

Mel Renfro played fourteen seasons for the Dallas Cowboys. The versatile defensive back spent his first six years as a free safety and his final eight as a cornerback.

Renfro was born on December 30, 1941, in Houston, Texas, and grew up in Portland, Oregon, where he was a high school football and track star. He was All-America at the University of Oregon, and then the 6-foot, 192-pound halfback was drafted by the Cowboys in 1964. Coach Tom Landry put him at safety until there was an opening on offense, but Renfro played defense too well. In his rookie year he excelled three ways—as pass defender, punt returner, and kickoff returner. He led the Cowboys in all three categories that year compiling 32 punt returns for 418 yards and 40 kickoff returns for 1,017 yards. His 7 interceptions accounted for 110 return yards and a touchdown.

Halfway through the 1969 season, Landry decided the Cowboys had given up too many touchdown passes, so he moved Renfro to cornerback to "shake up the defensive backfield." That season Renfro picked off 10 passes—a career high for one season—but in general his season interception totals declined after the move to cornerback because the opposition passers wouldn't throw in his direction.

In his last seasons Renfro's knees began to give out, and he retired in 1977. His career stats included a team-record 52 interceptions, returned for 626 yards and 3 touchdowns. He also returned 109 punts for 842 yards and 1 touchdown and 85 kickoffs for 2,246 yards and 2 touchdowns.

Renfro won All-NFL honors four times and All-NFC honors three times. Of his ten straight Pro Bowl invitations, he missed one because of injuries. He also played in eight conference championship games and four Super Bowls.

MEL RENFRO			
Interceptions	52	Average Gain	12.0
Yards	626	Touchdowns	3

Glossary of
Football Terms

GLOSSARY OF FOOTBALL TERMS

Audible A change of play called at the line of scrimmage. It is called an *audible* because it is shouted to the other players by the quarterback.

Backfield The area behind the line of scrimmage on both offense and defense. The *backfield* is also that part of the offensive team that consists of quarterbacks and running backs.

Blitz An all-out pass rush in which several defensive players leave their normal positions to rush the quarterback as he is preparing to pass.

Bomb A very long pass, usually thrown to score a touchdown or to gain big yardage.

"Bump and Run" A strategy used by defensive backs to throw off a pass receiver's timing. Usually, the back bumps the receiver just before a pass is thrown, then runs along with him on his pass pattern.

Center An offensive lineman whose main job is to block for the quarterback and running back on running and passing plays. A center also snaps the ball through his legs to the quarterback to start a play.

Clipping A blocking violation called when a player throws his body across the back of an opponent's legs or anywhere below the waist. Clipping can cause serious knee or leg injuries.

Conversion (also called try-for-point) Extra point or points made after a touchdown. One point is scored by kicking the ball over the crossbar. Two points are scored if the ball is thrown or run into the end zone.

Cornerback A defensive back who lines up on the line of scrimmage directly opposite a wide receiver and covers him on passing plays.

Dead ball A ball that is not in play.

Defensive backfield (also called the secondary) A defensive unit that consists of two cornerbacks and two safeties. They are the last line of defense against a ballcarrier.

Delay of game A violation called if the offensive team does not get a play off within 40 seconds after the referee's signal to begin the play.

Dime back A sixth defensive back brought into the game for certain pass situations.

Down One of four plays each offensive team has to move the ball 10 yards. If the offense moves the ball 10 or more yards, they get four more downs.

Drop back pass A play in which the quarterback runs back about 7 yards after taking the snap at the line of scrimmage. This gives his blockers time to form a protective "pocket" around him while he throws the ball.

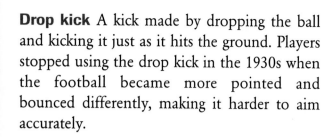

Drop kick A kick made by dropping the ball and kicking it just as it hits the ground. Players stopped using the drop kick in the 1930s when the football became more pointed and bounced differently, making it harder to aim accurately.

End A defensive lineman who lines up outside the defensive tackle. An end's main job is either to sack the quarterback before he can throw, or to tackle the ballcarrier after he has caught the ball.

Extra point(s) (also called point(s)-after-touchdown, PAT) Any point(s) made after a touchdown, either by kicking the ball into the end zone for 1 point, or by running or passing it in for 2 points.

Field goal A 3-point score made by placekicking the ball over the crossbar and through the goalposts.

Flanker Old-fashioned term for *wide receiver*.

Free ball A live ball that is not in any player's possession.

Fullback A running back whose main job is to take handoffs or catch passes from the quarterback. A fullback also blocks for the quarterback or other running backs.

Fumble When a player drops the ball or loses possession of it during play.

Guard An offensive lineman whose job is to block for the quarterback or running back on running and passing plays.

Halfback A running back whose main job is to take handoffs or catch passes from the quarterback.

Hail Mary pass A long, desperate pass downfield.

Handoff A play in which the quarterback hands the ball to the running back as the back runs past him.

Hang time The amount of time a punter's ball is in the air before it reaches the punt returner. Longer hang time is better because it gives the kicker's teammates time to race downfield and tackle the receiver.

Hashmarks Two short marks toward the middle of each yard line which line up with the uprights of both goal posts. Hashmarks show where to put the ball into play if it is near a sideline or out of bounds on the previous play.

Holding A violation of the rule that forbids a player from using his hands to grab or hold an opposing player.

Huddle A circle in which the offensive team gathers together to discuss the next play.

Incomplete pass A forward pass that hits the ground before it is caught, or any pass that is thrown out of bounds.

Interception A pass that is caught by a defensive player.

Interference When a player illegally or unfairly stops an opponent from catching a ball.

Lateral pass (also called a pitchout) A backward, sideways, or underhanded toss, usually made by the quarterback to a running back in the backfield.

Line of scrimmage An imaginary line running to both sidelines at the spot where the ball is placed on the field and snapped to start each play. The two teams line up on either side of the line and may not cross it until the ball is snapped.

Linebacker A defensive player who lines up 3 to 5 yards behind the linemen. There are usually three linebackers: one in the middle and two outside. They usually make the most tackles since they go after the ballcarrier.

Lineman An offensive or defensive player who lines up on the line of scrimmage. There are five offensive linemen: a center, two guards, and two tackles. They block for the quarterback and running backs on running and passing plays. There are usually four defensive linemen: two tackles and two ends. They try to sack the quarterback for a loss of yardage or they try to tackle the ballcarrier.

Man in motion An offensive player who runs behind the line of scrimmage before the snap.

Man-to-man defense A pass defense strategy in which a defensive player covers a particular opponent, as opposed to covering a zone or area of the field.

Neutral zone The space between the two ends of the football as it sits on the field before the snap. Offensive and defensive teams must stay behind their respective ends of the ball.

Nickel back A fifth defensive back sometimes brought in for certain pass situations.

Offsides A violation occurring when any part of a player's body is over the line of scrimmage before the ball is snapped.

Onside kick A bouncing kickoff used by a team that is behind to gain possession of the ball in a hurry. If the ball goes 10 yards it becomes a free ball, giving the kicking team a chance to recover it.

Option play A play in which a running back has a choice of running with the ball or passing it to a receiver.

Pass pattern A set route a receiver runs down the field to get in position to catch a pass.

Pass rush The defense's attempt to rush at the quarterback and tackle him behind the line of scrimmage before he can pass the ball.

Penalty A punishment for violating a rule of play, usually a loss of yardage or a loss of down.

Place kick A kick made with the ball held in a fixed position, either on the ground or sitting on a kicking tee. A place kick can be used as a kickoff to start the game or the half, to kick an extra point, or to score a field goal.

Plane The imaginary line above the goal line that the ball must cross to score a touchdown.

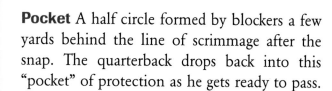

Pocket A half circle formed by blockers a few yards behind the line of scrimmage after the snap. The quarterback drops back into this "pocket" of protection as he gets ready to pass.

Punt A kick made by dropping the ball and kicking it before it hits the ground. A punt is usually made to move the ball downfield on fourth down.

Quarterback The leader of the offense who calls the signals. After receiving the ball from the center, the quarterback either runs with it, hands it to a running back, or passes it to a receiver.

Receiver An offensive player who catches passes thrown by the quarterback and then runs with the ball. There are three kinds of receivers: wide receivers, split ends, and tight ends. All three are fast runners, but tight ends are bigger and can block as well as run.

Roll-out pass A play in which the quarterback runs towards the sidelines away from defenders to give himself more time to find a receiver.

Running back A player in the offensive backfield who takes handoffs or catches passes from the quarterback. There are two kinds of running backs: halfbacks and fullbacks. Halfbacks are usually fast runners and fullbacks are usually good blockers.

Sack A term used when the defense tackles the quarterback behind the line of scrimmage while he is attempting to pass.

Safety A defensive back who plays 10 to 15 yards behind the line of scrimmage to protect against the long pass. There are two kinds of safeties: strong safeties and free safeties. A strong safety also covers running backs acting as receivers, while a free safety helps the cornerbacks cover wide receivers going long.

Safety A scoring play that occurs when the ballcarrier is tackled in his own end zone. The play is worth 2 points.

Scrambling A zigzagging running motion a quarterback uses to avoid getting tackled while trying to pass the ball.

Secondary See *defensive backfield*.

Signals The code the quarterback uses to tell his teammates what the play will be.

Snap The start of a play during which the center hands or passes the ball back to the quarterback.

Special teams Groups of players who come in to perform special kicking jobs–kickoffs, kickoff returns, place kicks, punts, and punt returns. Some special teams players are on regular offensive or defensive units as well, while others play only special teams. Special teams are sometimes called "suicide squads" because of the hard hits the kickers receive.

Split end See *receiver*.

Straight-arm A tactic used by a ballcarrier to push away a tackler by holding his free arm out straight.

Sudden death A term for overtime play that occurs when regulation play ends in a tie. The game ends as soon as one teams scores.

Sweep An offensive running play in which the running back "sweeps" wide around the far side of the field, carrying the ball and following one or more blocking linemen.

Tackle An offensive or defensive lineman. On offense, a tackle's main job is to block for the quarterback and running back on running and passing plays. On defense, his job is to stop the ballcarrier.

Tight end See *receiver*.

Touchback A non-scoring play that occurs when an interception, defensive fumble recovery, kickoff, or punt is downed inside a team's own end zone. The team's offense then must put the ball into play on its own 20-yard line.

Touchdown An offensive play in which the ball is carried or thrown over the goal line to score 6 points.

Two-point conversion An attempt to run or pass the ball into the end zone from the 2-yard line for 2 points following a touchdown, rather than kicking for 1 extra point.

Turnover An offensive mistake—either a fumble or an interception—that gives the ball to the defense.

Wide receiver See *receiver*.

Zone defense A pass defense strategy in which a defensive back covers an area of the field, or zone, instead of a single opponent.

Index
1979–1996

Bold page numbers denote main entry.

A

Adderley, Herb   **47**
Atkins, Doug   **51**

B

Badgro, Red   **48–49**
Barney, Lem   **122–123**
Bell, Bobby   **70**, 77
Biletnikoff, Fred   **86–87**
Blanda, George   40, **49–50**, 121
Blount, Mel   **101**, 104, 126
Bradshaw, Terry   **92–93**, 104, 126
Brown, Willie   **73**
Buchanan, Buck   **116**
Butkus, Dick   **34–35**, 107

C

Campbell, Earl   **108–109**, 132
Creekmur, Lou   **148–149**
Csonka, Larry   57, **82–83**

D

Davis, Al   40, 100, **123**, 130
Davis, Willie   **42–43**
Dawson, Len   **96**
Dierdorf, Dan   **149–150**
Ditka, Mike   **100**
Dorsett, Tony   **132–133**

F

Finks, Jim   128, **146-147**
Fouts, Dan   138, 140, 141, **142**

G

Gatski, Frank   **75**
Gibbs, Joe   114, 115, **150**
Gillman, Sid   **70–71**, 126, 127, 131
Grant, Bud   90, 91, **143–144**
Greene, Mean Joe   **84–85**, 104, 106, 126

Griese, Bob   38, 57, 66, **116–117**

H

Ham, Jack   **88–89**, 104, 107, 126, 127
Hannah, John   **110–111**
Harris, Franco   92, **104–105**, 126, 129
Hendricks, Ted   **117–118**
Hornung, Paul   29, **68–69**
Houston, Ken   **76**
Huff, Sam   **51–52**

J

Johnson, Jimmy   14, **144–145**
Johnson, John Henry   **96–97**, 119
Joiner, Charlie   138, **140–141**
Jones, Deacon   44, 45, **47–48**
Jones, Stan   **120**
Jordan, Henry   **147–148**
Jurgensen, Sonny   **71–72**

K

Kelly, Leroy   **145–146**

L

Lambert, Jack   **106–107**, 126
Landry, Tom   38, 39, 67, **118–119**, 132, 134, 150, 151
Langer, Jim   **97–98**, 143
Lanier, Willie   **76–77**
Largent, Steve   **136–137**, 140
Lary, Yale   **46**
Lilly, Bob   **38–39**
Little, Larry   **142–143**

M

Mackey, John   **112–113**
Maynard, Don   56, **98–99**, 140
McCormack, "Big Mike"   **74**, 137
Mitchell, Bobby   **72–73**
Mix, Ron   **46–47**
Musso, George   **52–53**

N

Namath, Joe   7, 10, 26, **60–61**, 78, 98, 115
Noll, Chuck   84, 88, 92, 104, **126–127**, 130

O

Olsen, Merlin   **44–45**
Otto, Jim   **40–41**

P

Page, Alan   **90–91**, 95
Payton, Walter   **128–129**, 132

R

Renfro, Mel   47, **150–151**
Riggins, John   **114–115**
Ringo, Jim   **50**
Rozell, Pete   6, 7, 9, 11, 13, **62–63**, 68, 147

S

Schramm, Tex   63, **120–121**
Shell, Art   **94–95**
Selmon, Lee Roy   **148**

Simpson, O.J.   **64–65**, 108, 128
Smith, Jackie   **145–146**
St. Clair, Bob   **118–119**
Staubach, Roger   **66–67**, 146
Stenerud, Jan   **121–122**

T

Tarkenton, Fran   **77–78**, 84, 142, 147
Taylor, Charley   56, **58–59**, 140

U

Unitas, Johnny   4, 29, **36–37**, 61, 93, 113, 142
Upshaw, Gene   94, 95, **99–100**

W

Walker, Doak   **78–79**
Walsh, Bill   12, **130–131**, 140, 141
Warfield, Paul   **56–57**
Weinmeister, Arnie   **74–75**
White, Randy   **134–135**
Winslow, Kellen   **138-139**
Wood, Willie   **101–102**

INDUCTEES BY POSITION

ADMINISTRATOR

Davis, Al   40, 100, **123**, 130

COACH/MANAGER

Davis, Al   40, 100, **123**, 130
Finks, Jim   128, **146-147**
Gibbs, Joe   114, 115, **150**
Gillman, Sid   **70–71**, 126, 127, 131
Grant, Bud   90, 91, **143–144**
Landry, Tom   38, 39, 67, **118–119**, 132, 134, 150, 151
Noll, Chuck   84, 88, 92, 104, **126–127**, 130

Schramm, Tex   63, **120–121**
Walsh, Bill   12, **130–131**, 140, 141

COMMISSIONER

Davis, Al   40, 100, **123**, 130
Rozell, Pete   6, 7, 9, 11, 13, **62–63**, 68, 147

CENTER

Gatski, Frank   **75**
Langer, Jim   **97–98**, 143
Otto, Jim   **40–41**
Ringo, Jim   **50**

CORNERBACK

Adderley, Herb   **47**

Barney, Lem   **122–123**

Blount, Mel   **101**, 104, 126

Brown, Willie   **73**

Johnson, Jimmy   14, **144–145**

Renfro, Mel   47, **150–151**

DEFENSIVE END

Atkins, Doug   **51**

Davis, Willie   **42–43**

Jones, Deacon   44, 45, **47–48**

Selmon, Lee Roy   **148**

DEFENSIVE TACKLE

Buchanan, Buck   **116**

Greene, Mean Joe   **84–85**, 104, 106, 126

Jones, Stan   **120**

Jordan, Henry   **147–148**

Lilly, Bob   **38–39**

Olsen, Merlin   **44–45**

Page, Alan   **90–91**, 95

Weinmeister, Arnie   **74–75**

White, Randy   **134–135**

END

Badgro, Red   **48–49**

FULLBACK

Csonka, Larry   57, **82–83**

Johnson, John Henry   **96–97**, 119

GUARD

Creekmur, Lou   **148–149**

Hannah, John   **110–111**

Little, Larry   **142–143**

Musso, George   **52–53**

Jones, Stan   **120**

Upshaw, Gene   94, 95, **99–100**

HALFBACK

Mitchell, Bobby   **72–73**

Walker, Doak   **78–79**

LINEBACKER

Bell, Bobby   **70**, 77

Butkus, Dick   **34–35**, 107

Ham, Jack   **88–89**, 104, 107, 126, 127

Hendricks, Ted   **117–118**

Huff, Sam   **51–52**

Lambert, Jack   **106–107**, 126

Lanier, Willie   **76–77**

OFFENSIVE TACKLE

Mix, Ron   **46-47**

PLACEKICKER

Blanda, George   40, **49–50**, 121

Hornung, Paul   29, **68–69**

Stenerud, Jan   **121–122**

PUNTER

Lary, Yale   **46**

QUARTERBACK

Blanda, George   40, **49–50**, 121

Bradshaw, Terry   **92–93**, 104, 126

Dawson, Len   **96**

Fouts, Dan   138, 140, 141, **142**

Griese, Bob   38, 57, 66, **116–117**

Jurgensen, Sonny   **71-72**

Namath, Joe   7, 10, 26, **60–61**, 78, 98, 115

Staubach, Roger   **66–67**, 146

Tarkenton, Fran   **77–78**, 84, 142, 147

Unitas, Johnny   4, 29, **36–37**, 61, 93, 113, 142

RUNNING BACK

Campbell, Earl   **108**–109, 132

Dorsett, Tony   **132-133**

Harris, Franco   92, **104–105**, 126, 129

Hornung, Paul   29, **68–69**
Kelly, Leroy   **145–146**
Payton, Walter   **128–129**, 132
Riggins, John   **114–115**
Simpson, O.J.   **64–65**, 108, 128

SAFETY
Houston, Ken   **76**
Lary, Yale   **46**
Renfro, Mel   47, **150–151**
Wood, Willie   **101-102**

TACKLE
Creekmur, Lou   **148–149**
Dierdorf, Dan   **149–150**
McCormack, "Big Mike"   **74**, 137
Musso, George   **52–53**

Shell, Art   **94–95**
St. Clair, Bob   **118-119**

TIGHT END
Ditka, Mike   **100**
Mackey, John   **112–113**
Smith, Jackie   **145–146**
Winslow, Kellen   **138–139**

WIDE RECEIVER
Biletnikoff, Fred   **86–87**
Joiner, Charlie   138, **140–141**
Largent, Steve   **136–137**, 140
Maynard, Don   56, **98–99**, 140
Mitchell, Bobby   **72–73**
Taylor, Charley   56, **58–59**, 140
Warfield, Paul   **56-57**

INDUCTEES BY LEAGUE/TEAM

BALTIMORE COLTS
Hendricks, Ted
Mackey, John
Unitas, Johnny

BROOKLYN DODGERS
Badgro, Red

BUFFALO BILLS
Simpson, O.J.

CHICAGO BEARS
Atkins, Doug
Blanda, George
Butkus, Dick
Ditka, Mike
Finks, Jim
Jones, Stan

Musso, George
Page, Alan
Payton, Walter

CINCINNATI BENGALS
Joiner, Charlie

CLEVELAND BROWNS
Atkins, Doug
Davis, Willie
Dawson, Len
Gatski, Frank
Jordan, Henry
Kelly, Leroy
McCormack, "Big Mike"
Mitchell, Bobby
Warfield, Paul

DALLAS COWBOYS
Adderley, Herb
Ditka, Mike
Dorsett, Tony
Landry, Tom
Lilly, Bob
Renfro, Mel
Schramm, Tex
Smith, Jackie
Staubach, Roger
White, Randy

DALLAS TEXANS
Dawson, Len

DENVER BRONCOS
Brown, Willie
Dorsett, Tony

DETROIT LIONS
Barney, Lem
Creekmur, Lou
Gatski, Frank
Johnson, John Henry
Lary, Yale
Walker, Doak

GREEN BAY PACKERS
Adderley, Herb
Davis, Willie
Hendricks, Ted
Hornung, Paul
Jordan, Henry
Ringo, Jim
Stenerud, Jan
Wood, Willie

HOUSTON OILERS
Blanda, George
Campbell, Earl
Gillman, Sid

Houston, Ken
Johnson, John Henry
Joiner, Charlie

KANSAS CITY CHIEFS
Bell, Bobby
Buchanan, Buck
Dawson, Len
Lanier, Willie
Stenerud, Jan

LOS ANGELES CHARGERS
Gillman, Sid
Mix, Ron

LOS ANGELES RAIDERS
Davis, Al
Hendricks, Ted
Shell, Art

LOS ANGELES RAMS
Gillman, Sid
Jones, Deacon
Namath, Joe
Olsen, Merlin

MIAMI DOLPHINS
Csonka, Larry
Griese, Bob
Langer, Jim
Little, Larry
Warfield, Paul

MINNESOTA VIKINGS
Finks, Jim
Grant, Bud
Langer, Jim
Page, Alan
Stenerud, Jan
Tarkenton, Fran

NEW ENGLAND PATRIOTS
Hannah, John

NEW ORLEANS SAINTS
Atkins, Doug
Campbell, Earl
Finks, Jim

NEW YORK GIANTS
Badgro, Red
Csonka, Larry
Huff, Sam
Maynard, Don
Tarkenton, Fran
Weinmeister, Arnie

NEW YORK JETS
Maynard, Don
Namath, Joe
Riggins, John

NEW YORK TITANS
Maynard, Don

NEW YORK YANKEES
Badgro, Red
McCormack, "Big Mike"
Weinmeister, Arnie

OAKLAND RAIDERS
Biletnikoff, Fred
Blanda, George
Brown, Willie
Davis, Al
Hendricks, Ted
Mix, Ron
Otto, Jim
Shell, Art
Upshaw, Gene

PHILADELPHIA EAGLES
Ditka, Mike
Jurgensen, Sonny
Ringo, Jim

PITTSBURGH STEELERS
Blount, Mel
Bradshaw, Terry
Dawson, Len
Greene, Mean Joe
Ham, Jack
Harris, Franco
Johnson, John Henry
Lambert, Jack
Noll, Chuck

SAN DIEGO CHARGERS
Fouts, Dan
Gillman, Sid
Joiner, Charlie
Jones, Deacon
Little, Larry
Mackey, John
Mix, Ron
Winslow, Kellen
Unitas, Johnny

SAN FRANCISCO 49ERS
Johnson, Jimmy
Johnson, John Henry
Simpson, O.J.
St. Clair, Bob
Walsh, Bill

SEATTLE SEAHAWKS
Harris, Franco
Largent, Steve

ST. LOUIS CARDINALS
Dierdorf, Dan
Maynard, Don
Smith, Jackie

TAMPA BAY BUCHANEERS
Selmon, Lee Roy

WASHINGTON REDSKINS
Houston, Ken
Gibbs, Joe
Huff, Sam
Jones, Deacon
Jones, Stan
Jurgensen, Sonny
Mitchell, Bobby
Riggins, John
Taylor, Charley